Lecture Notes in Computer Science   12660

More information about this subseries at http://www.springer.com/series/7409

Fred S. Roberts · Igor A. Sheremet (Eds.)

Resilience in the Digital Age

Editors
Fred S. Roberts 🆔
DIMACS Center
Rutgers University
Piscataway, NJ, USA

Igor A. Sheremet 🆔
Russian Foundation
for Basic Research
Moscow, Russia

ISSN 0302-9743   ISSN 1611-3349   (electronic)
Lecture Notes in Computer Science
ISBN 978-3-030-70369-1   ISBN 978-3-030-70370-7   (eBook)
https://doi.org/10.1007/978-3-030-70370-7

LNCS Sublibrary: SL3 – Information Systems and Applications, incl. Internet/Web, and HCI

Foreword

We live in a more and more complex society, where science also reveals layer after layer of underlying complexity in physical and biological systems. Once we discovered this complexity we needed to deal with it, and this means that large volumes of data and the structural assistance of high-performance computers is now an intrinsic part of science, innovation and society as a whole. All of the major challenges, such as for instance formulated in the United Nations Sustainable Development Goals, will require complex, yet fast, research and development processes. The rapid development and roll out of COVID-19 vaccines is just one recent example of how advanced science and global collaboration are a day-to-day reality and how 'retractive nationalism' is in essence ignoring the unavoidable reality of a global society. Digital Objects populating the Internet increasingly go way beyond the current 'Web' of mostly narrative documents and comprise anything from single Unique Identifiers for concepts, to single, published assertions, to entire large data collections, as well as algorithms dealing with these vast amounts of data and information. This means that computers have become pivotal in the processing of data and need to be fully integrated in the research and innovation process.

This increasingly digital representation of reality should serve us by leading mankind to substantially improved and equally distributed quality of life and moving countries toward achieving the sustainable development goals established by the United Nations. By constructing, implementing, maintaining, and applying an Internet supporting an Internet-based global information infrastructure, we have already created, over the past 30 years or so, a new reality where billions of people and hundreds of billions of devices operate as a whole, interacting and cooperating with one another online. The vision of an Internet of FAIR data and services, as briefly described in [chapter 6] of this book, is in fact a realization of the vision recently expressed by George Strawn in his article [1]: *"The first generation [of the IT revolution] consisted of many independent computers. The second generation consists of 'one computer' (the Internet network of computers) with many non-interoperable datasets [......], the third generation will consist of one computer and one dataset."* What is meant here is that data will increasingly 'stay where they are' and will be visited for high performance analysis 'in situ'. For this to happen, data and the algorithms and workflows encapsulated in virtual machines should find, access and re-use interoperable and machine actionable data.

However, the explosive growth of interconnectivity and complexity of digitalized sociotechnological systems also pose significant threats. One accidental or deliberate local malfunction of hardware or software may generate a flow of failures and damage, amplified by cascading effects and reaching objects and systems far beyond the place of the initial breakdown. The most dangerous threat is that consequences of such technological incidents may reach not only information objects and their storage, but transpose to physical space, producing cyberkinetic impacts on people, urban systems, and entire countries or regions. Similar issues arise with respect to complex linked natural and social systems at the center of changing climates, evolving urban environments, and questions about availability and equal access to food, water, and energy. The COVID-19 pandemic illustrates the interconnectedness of today's networks of trade, technology and medicine, and the importance of resilience of our infrastructure, supply chains, and human and social systems. That is why it is extremely necessary to support research efforts aimed at the development of better data stewardship, mathematical tools and models, providing assessment of resilience of the digitalized sociotechnological systems and their smart behavior, also under extreme and critical situations. Data science might help these systems to become more resilient, but only if a variety of challenges can be addressed. Examples of such challenges include the rapidly increasing need to re-use and combine data from numerous, distributed sources, the development of tools to address the explosion of alternatives available to policy makers, the need for algorithms to find anomalies in real-time in order to make instantaneous decisions to protect infrastructure, and the need to protect against the very vulnerabilities that the use of massive amounts of data introduce into sociotechnological systems.

The Committee on Data (CODATA) associated with the International Science Council provides multiple activities in the global data realm, organizing and supporting various international research groups whose scope is smart and sustainable operation of complex systems in the modern technosphere. CODATA is currently building a 'decadal programme' to systematically address the challenges associated with a global and data intensive society. The Task Group "Advanced mathematical tools for data-driven applied systems analysis" was established by the CODATA General Assembly in November, 2018, and has since worked out deep and widely applicable results, which were reported at a Workshop on Big Data and Systems Analysis hosted by the International Institute of Applied Systems Analysis (IIASA) in February, 2020. Papers from the Workshop, supplemented by a variety of contributions from relevant experts, form the basis for the book *Resilience in the Digital Age*, which is presented to your attention. Co-editors of this book are Prof. Fred Roberts from the United States and his Russian colleague Prof. Igor Sheremet.

I am sure that the theoretical basis and collection of applications established by the CODATA Task Group and described in this book will be of worldwide application and benefit. I hope you will enjoy reading and using it.

January 2021   Barend Mons
                                                          President of CODATA

Reference

1. Strawn, G.: 75 Years of IT: 1946–2021. IEEE magazine IT Professional (To appear)

Preface

Today mankind is seeing both great benefits and frightening potential difficulties resulting from the development of the modern digitalized technosphere. On the one hand, digitalization provides a new level of life to people through simplified and accelerated access to information, goods and services. This is the result of the Internet-based global interconnectivity of humans and devices joined to various sociotechnological systems (STSs). On the other hand, total digitalization and robotization make modern STSs extremely vulnerable to possible destructive impacts (both accidental and deliberate), whose potential consequences may be compared with the aftermath of application of weapons of mass destruction. A main reason for this situation is the aforementioned interconnectivity and associated multiple chain effects disseminating initial damage through large-scale distributed critical infrastructures. Similar issues arise for complex systems involving interactions of people and man-made artifacts with the natural environment, exacerbated by destructive impacts from changing climates, droughts and floods, earthquakes, and other natural events. The world-wide COVID-19 pandemic illustrates the vulnerability of our human and economic systems, challenging the ability of our healthcare system to provide needed service, the resilience of our supply chains to provide needed goods, and the ability of our social infrastructure to provide for economic well-being.

Fundamental to the development of today's highly digitalized STSs is the availability of vast amounts of data, but the development of tools of AI and machine learning that depend on such data can lead to problems when unexpected events (such as pandemics) occur. On the other hand, the vast amounts of data available can also be used to make modern systems more resilient.

Resilience of digitalized STSs to various destructive impacts must be achieved as a basic designed-in property. However, design and maintenance of resilient sociotechnological systems requires consideration and solution of a great many complicated multi-dimensional problems. Any valuable STS may include millions of interconnected components (humans and devices), so to assess whether an STS is resilient or vulnerable to some kind of impacts, or to design an STS with a predefined level of resiliency, it is necessary to represent in some unambiguous formal way a system's structure and logic of operation, and to develop an appropriate mathematical and algorithmic toolkit that can provide for efficient search for solutions over the extra-large volumes of heterogeneous data associated with STSs in today's era of Big Data.

This book contains both new theoretical and applied results and surveys, applicable to many practically interesting cases in the area of resilience of digitalized STSs. Most of these were reported on at the Workshop on Big Data and Systems Analysis held at the International Institute for Applied Systems Analysis (IIASA) in Laxenburg, Austria in February, 2020. The authors of the papers in this book are associated with the Task Group "Advanced mathematical tools for data-driven applied systems analysis" created and sponsored by CODATA in November, 2018.

This monograph contains three sections. The first one is dedicated to novel methods of analysis and assessment of resilience of sociotechnological systems as well as their ability to recover after destructive impacts. Various issues of interconnection between data science and systems analysis on the one hand and resilience on the other are considered in the second section. The third section is dedicated to several applications of new analytical tools to some actual problems of STSs.

In the section on Resilience of Sociotechnological Systems, the paper by Roberts (Chapter 1) explores disruptions of complex networks due to disease events, fires, outages in the power grid, and damage to critical infrastructure, and describes algorithms for responding to a disruption that minimize the departure from a previous state – a central component of the notion of resilience. Sheremet's paper (Chapter 2) develops in detail a multigrammatical framework that provides a way to represent the technological and resource bases of today's large-scale industrial systems as well as the transformations resulting from destructive impacts of natural hazards, pandemics, terrorist events or technological glitches, and introduces general criteria for the resilience, recoverability, and supportability of an affected industrial system. The paper by Hassani, Komendantova and Unger (Chapter 3) introduces the use of an entropy weight method for assessing the vulnerability of digitalized sociotechnological systems, based on the principle that assessment of the weaknesses in the structure of such systems improves relative to the reduction in information redundancies and losses and the improvement in information accuracy and efficiency. Ermolieva et al. (Chapter 4) describe two-stage stochastic optimization and stochastic quasigradient (SQG) procedures to manage STSs under uncertainty and risk; two-stage optimization helps to design a robust portfolio of strategic and adaptive operational decisions making the systems robust with respect to potential uncertainty and risks, while SQG iterative algorithms define a kind of sequential adaptive learning search aimed at improvement of decisions from data and simulations. In the final paper in this section, Wang et al. (Chapter 5) discuss how robotics can be deployed to enhance pre-emptive measures or post-disaster responses and increase resiliency against disasters.

The section on Data Science and Resilience begins with a paper by Gvishiani, Dobrovolsky and Rybkina (Chapter 6) on Big Data and FAIR Data for Data Science. The availability of large amounts of data can aid in the development of resilient sociotechnological systems. This paper explores current directions in data processing and handling and describes principles of FAIRness to ensure that data are made available, can be analyzed and integrated with other data through the use of common terminology and reusable formats, and include detailed information about the origin of the data and explicit data use licenses. A second paper by Roberts (Chapter 7) points out that data science may hold the key to making our systems more resilient, for example by allowing us to monitor the state of the power grid, get early warning of emerging diseases, find ways to minimize the effect of flooding, identify looming problems in supply chains, provide early warning of anomalies, and receive alerts that a system may be approaching a critical threshold, thus allowing more time for mitigation that will minimize the effect of disruptions. However, for tools of data science to help us create more resilient systems, we will need to overcome a variety of challenges, and it is these challenges that he discusses in his paper. The third paper in this section, by Panfilov and Suleykin (Chapter 8), deals with the extract-transform-load

(ETL) processes that play a crucial role in data analysis in real-time data warehouse environments. This paper explores a special Metadata Framework designed to address the problem that ETL processes are becoming bottlenecks in warehouse environments and to provide resilience of the ETL process.

The final section of the book, the one on Applications, has two papers. The first, by Usman et al. (Chapter 9), deals with the interactions between humans and built environments, and focuses on how AI techniques can be used to inform the design and management of today's smart and connected buildings and make such buildings resilient. The second paper in this section starts with the observation that misinformation and its dissemination is one of the most pressing issues facing our world today, exacerbated by modern and emerging communications technologies and the rise of social media, and potentially leading to both national and global conflicts of all kinds. In this paper, Komendantova et al. (Chapter 10) discuss the need for sociotechnical solutions, in particular AI tools, to increase the overall societal resilience against misinformation, and explore misinformation detection tools in the context of immigration in Austria.

The editors would like to thank Amy Luers, Global Lead for Sustainability Science at Microsoft, for the inspiration for the title. The idea that the world of Big Data and digitalization could contribute to sustainability emerged from the work of Dr. Luers that eventually expanded to become the initiative called Sustainability in the Digital Age (https://sustainabilitydigitalage.org). That initiative "works to leverage the digital age to drive societal transformations toward a more sustainable and equitable world." The editors are grateful to Dr. Luers for her encouragement to use a title that reflects her leadership and hopefully contributes to the initiative she started.

The editors are thankful to the CODATA President Prof. Barend Mons, Vice President Dr. John Broome, and Executive Director Dr. Simon Hodson for their continuous support and sponsorship of the Task Group (TG). Also the editors are grateful to the IIASA Director General Dr. Albert van Jaarsveld, his Deputy Director for Science Dr. Leena Srivastava, Prof. Nebojsa Nakicenovic, and Dr. Elena Rovenskaya for their effort in hosting the TG Workshop at IIASA. Numerous reviewers contributed to the success of this volume by reading the papers and suggesting changes. Kenneth Spassione, Esq., read over every paper, proposed changes in the language, suggested changes in organization and presentation, and asked the authors for clarification and modifications when things were unclear. He also helped format all of the papers in the volume, and the editors are extremely thankful for his help.

December 2020   Fred S. Roberts
                                                                   Igor A. Sheremet

Contents

Applications

Resilience of SocioTechnological Systems

Resilience of Social-Technological Systems

Chapter 1
Resilience Algorithms in Complex Networks

Fred S. Roberts(✉)

DIMACS Center, Rutgers University, Piscataway, NJ 08854, USA
froberts@dimacs.rutgers.edu

Abstract. Today's complex systems are vulnerable to disruptions from natural, deliberate, and accidental events. The paper explores resilience of systems under disruptions due to disease events, fires, outages in the power grid, and damage to critical infrastructure, and describes algorithms for responding to a disruption that minimize the departure from a previous state.

Keywords: Resilience · Disease spread · Power grid · Infrastructure repair

1 Resilience

Today's society has become dependent on complex systems, enabled by increased digitization of our world and the increasingly ubiquitous nature of intelligent machines, that have had a great impact on virtually all facets of our lives and our societies: enabling our financial transactions, running our power grid, underpinning our transportation systems, empowering our health care, supporting the rapid delivery of supplies and materials. Yet these changes have made us vulnerable to natural disasters, deliberate attacks, just plain errors. In recent years, *"resilience"* of complex natural and social systems has become a major area of emphasis; resilience in response to hurricanes, disease events, floods, earthquakes, cyber attacks, ...

The general concept of resilience is the ability of a system to recover from disasters or attacks and avoid catastrophic collapse. We can think of a system existing within a "normal healthy range" as measured under some parameter or parameters. In a resilient system, values will return to the normal healthy range after a disruption. Or they might establish a new healthy range – one that is not that far from the previous one. See Fig. 1.

There are many parameters that measure a "healthy" system. Some will get back into their normal healthy range faster than others. Do we ask that the longest time to return to this range be small? Or that the average time to return to this range be small? There are many such questions that we need to answer before being able to define resilience precisely.

One approach to resilience is to develop algorithms for responding to a disruption that will minimize the departure from the previous state when things settle down. Another is to design systems that can bounce back from disruptions quickly. In this paper we will emphasize the former. We will illustrate this with four examples built around models

© Springer Nature Switzerland AG 2021
F. S. Roberts and I. A. Sheremet (Eds.): Resilience in the Digital Age, LNCS 12660, pp. 3–15, 2021.
https://doi.org/10.1007/978-3-030-70370-7_1

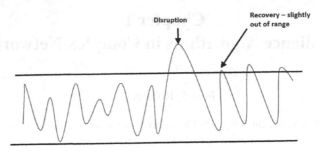

Fig. 1. A resilient system returns to its normal healthy range or one close to it.

using graphs and networks and will present "toy" examples that illustrate the main points about how algorithms might help in creating more resilient systems: containing the spread of disease, mitigating the effect of fires, controlling cascading outages in the power grid, and reopening a damaged infrastructure network.

2   Spread and Control of Disease

The spread of the new Coronavirus COVID-19 is the latest (and most drastic) example of a newly emerging disease that threatens not only lives but our economy and our social systems. SARS, MERS, Ebola, and Zika are other recent examples.

Modern transportation systems allow for rapid spread of diseases. Diseases are spread through social networks. "*Contact tracing*" is an important part of any strategy to combat outbreaks of infectious diseases, whether naturally occurring or resulting from bioterrorist attacks. We will illustrate the ideas with some fairly simple "toy" models that will illustrate concepts of resilience.

We model a social network as an undirected graph. The vertices of the graph represent people and there is an edge between two people if they are in contact. We imagine that the vertices are in different states at different times. In the simplest "toy" model, there are two states, a susceptible state that we will represent with a green vertex and an infected state that we will represent with a red vertex. Times are discrete: $t = 0, 1, 2, \ldots$ Let $s_i(t)$ give the state of vertex i at time t. This is sometimes called an SI model. More complex models might include susceptible S, exposed E, infected I, recovered R, and possibly split by age group, sex, etc.: SI, SEI, SEIR models,...

We will consider a very simple process called an *Irreversible k-Threshold Process* in which an individual changes their state from green to red at time $t + 1$ if at least k of their neighbors are in state red at time t. Moreover, an individual never leaves state red. The disease interpretation is that an individual is infected if sufficiently many of their neighbors are infected. In the special case $k = 1$, an individual is infected if any of their neighbors is infected. Figure 2 describes an irreversible 2-threshold process. It shows how the disease spreads from two infected vertices at time 0 to four at time 1, because each of the two new infected vertices had two infected neighbors. After that, no more spread can occur since the remaining uninfected vertices have only one infected neighbor. Figure 3 describes an irreversible 3-threshold process. Two of the green vertices turn red at time 1 since they have three red neighbors at time 0, but the third does not. It turns red at time 2 because at time 1 it now has three red neighbors.

A great deal of attention has been paid to a saturation problem, the *Attacker's Problem*: Given a graph, what subsets S of the vertices should we plant a disease with so that ultimately the maximum number of people will get it? This has an economic interpretation: What set of people do we place a new product with to guarantee "saturation" of the product in the population?

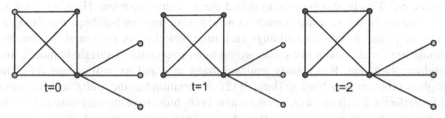

Fig. 2. An irreversible 2-threshold process. (Color figure online)

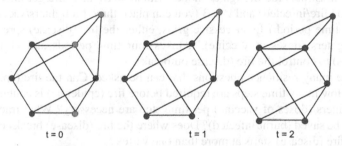

Fig. 3. An irreversible 3-threshold process. (Color figure online)

These problems are hard in a formal sense. Consider the problem called *IRRE-VERSIBLE k-CONVERSION SET*: Given a positive integer p and a graph G, does G have a set S of size at most p so that if all vertices of S are infected at the beginning, then all vertices will ultimately be infected? Dreyer and Roberts [1] showed that IRRE-VERSIBLE k-CONVERSION SET is NP-complete for fixed $k > 2$. For many more results about irreversible k-conversion sets, see [1].

There are various complications that have been considered in this model. For example, one could take $k = 1$, but a person only gets infected with a certain probability. Or, a person is automatically cured after being in the infected state for d time periods. Or, a public health authority could have the ability to "vaccinate" a certain number of vertices, making them immune from infection. It is the vaccination strategy that relates to the resilience question and it is natural to ask: Can we find vaccination strategies (algorithms) that minimize the number of people who get sick, i.e., minimize departure from the normal. It is also natural to ask: Can we find vaccination strategies that minimize the amount of time before an outbreak is controlled, i.e., minimize time to return to normal. We turn to these questions next.

3 Vaccination Strategies: Vaccinations and Fighting Fires

Mathematical models are very helpful in comparing alternative vaccination strategies. The problem is especially interesting if we think of protecting against deliberate infection by a bioterrorist attacker but applies if we think of "nature" as the attacker.

Another simple toy example considers an irreversible k-threshold model where a defender can vaccinate v people per time period but an attacker can only infect people at the beginning. We might ask: What vaccination strategy minimizes number of people infected? This is also sometimes called the *firefighter problem*. Here, we think of a forest or a city where a fire spreads to neighboring trees or buildings and firefighters can be placed at trees or buildings each time period to try to control the fire. We alternate fire spread which occurs according to an irreversible k-threshold model, and firefighter placement. It is usually assumed that $k = 1$ and we will assume this. The firefighter problem goes back to Hartnell [2]. A variation has the firefighter/vaccinator and fire/infector alternate turns, having v new firefighters to place/vaccination doses to give per time period and i new fires/new doses of pathogen per period. What is a good strategy for the firefighter/vaccinator?

Figure 4 illustrates the firefighter model with $k = 1$ (catch fire/get infected if one neighbor is on fire/infected) and $v = 3$ (you can place three firefighters/vaccinate three people each time period.) In successive grids, either the fire (disease) spreads or one places firefighters (doses of vaccine). It takes four time periods and 11 firefighters (vaccinations) to control the fire (disease outbreak).

There are many resilience questions that can be asked. Can the fire (epidemic) be contained? How many time steps are required before fire (epidemic) is contained? How many firefighters (doses of vaccine) per time step are necessary? What fraction of all vertices will be saved (burnt/infected)? Does where the fire (disease) breaks out matter? What if the fire (disease) starts at more than one vertex?

Consider the case of an infinite d-dimensional grid. With $d = 2$ (similar to the grids in Fig. 4), it is easy to see that a fire (disease outbreak) cannot be controlled with one firefighter (vaccine dose) per time period. With $d = 2$ and $v = 2$ (two firefighters or vaccinations per time period), one can show that a fire (disease) starting at one vertex can be controlled in eight time steps, with 18 trees burned (people infected). Develin and Hartke [3] showed that one cannot do better than 18 steps and Wang and Moeller [4] that one cannot contain the fire (disease outbreak) in less than eight steps. If $d \geq 3$, note that every vertex has 2d neighbors. Thus: 2d-1 firefighters (vaccine doses) per time step are sufficient to contain any outbreak starting at a single vertex. Develin and Hartke [3] showed that if $d \geq 3$, $2d - 2$ firefighters (vaccine doses) per time step are not enough to contain an outbreak. However, with $2d - 1$ firefighters (doses) per time step containment can be attained in two time steps. This is just one example of a result, and there is an extensive literature on the firefighter problem by now.

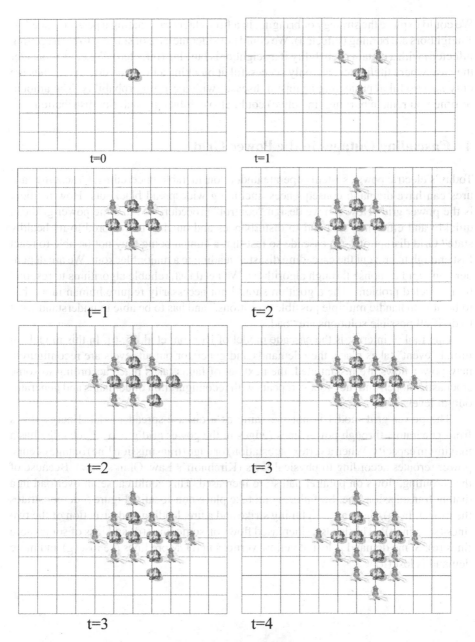

Fig. 4. The firefighter model with $k = 1$, $v = 3$. Thanks to Kah Loon Ng for help with this figure.

There are many variants of the irreversible k-threshold model that would make the firefighter problem more realistic. A vertex could stay in the burning (infected state) for T time periods after entering it and then go back to the non-burning (uninfected) state – which is more appropriate for the disease application than the firefighting application.

We could explore the strategy of bringing in a firefighter (vaccinating a person) once $k - 1$ neighbors are burning (infected). We could consider the case of starting to burn (getting infected) with a certain probability if a neighbor is burning (infected). We could consider the case where firefighters are only successful at blocking a fire at a vertex (vaccines are only successful at protecting against a disease) with a certain probability. The amount of time you remain burning (infective) could also exhibit a probability distribution.

4 Cascading Outages in the Power Grid

Today's electric power systems operate under considerable uncertainty. Cascading failures can have dramatic consequences, including widespread blackouts. How resilient is the power grid? How can we design "control" procedures so that the power grid can quickly and efficiently respond to disturbances and quickly be restored to its healthy state? Grid disruptions can cascade so fast that a human being may not be able to react fast enough to prevent the cascading disaster, leading to a major blackout. We are dependent on rapid response through algorithms. We need fast, reliable algorithms to respond to a detected problem. The algorithm should not necessarily require human input, has to be able to handle multiple possible "solutions," and has to be able to understand what to do if all possible solutions are "bad."

One tool of interest is the cascade model of Dobson, et al. [5, 6]. In this model, an initial "event" takes place, then demands and generator output levels are reconfigured, new power flows are instantiated, the next set of faults takes place according to some stochastic model, and the process repeats with reconfiguration of demands and generator output levels.

The power grid model is not the same as a disease-spread model. Energy flows from generators through power lines (edges in the power grid graph). Each edge has a maximum capacity. When a vertex (substation) or edge (transmission line) outage occurs, power reroutes according to physical laws (Kirchhoff's Law, Ohm's Law). Because of the rerouting, flows on parallel paths are increased. This could cause an overload in a distant transmission line. So failures can take place non-locally. Figure 5 demonstrates the model. In (b), there are a lightning strike and a fire, leading to destruction of the two lines (seen in (c)). This leads to increased flows on some lines (d) and loss of some more lines (e). Some demand is lost at yellow vertices in (f). More lines are lost (g) and more demand is lost (h).

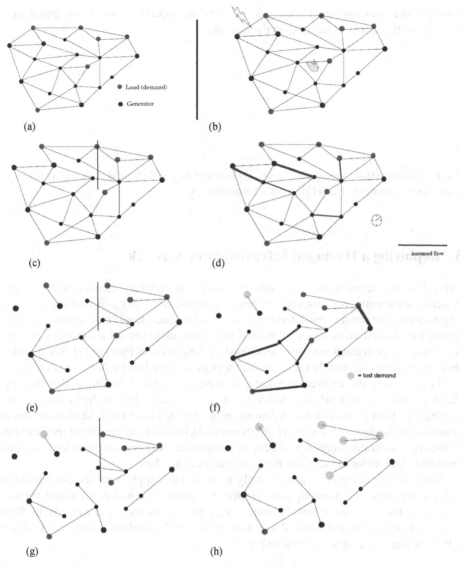

Fig. 5. The cascade model for power grids. Red edges show increased flow. Yellow nodes show lost demand. Thanks to Daniel Bienstock for the figures (Color figure online).

The cascade model shows what might happen if a system is left alone. However, it can be used to develop algorithms to "take control." Instead of waiting for the next set of faults to take place according to some stochastic process, one can use the cascade model to learn how to take measurements and apply control to shed demand and to reconfigure generator outputs and get new power flows. One can also use the model to learn how best to create islands to protect part of the grid. Hopefully the islands are small and in the rest of the grid, supply is greater than demand. Figure 6 illustrates the point. By cutting some lines, one divides the grid into islands, hopefully a small one and a large one, where the supply is larger than the demand.

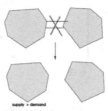

Fig. 6. Cutting out lines creates islands and in the rest of the grid (left-most part), supply is greater than demand. Thanks to Daniel Bienstock for the figures.

5   Repairing a Damaged Infrastructure Network

Critical infrastructure systems include transportation systems, telecom, water supply systems, wastewater systems, electric power systems, etc. After a disruption, a system begins to restore service until returning to a performance level *at or below* the level before the disruption. A series of models that allow us to reason about infrastructure resilience under disruptions were developed by Sharkey and Pinkley [7]. We describe their ideas in this section. In these models, service is described by flows in networks.

In contrast to the undirected graphs we have worked with so far, in the Sharkey-Pinkley models, a network now has vertices and directed edges (called *arcs*). A flow can only go from vertex i to vertex j along an arc directed from i to j. Vertices represent components that generate services (supply vertices), locations where one alters the routes of the services (transshipment vertices), or components that consume services (demand vertices). Arcs move the services from one vertex to another.

Consider for example a water supply system. The supply vertices correspond to water companies, the transshipment vertices to substations, and the demand vertices to households, factories, hospitals, malls, etc. Pipes are the arcs, and water is the flow. Meeting as much demand as possible is modeled as the classical maximum flow problem – both before and after a disruption (Fig. 7).

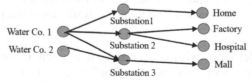

Fig. 7. A water supply system with two supply vertices, three transshipment vertices, and four demand vertices.

Consider a network $G = (V,A)$ where V is a set of vertices and A a set of arcs. The arc i to j has a *capacity* u_{ij}. In the simplest case, we have one supply vertex s and one demand vertex t. There is a *supply A(s)* at s and a *demand B(t)* at t. We seek to assign a *flow x_{ij}* to the arc from i to j. The flow along that arc must be at most the capacity:

$$x_{ij} \leq u_{ij}.$$

The classic maximum flow problem assumes that we have *flow conservation*: The sum of flows on arcs into a vertex equals the sum of flows out of the vertex. If $A(i) = \{j: (i,j) \in A\}$, then this says:

$$\sum_{j \in A(i)} x_{ij} = \sum_{j:i \in A(j)} x_{ji}$$

We also assume that the total flow out of s cannot exceed the supply $A(s)$ and the total flow into t cannot exceed the demand $B(t)$. We seek to maximize the total flow that reaches t. Thus, the *Maximum Flow Problem* seeks to determine the largest amount of flow that can reach t while keeping the flow on each arc at most the capacity, not exceeding total supply and demand, and satisfying the flow conservation requirement at each vertex. The famous augmenting path algorithm (Ford-Fulkerson Algorithm) finds the maximum flow.

Note that the maximum flow problem is a simplification. It assumes that there are no other constraints on flow. This might apply to supply chain networks, for example when physical goods move through intermediate warehouses and distribution centers.

For more complicated infrastructure, there are things like physical laws offering additional constraints. For example, there are Kirchhoff's and Ohm's Laws for power grid networks. In water distribution networks, there are constraints involving the relation between flow of water and pressure.

Figure 8 shows a network with capacities on arcs and supply and demand at the supply and demand vertices and Fig. 9 shows the maximum flow in the network. The flow is maximum because the flow from x to y is at most 2, so s to x is at most 2, so out of s is at most 40.

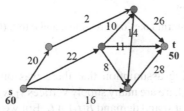

Blue: supply and demand
Black: Capacity

Fig. 8. A network with capacities on arcs and supply and demand at supply and demand vertices. (Color figure online)

If some of the arcs in a network are destroyed, we might ask in what order we should reopen them. There are various possible objectives. One goal might be to get closest to the original maximum flow as early as possible. Consider the example of Fig. 10 where

12   F. S. Roberts

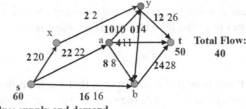

Blue: supply and demand
Black: Capacity
Red: Flow

Fig. 9. The flow in this network is maximum. (Color figure online)

a lightning storm has taken out two arcs of the network of Fig. 9. Assume that the arc b to t can be repaired fully but the arc s to a can only be repaired to a lower capacity of 15, as shown in Fig. 11. That figure also shows the maximum flow if arc s to a is fixed first and arc b to t is not yet repaired so has no capacity. The maximum flow is 17. Figure 12 shows the maximum flow if arc b to t is fixed first and arc s to a is not yet repaired so has no capacity. That flow is 18, which is better, so to obtain the best flow after one repair we would repair the arc b to t first. Figure 13 shows the maximum flow once both arcs are repaired, but arc s to a only to reduced capacity. We only regained a reduced max flow of 33 so didn't fully restore the flow of 40.

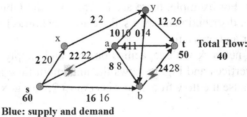

Blue: supply and demand
Black: Capacity
Red: Flow

Fig. 10. A lightning storm takes out arcs s to a and b to t. (Color figure online)

We made the simplifying assumption that there was one supply vertex and one demand vertex. In practice, there are many supply vertices $s_1, s_2, \ldots,$ and demand vertices $t_1, t_2, \ldots,$ with supply $A(s_i)$ at s_i and demand $B(t_i)$ at t_i. But we can reduce this to a single supply and demand vertex by adding a supply vertex S with supply $A(S) = \sum A(s_i)$ and an arc from S to each s_i with capacity $A(s_i)$ and a demand vertex T with demand $B(T) = \sum B(t_i)$ and an arc from each t_i to T with capacity $B(t_i)$.

As different components of a network are repaired (to the extent possible), the maximum flow increases. How far off it is from the original max flow when repairs are done is one metric for resilience. How long it takes to complete the repairs is another metric for resilience. We turn next to the repair process.

A different approach to reopening damaged components uses the theory of machine scheduling. After a disruption, repairs are made so services can be restored. Repairs use

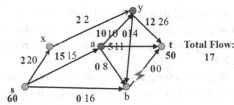

Blue: supply and demand
Black: Capacity
Red: Flow
Purple: Reduced Capacity

Fig. 11. Maximum flow if arc s to a is repaired to reduced capacity of 15 while arc b to t is not yet repaired. (Color figure online)

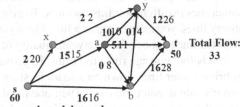

Blue: supply and demand
Black: Capacity
Red: Flow
Purple: Reduced Capacity

Fig. 12. Maximum flow if arc b to t is repaired to original capacity while arc s to a is not yet repaired. (Color figure online)

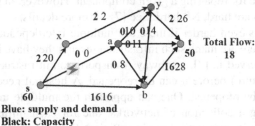

Blue: supply and demand
Black: Capacity
Red: Flow
Purple: Reduced Capacity

Fig. 13. Maximum flow if arcs s to a and b to t are repaired, the former to reduced capacity. (Color figure online)

scarce *resources*: work crews, equipment. Let us make the simplifying assumption that one can only repair one *component at a time (one vertex or arc). We need a schedule for when a resource will be repairing* a component. In the scheduling literature, we talk about jobs on a set of machines, and processing them. *Jobs* here correspond to damaged components. *Machines* correspond to work crews. Each job (damaged component) k has a different level of *importance* w_k. Each job also has a *duration* p_k. In the scheduling literature, each job k is assigned to a machine (work crew) m_k. The jobs assigned to a machine (work crew) m are given an order. So the *completion time* C_k of job k is the sum of the durations of all jobs assigned to the machine (crew) m_k that precede job k plus the duration of job k.

There are various objectives for a good repair schedule. One might be to minimize the weighted average completion time over all jobs, with the weight measuring the importance of the job:

$$\min \sum_k w_k C_k$$

This is sometimes called the *restoration performance*. If there is just one work crew, a greedy algorithm minimizes this: Repair component k in non-increasing order of the ratio w_k/p_k. A similar algorithm works if there many machines but each has the same processing time for repairing a given component. However, in general, most such scheduling problems are hard, NP-hard. See [7] for more details.

The problem gets even harder if there are multiple interdependent infrastructures. In a complex city, there are many such infrastructures and they have interdependencies. For example, as observed in [7], a subway (transportation infrastructure) needs power (electrical infrastructure) before it can be reopened. A hospital needs both power and water before it can be reopened. One can approach the multiple infrastructure repair problem by studying a collection of networks, one for each infrastructure. A given infrastructure cannot operate until there is sufficient level of service (flow) on certain specific vertices in other infrastructures. Scheduling repair of different infrastructures will therefore depend on these interdependencies. There is a considerable literature on this topic. Another complication: There could be interdependencies among repair jobs, sometimes in different infrastructures. Scheduling repair of different infrastructures will therefore depend on these interdependencies. Another complication: interdependencies among repair jobs – sometimes in different infrastructures. To give an example from [7], note that to reopen subway lines, you need to repair a line. Once you repair the lines, you need to run a test train on the line to check for safety and quality of the repair. But power to the line must be restored before you can run a test train. To give another example from [7], suppose that trees bring power lines down on a road. First one needs to do a safety inspection to make sure it's safe to enter the road. Then one must clear debris from the road. Then one can repair downed power lines. There is a considerable literature on this and related topics. See [7] for a discussion.

6   Closing Comments

We have presented several simple examples of how to generate responses to disruptive events. Even these simple examples lead to problems that are "hard" in a precise sense.

Another approach is to study ways to design graphs or networks so as to make them more resilient in case of disruption. That is a topic for another paper.

Acknowledgement. The author thanks the National Science Foundation for support under grants CCF-1934924 and DMS-1737857 to Rutgers University.

References

1. Dreyer, P.A., Jr., Roberts, F.S.: Irreversible k-threshold processes: graph-theoretical threshold models of the spread of disease and of opinion. Discrete Applied Mathematics **157**, 1615–1627 (2009)
2. Hartnell, B.: Firefighter! An application of domination. In: Presentation. 20th Conference on Numerical Mathematics and Computing, University of Manitoba, Winnipeg, Canada, September 1995
3. Develin, M., Hartke, S.G.: Fire containment in grids of dimension three and higher. Discrete Appl. Math. **155**, 2257–2268 (2007)
4. Wang, P., Moeller, S.A.: Fire control on graphs. J. Combin. Math. Combin. Comput. **41**, 19–34 (2002)
5. Dobson, I., Carreras, B.A., Lynch, V.E., Newman, D.E.: Complex systems analysis of series of blackouts: cascading failure, critical points, self-organization. Chaos **17**, 026103 (2007). https://doi.org/10.1063/1.2737822
6. Dobson, I., Carreras, B.A., Newman, D.E.: A loading-dependent model of probabilistic cascading failure. Probab. Eng. Inform. Sci. **19**(1), 15–32 (2005)
7. Sharkey, T.C., Pinkley, S.G.N.: Quantitative models for infrastructure restoration after extreme events: network optimization meets scheduling. In: Kaper, H.G., Roberts, F.S. (eds.) Mathematics of Planet Earth: Protecting Our Planet, Learning from the Past, Safeguarding for the Future, vol. 5, pp. 313–336. Springer, Cham (2019). https://doi.org/10.1007/978-3-030-22044-0_12

Chapter 2
Application of the Multigrammatical Framework to the Assessment of Resilience and Recoverability of Large – Scale Industrial Systems

Igor A. Sheremet$^{(\boxtimes)}$

Russian Foundation for Basic Research, Moscow, Russia
sheremet@rfbr.ru

Abstract. The present paper is dedicated to assessing the resilience and the possibility of recovery and support of large-scale industrial systems (*ISs*) affected by
destructive impacts such as natural hazards, technogenic catastrophes, acts of terror, pandemics, mutual sanctions, etc. The proposed approach to these problems
is based on the application of the multigrammatical framework that provides a
natural and flexible representation of the technological and resource bases of *ISs*
as well as their transformations after impacts. We introduce a general criteria for
the resilience, recoverability, and supportability of the affected industrial system
by other external *IS* with it's own technological and resource bases.

Keywords: Resilience · Vulnerability · Industrial systems · Recovery · Support ·
Multisets · Multiset grammars

1 Introduction

The problem of assessing the resilience/vulnerability of various classes of sociotechnological systems (*STSs*) to destructive impacts has been studied for a long time [1–15].
In the context of the applicability of mathematical tools, a comprehensive survey of the
different problems considered in this area was done in [16]. According to the ontology
proposed in [16], we can find the following cases of *STS*, orders completed by *STS*, and
impacts on *STS*:

1) an *STS* may be local (*LSTS*) or distributed (*DSTS*);
2) orders to an *STS* may be single or multiple (the last case covers flows of orders
   incoming to an *STS* sequentially);
3) impacts on an *STS* may affect the resource base (*RB*) of such *STS*, i.e., the set of
   resources available to the system while operating. They may also affect it's technological base (*TB*), i.e., the set of facilities (devices) that form the system and operate
   resources. In both cases, there might have cascade (or chain) effects that multiply

© Springer Nature Switzerland AG 2021
F. S. Roberts and I. A. Sheremet (Eds.): Resilience in the Digital Age, LNCS 12660, pp. 16–34, 2021.
https://doi.org/10.1007/978-3-030-70370-7_2

the consequences of the initial impact by transferring destructions or malfunctions through interconnections between subsystems (elements) of the *STS* in question. This phenomenon can be generalized to the case of multiple impacts or flows of impacts incoming to the *STS* in unpredicted moments.

The problems that single impacts pose to the resilience/vulnerability of local and distributed *STS* were considered by the author in [17–20] via the application of multiset grammars (multigrammars, *MGs*) developed objectively as a basic knowledge representation for large-scale *STSs* assessment and optimization [21, 22]. Primary multigrammatical criteria for the recognition of resilience of distributed industrial systems (*IS*) to the destructive impacts were formulated in [17]. A more sophisticated case of distributed *STS*, including not only production, but also consumption (where customers are the sources of the orders to the *IS*) was considered in [18]. In that paper, the criteria formulated in [17] were generalized for critical infrastructures (*Cis*) – multiple interconnected *DSTS* that produce and deliver to the consumers various basic resources, such as fuel, heat, electrical energy, etc. In addition, cases of partial completion of orders by affected *ISs* were studied in [18], and the relations to compute the maximal part of the order that can be completed given the *RB* and the *TB* remaining after an impact, were also derived. Those criteria define the *necessary* conditions for sustainability. Therefore, *STS* which do not satisfy these conditions are vulnerable. Since these conditions are only necessary but not *sufficient*, there may be additional conditions for the sustainability of these systems. However, not satisfying those necessary conditions guarantee the vulnerability of the *STS* considered.

All the aforementioned results concern the case of a so-called "closed" *STS*. This type of *STSs* cannot obtain resources that may help in mitigating the consequences of an impact. This may be done in two ways: (1) necessary resources and devices may be produced by some external industrial systems (*EISs*) and relocated to the resource and technological bases of the affected *STS*; (2) *EIS* may support the affected *STS* by completing an order partially, that was due to be completed entirely by the *STS* when the impact was applied. However, it is not clear a priori whether *EIS* capabilities are sufficient to recover and support the affected *STS* for the entire order completion after an impact has taken place. Accordingly, it is important to find criteria for assessing if the capabilities of the aforementioned *EIS* are sufficient.

This paper tackles this assessment with the application of the tool already used in [17–20]: unitary multiset grammars (*UMGs*), a simplified version of *MGs* with reduced computational complexity when it comes to searching solutions.

We shall limit our scope to affected *industrial* systems. Every such system includes only manufacturing (producing) facilities (devices), interacting and operating as a whole while completing orders entered by external customers. Let us remind that facilities (devices) form the technological base of an *IS*, while resources, which are available to the *TB* during it's operation, form the resource base of an *IS*. In general, an impact eliminates elements from both the resource and the technological bases of an *IS* and results in a reduced capability of the affected *IS* to complete the order.

As mentioned above, there are external industrial systems which may mitigate the consequences of an impact in two ways: (1) by the recovery of the affected *IS* and (2) by their support as described above. *EISs* have their own *RBs* and *TBs*, which are not accessible to any impacts. However, the capabilities of these *EISs* are also limited, and the question studied in this paper is to assess whether a given *EIS* may or may not complete the order due by the *IS* that was affected by an impact.

If an affected vulnerable *IS* can be recovered by an *EIS*, we say that such *IS* is *recoverable* by this *EIS*. We refer to this property as the *recoverability* of an *IS*. Similarly, if an affected vulnerable *IS* may be supported by an *EIS*, this *IS* is *supportable* by this *EIS* (i.e. the *IS* has the *supportability* property). We shall consider here only a core case of a *local IS* and *EIS*. This case can be generalized on distributed systems easily via the techniques introduced in [17, 18].

In what follows, Sect. 2 is dedicated to basic notions, definitions, and criteria that serve as a mathematical background for the next section. Section 3 contains the main results on the criterial base developed for the assessment of the capabilities of an external industrial system to recover the resource and technological bases of the affected *IS*. It also contains results that stem from the application of the joint *TB* and *RB* and that are aimed at supporting the *IS* to complete an order interrupted by a destructive impact.

2 Basic Notions, Definitions, and Criteria

2.1 Operations on Multisets and Sets of Multisets

A multiset (*MS*) is usually defined as a set of multiobjects (*MOs*), denoted as $n \cdot a$, where n is the multiplicity of object a. Therefore, this record denotes n indistinguishable (identical) objects a. In turn, the record

$$v = \{n_1 \cdot a_1, ..., n_m \cdot a_m\} \tag{1}$$

denotes a multiset that contains n_1 objects a_1, ..., n_m objects a_m, for every $i \neq j \; a_i \neq a_j$. Object a and multiobject $1 \cdot a$ are equivalent entities. In general, positive rational numbers may be used as multiplicities along with positive integer numbers [23, 24].

The symbols "$\in$" and "$\notin$" are used below for denoting that an object a enters or does not enter a multiset v (or, in other words, to claim that the *MS* v includes or does not include the *MO* a). Therefore, we will use notation such as $a \in v$ and $a \notin v$, respectively. The same symbols are used for a multiobject $n \cdot a$. Both $0 \cdot a \in v$ and $a \notin v$ mean that the object a does not enter the *MS* v. In other words, an object a with zero multiplicity is equivalent to an object absent in the *MS* v. The empty set and the empty multiset are denoted, as usually, by the symbol $\{\emptyset\}$. The set

$$\beta(v) = \{a_1, ..., a_m\}, \tag{2}$$

where v is defined by (1), is called the basis of *MS* v [23].

There are two main relations on multisets:

1. A *MS* $v = \{n_1 \cdot a_1, ..., n_m \cdot a_m\}$ is a submultiset of another *MS* $v' = \{n'_1 \cdot a'_1, ..., n'_m \cdot a'_m\}$ if for every $n \cdot a \in v$ the *MS* v' includes $n' \cdot a$ such that $n' \geq n$. This is denoted as

$$v \subseteq v', \tag{3}$$

where the bold symbol $\subseteq$ means a relation of inclusion of the *MS* v in the *MS* v'.

2. If for at least one $n \cdot a \in v$ the MS v' includes $n' \cdot a$ such that $n' > n$ or $\beta(v) \subset \beta(v')$, this is denoted by

$$v \subset v', \tag{4}$$

where the bold symbol $\subset$ indicates a relation of strict inclusion of the MS v in the MS v'. Let us illustrate these concepts with an example that we will use throughout this paper.

Example 1. Let
$v_1 = \{10 \cdot \langle eur \rangle, 3 \cdot \langle usd \rangle, 5 \cdot \langle rur \rangle\}$,
$v_2 = \{10 \cdot \langle eur \rangle, 5 \cdot \langle usd \rangle, 5 \cdot \langle rur \rangle\}$.
where objects names are represented by strings in angle brackets. Per the definitions introduced above, we have that $v_1 \subseteq v_2$ and $v_1 \subset v_2$. Also, if
$v_3 = \{10 \cdot \langle eur \rangle, 5 \cdot \langle usd \rangle, 5 \cdot \langle rur \rangle, 1 \cdot \langle computer \rangle\}$,
then it follows that $v_2 \subseteq v_3$ and $v_2 \subset v_3$. ■

Below we shall use some well-known operations on multisets, namely, addition, subtraction, and multiplication by a constant. We denote these operations by the bold symbols $+$, $-$ and $*$, respectively:

$$v + v' = \bigcup_{\substack{a \in \beta(v) \cup \beta(v') \\ n \cdot a \in v \\ n' \cdot a \in v'}} \{(n + n') \cdot a\}, \tag{5}$$

$$v - v' = \bigcup_{\substack{n \cdot a \in v \\ n' \cdot a \in v' \\ n > n'}} \{(n - n') \cdot a\}, \tag{6}$$

$$n * \{n_1 \cdot a_1, \ldots, n_m \cdot a_m\} = \{(n \times n_1) \cdot a_1, \ldots, (n \times n_m) \cdot a_m\}, \tag{7}$$

where the symbol $\times$ represents the multiplication of integer numbers.

We will also use set-theoretic operations on multisets, namely, join and intersection, which we shall denote by bold symbols $\cup$ and $\cap$:

$$v \cup v' = \bigcup_{\substack{a \in \beta(v) \cup \beta(v') \\ n \cdot a \in v \\ n' \cdot a \in v'}} \{max(n, n') \cdot a\}, \tag{8}$$

$$v \cap v' = \bigcap_{\substack{a \in \beta(v) \cup \beta(v') \\ n \cdot a \in v \\ n' \cdot a \in v'}} \{min(n, n') \cdot a\}, \tag{9}$$

Note that in Eqs. (3)–(7) we used the aforementioned equivalence between $a \notin v$ and $0 \cdot a \in v$.

Example 2. Let
$v_1 = \{10 \cdot \langle eur \rangle, 3 \cdot \langle usd \rangle\}$,
$v_2 = \{4 \cdot \langle usd \rangle, 5 \cdot \langle computer \rangle\}$.
Then
$v_1 + v_2 = \{10 \cdot \langle eur \rangle, 7 \cdot \langle usd \rangle, 5 \cdot \langle computer \rangle\}$,
$v_1 - v_2 = \{10 \cdot \langle eur \rangle\}$,
$3 * v_2 = \{12 \cdot \langle usd \rangle, 15 \cdot \langle computer \rangle\}$,
$v_1 \cup v_2 = \{10 \cdot \langle eur \rangle, 4 \cdot \langle usd \rangle, 5 \cdot \langle computer \rangle\}$,
$v_1 \cap v_2 = \{3 \cdot \langle usd \rangle\}$.   ■

All the operations defined use multisets as operands and are well known [23, 24].

The operations that follow are defined on sets on multisets (*SMSs*) and were introduced and applied in [17–20] for *STSs* modelling. As explained in [23, 24], the set of all possible multisets with the same basis is partially ordered by the $\subset$ relation. Given this fact, we shall use also two operations, denoted by **max** and **min**, defined on a finite set V of multisets such that

$$\mathbf{max}\, V = \{v | (\nexists v' \in V) v \subset v'\}, \tag{10}$$

$$\mathbf{min}\, V = \{v | (\nexists v' \in V) v' \subset v\}. \tag{11}$$

According to (10), **max** V includes all the *MSs* v entering *SMS* V that are not submultisets of any other *MS* v' from *SMS* V. Similarly, according to (11), **min** V includes all the *MSs* v entering *SMS* V such that there is not any other *MSs* v' from *SMS* V which is a submultiset of v.

Example 3. Let $V = \{v_1, v_2, v_3, v_4\}$, where
$v_1 = \{10 \cdot \langle eur \rangle, 5 \cdot \langle usd \rangle, 6 \cdot \langle computer \rangle\}$,
$v_2 = \{3 \cdot \langle eur \rangle, 2 \cdot \langle usd \rangle\}$,
$v_3 = \{5 \cdot \langle usd \rangle, 5 \cdot \langle computer \rangle\}$,
$v_4 = \{10 \cdot \langle usd \rangle, 12 \cdot \langle computer \rangle\}$.
Applying (10) and (11) to V and taking into account that $v_2 \subset v_1$ and $v_3 \subset v_1$, we obtain.
max $V = \{v_1, v_4\}$,
min $V = \{v_2, v_3, v_4\}$.   ■

(In general, some *MS* may enter both **max** V and **min** V, as v_4 in the above example). As seen, the **max** and **min** operations result in the selection of some subsets of *SMS*.

Boundary conditions (*BC*) have unified syntax $a\theta n$, where $\theta \in \{>, <, \leq, \geq, =\}$. An *MS* v satisfies the *BC* $a\theta m$ if both $n \cdot a \in v$ and $n\theta m$ are true. As stated above, $a \notin v$ is equivalent to $0 \cdot a \in v$.

On the other hand, *optimizing conditions* (*OC*) have syntax $a = opt$, where $opt \in \{max, min\}$ (note that both *max* and *min* differ from the bold **max** and **min** introduced above). An *MS* $v \in V$ satisfies the *OC* $a = max$ if $n \cdot a \in v$ and all $v' \in V - \{v\}$ satisfy the *BC* $a \leq n$. Similarly, an *MS* $v \in V$ satisfies the *OC* $a = min$ if $n \cdot a \in v$ and all $v' \in V - \{v\}$ satisfy the *BC* $a \geq n$.

Let V be an *SMS*. We define the *filtration* operation, denoted by the special symbol $\downarrow$, and by $V \downarrow F$ in infix notation, where the filter F is a set of boundary and optimizing conditions.

Let $F_\le = \{bc_1, ..., bc_m\}$ be a set of boundary conditions. Then, applying $F_\le$ to *SMS* V results in

$$V \downarrow F_\le = \bigcap_{i=1}^{m}(V \downarrow \{bc_i\}). \tag{12}$$

Example 4. Let V be the same as in Example 3. Then.
$V \downarrow \{\langle eur \rangle \le 2, \langle usd \rangle > 3\} = V \downarrow \{\langle eur \rangle \le 2\} \cap V \downarrow \{\langle usd \rangle > 3\}$.
By definition,
$V \downarrow \{\langle eur \rangle \le 2\} = \{v_3, v_4\}$,
$V \downarrow \{\langle usd \rangle > 3\} = \{v_1, v_3, v_4\}$.
Therefore, the result of the filtration is
$\{v_3, v_4\} \cap \{v_1, v_3, v_4\} = \{v_3, v_4\}$. ∎

Let $F_{opt} = \{oc_1, ..., oc_k\}$ be a set of optimizing conditions. Similarly to (12), the application of F_{opt} to *SMS* V results in

$$V \downarrow F_{opt} = \bigcap_{i=1}^{k}(V \downarrow \{oc_i\}). \tag{13}$$

Example 5. Let V be the same as in Example 2. Then, according to the definition of $V \downarrow F_{opt}$,
$V \downarrow \{\langle usd \rangle = max, \langle eur \rangle = min\} = (V \downarrow \{\langle usd \rangle = max\}) \cap (V \downarrow \{\langle eur \rangle = min\})$
and
$V \downarrow \{\langle usd \rangle = max\} = \{v_4\}$,
$V \downarrow \{\langle eur \rangle = min\} = \{v_3, v_4\}\}$,
where we used that $\langle eur \rangle \notin v_3$, $\langle eur \rangle \notin v_4$ in the last equation (i.e., $0 \cdot \langle eur \rangle \in v_3$, $0 \cdot \langle eur \rangle \in v_4$). Consequently, the result of the filtration is
$\{v_4\} \cap \{v_3, v_4\} = \{v_4\}$. ∎

In the case of a general filter F applied to *SMS* V we may include both boundary and optimizing conditions, i.e.,

$$F = F_\le \cup F_{opt}, \tag{14}$$

and the result of filtrating the *SMS* V with a filter F is

$$V \downarrow F = (V \downarrow F_\le) \downarrow F_{opt}. \tag{15}$$

As seen above, the syntax and semantics of filters inherit features from query languages, thus providing a selection of data from relational-like databases [25, 26].

Once we have introduced the basic operations on multisets and their sets, we may move to multiset grammars and their simplified modification – unitary *MG*, – which ultimately conform the main tool for solving the problems under consideration. By developing this set of tools, we have tried to unify it's background with the classical string-operating grammars, as introduced by N. Chomsky [27]. The family of *MGs* as a whole is the result of the combination of the most useful features of modern knowledge engineering [28, 29] and classical mathematical programming [30, 31] in one multiset-based formalism.

2.2 Multiset Grammars and Unitary Multiset Grammars

A *multiset grammar* is defined as a couple $S = \langle v_0, R \rangle$, where v_0 is a multiset called *kernel*, and R, called *scheme*, is a finite set of rules. A *rule* $r \in R$ is a construction

$$v \rightarrow v', \tag{16}$$

where "$\rightarrow$" is a divider and v and v' are multisets that conform the left and right parts of the rule, respectively. Rules are applied to multisets as follows. Let $\bar{v}$ be a multiset such that $v \subseteq \bar{v}$. Then, the result of the application of rule r to the *MS* $\bar{v}$ is an *MS*

$$\bar{v}' = \bar{v} - v + v'. \tag{17}$$

Therefore, the *MS* v, being a submultiset of the *MS* $\bar{v}$, is replaced by the *MS* v'. The set of all objects contained in rules $r \in R$ is denoted by A_S.

Applying rule $r \in R$ to *MS* $\bar{v}$ is denoted as

$$\bar{v} \overset{r}{\Rightarrow} \bar{v}', \tag{18}$$

and we say that the *MS* $\bar{v}'$ is *generated* from the *MS* $\bar{v}$ by the application of rule r.

An *MG* $S = \langle v_0, R \rangle$ defines a set of multisets V_S such that:

$$V_{(0)} = \{v_0\}, \tag{19}$$

$$V_{(i+1)} = V_{(i)} \cup \left(\bigcup_{\bar{v} \in V_{(i)}} \bigcup_{r \in R} \left\{ \bar{v}' \middle| \bar{v} \overset{r}{\Rightarrow} \bar{v}' \right\} \right), \tag{20}$$

$$V_S = V_{(\infty)}. \tag{21}$$

The above means that V_S includes all multisets, which may be generated from kernel v_0 by the sequential application of the rules contained in R, until at least one rule can be applied to the current multiset. V_S is therefore a fixed point of the sequence $V_{(0)}, V_{(1)}, ..., V_{(i)}, ...$ A multiset $\bar{v} \in V_S$ is called *terminal* (*TMS*) if there is not any rule $r \in R$ that can be applied to $\bar{v}$. The set of terminal multisets (*STMS*) generated by the *MG* S is denoted by $\overline{V_S}$. Naturally, it follows that $\overline{V_S} \subseteq V_S$.

Example 6. Let $S = \langle v_0, R \rangle$, where
$v_0 = \{10 \cdot \langle eur \rangle, 5 \cdot \langle usd \rangle, 3 \cdot \langle rur \rangle\}$.
Also let $R = \{r_1, r_2\}$, where r_1 is
$\{3 \cdot \langle eur \rangle\} \rightarrow \{4 \cdot \langle usd \rangle\}$,

and r_2 is

$\{3 \cdot \langle usd \rangle, 1 \cdot \langle rur \rangle\} \rightarrow \{2 \cdot \langle eur \rangle\}$.

Then, according to Eqs. (19)–(21),

$V_{(0)} = \{\{10 \cdot \langle eur \rangle, 5 \cdot \langle usd \rangle, 3 \cdot \langle rur \rangle\}\}$,

$V_{(1)} = V_{(0)} \cup \{\{7 \cdot \langle eur \rangle, 9 \cdot \langle usd \rangle, 3 \cdot \langle rur \rangle\}, \{12 \cdot \langle eur \rangle, 2 \cdot \langle usd \rangle, 2 \cdot \langle rur \rangle\}\}$,

$V_{(2)} \quad = \quad V_{(1)} \quad \cup \quad \{\{4 \cdot eur, 13 \cdot \langle usd \rangle, 3 \cdot \langle rur \rangle\}, \{9 \cdot \langle eur \rangle, 6 \cdot \langle usd \rangle, 2 \cdot \langle rur \rangle\}$,

$\{9 \cdot \langle eur \rangle, 6 \cdot \langle usd \rangle, 2 \cdot \langle rur \rangle\}, \{11 \cdot \langle eur \rangle, 3 \cdot \langle usd \rangle, 1 \cdot \langle rur \rangle\}\}$,

...

As seen above, this *MG* describes all possible ways of currency exchange, starting from an initial collection of euros, dollars, and rubles. The rules define how such exchange may be implemented, i.e., what amounts of various currencies may be replaced by the associated amounts of other currencies. ∎

By analogy with the aforementioned string-operating grammars, multiset grammars may be classified by their left part. Namely, if the left part of any rule of an *MG* is the multiset $\{1 \cdot a\}$, $a \in A_S$, then this *MG* is called *context-free* (*CF*). Otherwise, if there exists at least one rule $v \rightarrow v'$, where v differs from $\{1 \cdot a\}$, this *MG* is called *context-sensitive*, or *general*.

Filtering multiset grammars (*FMG*) are a generalization of *MG*. A *filtering multiset grammar* is a triple $S = \langle v_0, R, F \rangle$, where v_0 and R are the same as in *MGs* and F is a filter that provides a selection of *MGs* generated by the core *MG* $S' = \langle v_0, R \rangle$, i.e.,

$$V_S = V_{S'} \downarrow F. \tag{22}$$

In other words, V_S is subset of $V_{S'}$ including only those elements in this set that satisfy filter F.

Example 7. Let $S = \langle v_0, R, F \rangle$, where v_0 and R are the same as in Example 6, and $F = \{\langle eur \rangle \geq 30, \langle usd \rangle = max\}$.

This means that V_S will include those collections created by all possible chains of currency exchange that contain at least 30 euros and are a maximal of the sum of dollars. According to the definition of filter, $V_{S'}$ will be filtered by $F_\leq = \{\langle eur \rangle \geq 30\}$. Thus, the resulting *SMS* will be filtered by $F_{opt} = \{\langle usd \rangle = max\}$. ∎

We shall use context-free multiset grammars as a basic formalism providing natural formal representation of hierarchical technological and sociotechnological systems and processes of their creation and operation. We shall use a simplified record of rules entering a scheme of *CF MG*:

$$a \rightarrow n_1 \cdot a_1, ..., n_m \cdot a_m, \tag{23}$$

where the left part, called *header*, is used instead of the multiset $\{1 \cdot a\}$ and right part, called *body*, is a record of the multiset $\{n_1 \cdot a_1, ..., n_m \cdot a_m\}$. Let us remind that the set of all objects contained in scheme R is denoted by A_S. The set $\overline{A_S} \subseteq A_S$ includes the *terminal objects*, which present only in the bodies of the rules. Therefore, the set $A_S - \overline{A_S}$ is formed by *non-terminal objects*, each being the header of at least one rule. The set of rules with the same header a is denoted R_a. It follows that $R_a \subseteq R$.

Rules like (23) are called *unitary* (*UR*) and any *MG* whose scheme is a set of *URs* is called *unitary multiset grammar*. The most natural interpretation of (23) is that a system (device) a consists of n_1 subsystems (subdevices, spare parts) a_1, ..., n_m subsystems a_m. This interpretation, called *structural*, is illustrated in the following example.

Example 8. Let us consider a computer, consisting of 4 processors, memory, power supply, a monitor, and a keyboard. Each processor, in turn, consists of 16 cores, and memory is made of 64 1-Gbit modules. This device may be represented by the *UMG* $S = \langle v_0, R \rangle$, where $v_0 = \{1 \cdot \langle computer \rangle\}$ and $R = \{r_1, r_2, r_3\}$, with

r_1: $\langle computer \rangle \rightarrow 4 \cdot \langle processor \rangle, 1 \cdot \langle memory \rangle, 1 \cdot \langle power\text{-}supply \rangle, 1 \cdot \langle monitor \rangle, 1 \cdot \langle keyboard \rangle$,
r_2: $\langle processor \rangle \rightarrow 16 \cdot \langle core \rangle$,
r_3: $\langle memory \rangle \rightarrow 64 \cdot \langle 1gbit \rangle$. ∎

When we consider industrial systems that manufacture various devices and complexes we use a *technological interpretation* of unitary rules obtained from the structural interpretation after including to the *UR* multiobjects representing resources necessary for manufacturing or assembling object a from n_1 objects a_1, ..., n_m objects a_m. Consequently, any *UR* in the technological interpretation can be written as

$$a \rightarrow n_1 \cdot a_1, ..., n_m \cdot a_m, n_1' \cdot a_1', ..., n_l' \cdot a_l', \tag{24}$$

where the aforementioned amounts of resources (electrical energy, fuel, money, etc.) are n_1' units of resource a_1', ..., n_l' units of resource a_l'. It is worth mentioning that the term "object" can be used both in multiset theory and in applications. In the latter case, it refers to some manufactured device or complex, or a unit of a given resource consumed during manufacturing. From now on, we shall use the term *"object/resource"* (*OR*) to denote all entities having place in *URs*. Note that *ORs* like $a_1', \ldots, a_l'$ from (24) may also be headers of some *UR*, meaning that they are produced by some devices [18].

Example 9. Let us consider the same computer from Example 8 and the following unitary rules in technological interpretation describing it's production:

r_1': $\langle computer \rangle \rightarrow 4 \cdot \langle processor \rangle, 1 \cdot \langle memory \rangle, 1 \cdot \langle power\text{-}supply \rangle, 1 \cdot \langle monitor \rangle, 1 \cdot \langle keyboard \rangle, 5 \cdot \langle mnt\text{-}asm\text{-}comp \rangle, 100 \cdot \langle wh \rangle, 300 \cdot \langle usd \rangle$,
r_2': $\langle processor \rangle \rightarrow 16 \cdot \langle core \rangle, 3 \cdot \langle mnt\text{-}asm\text{-}proc \rangle, 30 \cdot \langle wh \rangle, 500 \cdot \langle usd \rangle$,
r_3': $\langle memory \rangle \rightarrow 64 \cdot \langle 1gbit \rangle, 1 \cdot \langle mnt\text{-}asm\text{-}mem \rangle, 20 \cdot \langle wh \rangle, 100 \cdot \langle usd \rangle$.

In this case, *UR* r_1' defines that to produce one computer it is necessary to assemble spare parts by the assembly line (*AL*) for 5 min, consume 100 W · h of electrical energy, and spend 300 dollars. Similarly, *UR* r_2' defines that to produce processors from cores it is necessary to apply 3 min of the *AL* operation, 30 W · h of electrical energy, and 500 dollars. Finally, *UR* r_3' defines that to produce memory from 64 1-Gigabit modules it is necessary to apply 1 min of the *AL* operation, 20 W · h of electrical energy, and 100 dollars. ∎

Let us note that an *UMG* may be alternating or non-alternating [19, 20]. An *UMG* is called *alternating* if there exists at least one non-terminal *OR* a which is the header of more than one *UR* in the scheme of *UMG*. This is important because it means that there are at least two ways of manufacturing the *OR* a. As it will be shown below, this possibility is a background for the resilience of the affected industrial systems, represented by their own *UMGs*. Formally, an *UMGs* is alternating, if $|R| > |A_S - \overline{A_S}|$ or, in other words, if there exists a non-terminal *OR a* such that $|R_a| > 1$. Otherwise, we say that an *UMG* is *non-alternating*. Below we shall consider the general case, i.e., that of an alternating *UMG*.

In addition, an *UMG* may be also *acyclic* and *cyclic, finitary* and *infinitary* [19, 20]. For simplicity we shall consider only acyclic and finitary *UMG* generating finite *STMS*.

A technological interpretation of unitary rules makes it easy to assess amounts of *OR* necessary for an *IS* to complete an order, as well as to evaluate the sufficiency of the amounts of *OR* available during this completion. The application of *UMG* also makes the representation of an "added value" (as defined by K. Marx [32]) easy and natural. In fact, this application is declared by multiobjects representing money in the bodies of *UR* in technological interpretation (e.g. $300 \cdot \langle usd \rangle$, $500 \cdot \langle usd \rangle$, $100 \cdot \langle usd \rangle$ in *URs* r'_1, r'_2, r'_3 respectively in Example 9). On the other hand, *UMG* provide just a simple representation of input-output models of mathematical economy, as formulated by V. Leontief with the application of conventional matrix-vector toolkits [33].

2.3 Application of UMGs to the Assessment of Vulnerability of Industrial Systems

We shall represent an order as a multiset $q = \{m_1 \cdot b_1, ..., m_k \cdot b_k\}$. The aim of an order is to have m_1 *ORs* b_1, ..., m_k *ORs* b_k manufactured by an *IS*. Similarly, we shall represent the collection of resources available to the *IS* in question during the completion of an order as a multiset $v = \{l_1 \cdot c_1, ..., l_p \cdot c_p\}$. This means that l_1 *ORs* c_1, ..., l_p *ORs* c_p are available to the *IS* at the beginning of the manufacturing process. In what follows, this *MS* will be the resource base of *IS*, whereas the set *R* of unitary rules in the technological interpretation will be the technological base of *IS*. Also, we shall assume that the set $\{c_1, ..., c_p\}$ represents *primary ORs* that are not produced by the *IS* from another *ORs*.

The triple $I = < q, R, v >$ will be referred to as the *industrial system, assigned to order q* (for short, *AIS*), while the triple $I = \langle \{\emptyset\}, R, v \rangle$ will be referred to as the *free industrial system (FIS)*.

As mentioned in previous works [17, 18], an *AIS* $I = \langle q, R, v \rangle$ is *capable* to complete the assigned order *q* if

$$(\exists \overline{v} \in \overline{V_S})\overline{v} \subseteq v, \tag{25}$$

where $S = < q, R >$ is the *UMG associated with this IS*. (25) means that there exists at least one way to complete an order that needs that the collection of resources $\overline{v}$ is a submultiset of the resource base of *IS v*. In other words, the amount of resources in the *RB* is sufficient for the *TB* to complete the order.

Example 10. Consider the *IS* with technological base $R = \{r'_1, r'_2, r'_3\}$, where *URs* r'_1, r'_2, r'_3 are the same as in Example 9. Also, consider the resource base
$v = \{600 \cdot \langle core \rangle, 5 \cdot \langle power\text{-}supply \rangle, 13 \cdot \langle monitor \rangle, 12 \cdot \langle keyboard \rangle,$
$300 \cdot \langle 1gbit \rangle, 60 \cdot \langle mnt\text{-}asm\text{-}comp \rangle, 200 \cdot \langle mnt\text{-}asm\text{-}proc \rangle,$
$10 \cdot \langle mnt\text{-}asm\text{-}mem \rangle, 10000 \cdot \langle wh \rangle, 300000 \cdot \langle usd \rangle\}$.

Let $q = \{3 \cdot \langle computer \rangle\}$ be assigned to this *IS*. Then, $\overline{V_S} = \{\bar{v}_1\}$, where
$\bar{v}_1 = \{192 \cdot \langle core \rangle, 3 \cdot \langle power\text{-}supply \rangle, 3 \cdot \langle monitor \rangle, 3 \cdot \langle keyboard \rangle,$
$192 \cdot \langle 1gbit \rangle, 15 \cdot \langle mnt\text{-}asm\text{-}comp \rangle, 36 \cdot \langle mnt\text{-}asm\text{-}proc \rangle,$
$3 \cdot \langle mnt\text{-}asm\text{-}mem \rangle, 4500 \cdot \langle wh \rangle, 45300 \cdot \langle usd \rangle\},$
and because $\bar{v}_1 \subset v$, we have that the *AIS* is capable of completing the assigned order q.

If the resource base includes only 2 power supplies instead of 5, then the *AIS* would not be not capable of completing this order, as it would lack one power supply. ∎

It is important to remark that, in general, there may be more than one multiset in an *STMS* $\overline{V_S}$, as the technological base of an *AIS* may produce one and the same *OR* in several ways. This may be true for any *OR* produced by this *AIS* and is the case when representing an *IS* by an alternating *UMG* with a scheme that may include more than one *UR* with the same header and any of those *URs* defines a possible way of manufacturing the *OR*.

To select some preferable ways for order completion that differ in the amounts of resources consumed, we can use filtering multiset grammars. A *filtering UMG (FUMG)* is a triple $S = \langle v_0, R, F \rangle$ that defines the *STMS*.

$$\overline{V_S} = \overline{V_{S'}} \downarrow F, \qquad (26)$$

where, similarly to (22), $S' = \langle v_0, R \rangle$ is a *core UMG* of *FUMG* S. The only difference from the definition given by (22) is that in an *FUMGs* only the terminal multisets are filtered, whereas in an *FMGs* all generated multisets are filtered. This difference has an evident background: in *FMGs* we do not split the set A_S of objects that take place in rules between terminal and non-terminal; in contrast, such splitting does exist in *FUMGs*. Thus, the resources consumed while completing an order are represented by terminal multisets. As mentioned before, when it comes to completing an order, the application of filters provides an opportunity to select different options which are better than others in the sense of the consumed resources.

Every *AIS* $S = \langle q, R, v \rangle$ may be represented by a *FUMG* $S = \langle q, R, F \rangle$ if we replace the *RB* $v = \{l_1 \cdot c_1, \ldots, l_p \cdot c_p\}$ by an equivalent filter $F_v = \{c_1 \leq l_1, \ldots, c_p \leq l_p\} \cup F_0$, where

$$F_0 = \{c = 0 | c \in \overline{A_S} - \{c_1, \ldots, c_p\}\}. \qquad (27)$$

F_0 states that all but $c_1, \ldots, c_p$, primary *ORs* are not available while completing order q (i.e. the amounts of such *ORs* in the *AIS RB* are zero). So the criterion expressed in (25) for the capability of *AIS* $S = \langle q, R, v \rangle$ to complete order q may be reformulated by the application of an equivalent *FUMG* $S = \langle q, R, F \rangle$. This is, the aforementioned *AIS* is capable of completing q if the *STMS* generated by an equivalent *FUMG* is non-empty:

$$\overline{V_S} \neq \{\emptyset\}. \qquad (28)$$

In other words, there exists at least one *TMS* $\bar{v} \in \overline{V_S}$ representing the collection of resources necessary for completing q. The *STMS* $\overline{V_S}$ represents all such collections, each corresponding to some specific way to complete this order (or several ways with the same consumption of resources).

Example 11. Consider the *AIS* from Example 10. It can also be represented by the *FUMG* $S = \langle q, R, F \rangle$, where
$F_v = \{\langle core \rangle \leq 600, \langle power\text{-}supply \rangle \leq 5, \langle monitor \rangle \leq 13, \langle keyboard \rangle \leq 12,$
$\langle 1\text{-}Gbit\text{-}module \rangle \leq 300, \langle mnt\text{-}asm\text{-}comp \rangle \leq 60, \langle mnt\text{-}asm\text{-}proc \rangle \leq 200,$
$\langle mnt\text{-}asm\text{-}mem \rangle \leq 10, \langle wh \rangle \leq 10000, \langle usd \rangle \leq 300000\}.$ ∎

Once we have introduced the necessary notions and criteria, we shall pay attention to an obstacle of practical importance: the case in which at any moment during the operating process the resource base of any *AIS* may contain not only primary *ORs*, represented by terminal multiobjects, but also produced (secondary) *ORs*, represented by non-terminal multiobjects. These *secondary ORs* have been manufactured by the *AIS* from primary *ORs* or transferred to the *AIS RB* from external systems. In Example 11, the *RB* v may contain the non-terminal multiobjects $1 \cdot \langle computer \rangle$, $3 \cdot \langle processor \rangle$ and $8 \cdot \langle memory \rangle$, so, in reality, the resource base of this *AIS* contains one computer, three processors, and eight memory blocks already manufactured.

Taking into account this obstacle, the notion of the capability of an *IS* to complete orders was generalized in [18] by an extension of the concept *UMG* called unitary multiset grammars with reduced generation (*UMGs RG*). For handling manufactured *ORs*, let us consider both this extension and a new technique called *terminalization*.

2.4 Terminalization

A *unitary multigrammar with reduced generation* is triple $S = \langle v_0, R, v \rangle$, where v_0 and R are a kernel and a scheme, respectively (or the order and the technological base in the considered problem area), while multiset v is called *storage*. In general, this multiset contains (along with terminal multiobjects) non-terminal *MOs* used for the reduction of generation steps. Naturally, storage represents the resource base containing not only initial *ORs* (represented by terminal *MOs*), but also produced *ORs* (represented by non-terminal *MOs*).

This makes the semantics of *UMGs RG* a little different from the semantics of *UMGs*. Before applying any *UR* r $a \rightarrow n_1 \cdot a_1, \ldots, n_m \cdot a_m$ to the current multiset v, including *MO* $n \cdot a$, we test, whether the current storage contains the *MO* $n' \cdot a$. If such *MO* exists, further actions depend on the relation between n and n'. In the simplest case ($n' \geq n$) all n *OR*, represented by the *MO* $n \cdot a$, are already in the storage (resource base) and there is no need to produce them and spend another *ORs* from the *RB*. Hence, for further generation it is sufficient to exclude the *MO* $n \cdot a$ from the storage (i.e., n *ORs* a from the resource base) and apply scheme R to the rest of the current *MS*. In the more complicated case ($n' < n$), only n' *ORs* a may be taken from the resource base, and the remaining $n - n'$ *ORs* a must be produced. This requires that the *MO* $n' \cdot a$ is excluded from the storage first and then the *UR* r must be applied to the *MO* $(n - n') \cdot a$, hence transforming the current multiset in accordance with the semantics of *UMGs* (namely, according to relation (20)). Thus, the presence of some already manufactured objects in the resource base provides a reduction of amounts of the resources consumed for completing an order.

However, the application of *UMGs RG* is rather sophisticated both from semantical and algorithmic (computational complexity) points of view. Here we propose a technique that aims at replacing *UMGs RG* and simplifying the algorithm for the assessment of the vulnerability of an *IS* with the use of the regular procedure that stems directly from (19)–(21).

This technique, referred above as *terminalization*, is simply the inclusion of additional $|A_S - \overline{A_S}|$ unitary rules in the scheme R, representing the technological base of the *IS*:

$$a \to 1 \cdot a', \tag{29}$$

each corresponding to a non-terminal object (i.e., to a produced or secondary *OR*) a. Here a' is an additional terminal object representing the produced *OR* a. This makes it possible to include the multiobject $n \cdot a'$ in the *IS* resource base if there are n already produced *OR* a. This inclusion adds another alternative way of manufacturing *OR* a: the extraction of this *OR* from the resource base, as long as it takes places in that base. Such *UR* are called *terminalizing*.

The proposed simplification provides a direct application of criterion (28) to the case of *RB* containing both primary and produced *ORs*. Hence, there is no need to extend the mathematical and algorithmic background of the assessment of the resilience of *IS* in this case.

2.5 Criteria of AIS Vulnerability to the Destructive Impacts

Following [17, 18], we shall represent the impact induced by multiset Δv, which includes *MOs* representing *ORs*. These *ORs* are eliminated from the resource base as a result of this impact. Therefore, after the impact this *RB* becomes $v - \Delta v$. Consequently, the criteria for the recognition of the vulnerability of an *AIS* $I = \langle q, R, v \rangle$ to impact Δv follows directly from (23).

Namely, an *AIS I* is *vulnerable* to impact Δv if *AIS* $I' = q, R, v - \Delta v$ is not capable to complete this order given a resource base reduced by this impact:

$$\{\bar{v}|\bar{v} \in \overline{V_S} \,\&\, \bar{v} \subseteq v - \Delta v\} = \{\emptyset\}, \tag{30}$$

where, as above, $S = \langle q, R \rangle$.

Let us note that, in general, an impact may affect not only the resource base, but also the technological base of an *AIS*. However, there is no need to make the vulnerability criteria more sophisticated. As it was shown in [17, 18], the impact on the *TB* may be fully modelled by including to *MSs* v and Δv, as well as by adding to the bodies of the *URs* multiobjects of the form $n \cdot \langle t\text{-}d \rangle$ (where t is expressed in units of time and denotes the duration of the operation performed by device d that belongs to the manufacturing *OR*). In Example 10, such *MO* entering the *RB* v are $60 \cdot \langle mnt\text{-}asm\text{-}comp \rangle$, $200 \cdot \langle mnt\text{-}asm\text{-}proc \rangle$, and $10 \cdot \langle mnt\text{-}asm\text{-}mem \rangle$. In this example the unit for t is minutes, while d are *asm-comp*, *asm-proc* and *asm-mem*, respectively. Applying *FUMGs* as the knowledge representation model, if the *MS* Δv includes the *MO* $N \cdot \langle t\text{-}d \rangle$ (where N is the maximal integer number in the current implementation of knowledge-based decision support system), then the presence of this *MO* $N \cdot \langle t\text{-}d \rangle$ in this *MS* means that the impact destroys device d completely. This happens because for any $n < N$ $\{n \cdot \langle t\text{-}d \rangle\} - \{N \cdot \langle t\text{-}d \rangle\} = \{0 \cdot \langle t\text{-}d \rangle\} = \{\emptyset\}$. This occurs as well if Δv includes $n' \cdot \langle t\text{-}d \rangle$, where $n' \geq n$. On the contrary, if $n' < n$, then the impact produces some damage to the affected device and its operation resource is reduced from $n \cdot \langle t\text{-}d \rangle$ to $(n - n') \cdot \langle t\text{-}d \rangle$.

Example 12. Consider an *AIS* whose technological base R is the same as in Example 9. Let the resource base v and the order q be the same as in Example 10. It turns out that this *AIS* is not vulnerable to impact $\Delta \cdot v = \{3 \cdot \langle monitor \rangle, 30 \cdot \langle mnt\text{-}asm\text{-}proc \rangle, 500 \cdot \langle wh \rangle\}$, which affects this system before order completion. This is because the reduced amounts of monitors, available electrical energy, and available operation time in the processors assembling line are sufficient for order q to be completed. On the contrary, if $\Delta v = \{10 \cdot \langle keyboard \rangle\}$, then the *AIS* is vulnerable to this impact, because the remaining number of keyboards (two) is not sufficient for completing the order. ∎

This subsection marks the end of our study of basic issues in the assessment of the vulnerability in closed *AISs*. The following section will tackle the case of an external industrial system assigned to recover eliminated resources or to support the affected *AIS* in completing the initial order by joining their capabilities.

3 Assessment of Recovery and Support Capabilities of External Industrial Systems

3.1 Recovery

Consider the case, where a destructive impact Δv is applied to an *AIS* $I = \langle q, R, v \rangle$ and that, as a result of this impact, the *AIS* becomes vulnerable (i.e., not capable of completing order q with a reduced *RB* $v - \Delta v$). An external industrial system, in turn, may be or may not capable of recovering this reduced *RB*. There is a set.

$$Q = \left\{ \bar{v} - (v - \Delta v) | \bar{v} \in \overline{V_S} \right\}, \tag{31}$$

of orders assigned to the *EIS*, such that, if completed, would recover some part of the *RB* of the affected *AIS*. In this case, the *AIS* would be capable of completing the assigned order q.

Let $S' = \langle \{\emptyset\}, R', v' \rangle$ be a *free external industrial system*. Obviously, the resource base of the *AIS* S may be recovered if at least one order $q' \in Q$ may be completed by the assigned *EIS* $S_{q'} = \langle q', R', v' \rangle$, i.e.,

$$\left(\exists q' \in Q\right)\left(\exists \bar{v} \in \overline{V}_{S_{q'}}\right)\bar{v} \subseteq v', \tag{32}$$

or in set-theoretic representation

$$\overline{Q} = \bigcup_{q' \in Q} \left\{ \bar{v} | \bar{v} \in \overline{V}_{S_{q'}} \,\&\, \bar{v} \subseteq v' \right\} \neq \{\emptyset\}. \tag{33}$$

Relations (31)–(33) form the *criterion of capability of an external industrial system to recover the resource base of an AIS that has received an impact* Δv.

However, generally the number of orders $q' \in Q$ (i.e., the different ways for recovery) which may be completed by an *EIS* may be more than one. This poses a problem when it comes to selecting one order $q' \in Q$ to be completed by an *EIS* for the recovery of the *RB* of the affected *AIS*.

This problem is solved rather evidently. First of all, it is reasonable to reduce the number of the considered orders from $|\overline{Q}|$ to $|\mathbf{min}\ \overline{Q}|$, thus extracting from the set $\overline{Q}$ all terminal multisets for which there are submultisets in $\overline{Q}$. It is clear that every excluded *TMS* that is an order for the *EIS* would require additional amounts of resources regarding its submultiset. If it is not necessary to reduce (or even to minimize) the amounts of resources consumed by the *EIS* during the recovery, then this step may be omitted. In any case, it is sufficient to define a filter $\overline{F}$ for selecting exactly one *TMS* from $\overline{Q}$ (or $\mathbf{min}\ \overline{Q}$). Thus,

$$\{q'\} = \overline{Q} \downarrow \overline{F}. \tag{34}$$

This order q' would be completed by the *EIS* and represented by a collection of resources produced as a result of its completion, thus recovering the affected *AIS*.

3.2 Support

As previously mentioned, supporting the affected *AIS* by an external industrial system is an attempt to complete an order assigned to this *AIS* by applying joint capabilities of both systems (i.e., their technological and resource bases). Let us consider the case in which a destructive impact Δv is applied to an *AIS* $I = \langle q, R, v \rangle$, and the affected *AIS* $\langle q, R, v - \Delta v \rangle$ is not capable of completing this order.

Joining the capabilities of the affected *AIS* and a free *EIS* $I' = \langle \{\emptyset\}, R', v' \rangle$ means the creation of a new industrial system with a technological base $R \cup R'$ that includes all the manufacturing devices from both systems, and a resource base $v - \Delta v + v'$ that includes the *ORs* that are present in the *RBs* from both systems. Note that when there are identical devices (unitary rules) in both R and R', the resulting *TB* (scheme) will not include two devices (*URs*), but only one device (*UR*). However, the real capabilities of the *TB* are represented by the multiobjects $n \cdot \langle t{-}d \rangle$, so the *RB* $v - \Delta v$ and v' result will be $(n + n') \cdot \langle t{-}d \rangle$, where $n \cdot \langle t{-}d \rangle \in R$, $n' \cdot \langle t{-}d \rangle \in R'$. Thus, the real capabilities of the joint technological base will be the sum of the capabilities of the united *IS*, despite the fact that the scheme of the resulting *UMG* contains only one *UR* for every type of manufacturing devices.

The criterion for the capability of an external *IS* to support an affected *AIS* is rather evident. Let

$$\overline{I} = \langle q, R \cup R', v - \Delta v {+} v' \rangle \tag{35}$$

be the joint *AIS*. Then, the *EIS* would be capable of supporting the affected *AIS* if it satisfies criterion (25), in which *S* is replaced by $\overline{S} = \langle q, R \cup R' \rangle$ and v is replaced by $v - \Delta v {+} v'$.

There is one hidden nuance in this criterion: terminal objects $a \in \overline{A_S}$ may become non-terminal $a \in A_{\overline{S}} - \overline{A_{\overline{S}}}$ because there may be *URs* with head a in R' (i.e., they represent *OR* manufactured by the *EIS*, but having place in the initial *RB* of the *AIS*). Since R' also contains terminalizing rules for all non-terminal objects, this case does not require any additional actions.

Let us note that an impact may be applied to an *AIS* not only before the beginning of order completion but also when a portion of such order was already completed. If this is the case, the criteria introduced can also be applied to the remaining parts of the order and the resource base of *AIS*.

4 Conclusion

This paper continues a series of publications dedicated to the development and the application of a multiset-based approach to modelling, assessment, and optimization of large-scale sociotechnological systems. Here we have discussed an extremely important area: the resilience of such systems and the recovery of *STS* affected by destructive impacts. The main tool for solving these problems is the family of unitary multiset grammars, for they have declarative capabilities that make the representation of industrial systems and their technological and resource bases, as well as the representation of destructive impacts, natural and easy.

This paper's approach is focused only on industrial systems, but the application to *STSs* of the techniques introduced in [18] for industrial systems makes it rather simple to establish criteria for the vulnerability of *STS* and the capability of external *IS/STS* to recover and/or support vulnerable *STS*.

We did not delve here into the algorithmics that aid in providing with the implementation of the developed criteria. However, as shown in [19, 20], *UMG* and *UMG*-like knowledge representation models are efficiently implemented due to the natural application of "branch–and–bound" techniques, which provide cut–off non-perspective generation chains at the very early steps, as well as natural parallelization of alternative chains in parallel computing environments.

A cut–off is efficiently applied because of the information contained in filters (with the representation of a resource base being the simplest of them) and the non-decreasing monotonicity of the multiplicities of the objects during the generation of multisets. This, in turn, is a consequence of the additivity of the resources used in the manufacturing process. Such additivity has been taken into account when we proposed to apply *UMGs* instead of general multiset grammars in this problem area.

We have used here the *UMGs* as the simplest form of multiset grammars, containing, among others, time as an additive resource. The total amount consumed of this resource can be computed only for one device. However, time is not a fully additive resource because of the operation of some devices, entering *IS (STS)*, in parallel. In order to describe this interconnected operation, a more general and adequate tool was developed: *temporal multiset grammars* [17]. We will tackle this topic in future publications. Nevertheless, assessing the vulnerability and evaluating ways to recover the affected systems using only additive resources in many non–trivial practical cases can be done efficiently.

The author will appreciate any future collaboration with researchers who may become interested in the approach and main results presented in this paper.

Acknowledgments. The author is grateful to Prof. Fred Roberts for his useful advice and support, to Prof. Javier Rubio-Herrero for his thorough and careful editing of this paper, and to Prof. Alexey Gvishiani for his permanent collaboration.

List of Acronyms

AIS	Assigned industrial system
BC	Boundary condition
CF	Context-free
CI	Critical infrastructure
DSTS	Distributed sociotechnological system
EIS	External industrial system
FIS	Free industrial system
FMG	Filtering multiset grammar
FUMG	Filtering unitary multiset grammar
STS	Sociotechnological system
IS	Industrial system
LSTS	Local sociotechnological system
MG	Multiset grammar
MO	Multiobject
MS	Multiset
OC	Optimizing condition
OR	Object-resource
RB	Resource base
SMS	Set of multisets
STMS	Set of terminal multisets
TB	Technological base
TMS	Terminal multiset
UMG	Unitary multiset grammar
UMG RG	Unitary multiset grammar with reduced generation
UR	Unitary rules

References

1. Alcaraz, C., Zeadally, S.: Critical infrastructure protection: requirements and challenges for the 21st century. Int. J. Critical Infrastruct. Prot. **8**, 53–66 (2015). https://doi.org/10.1016/j.ijcip.2014.12.002
2. Rinaldi, S., Peerenboom, J.P., Kelly, T.K.: Identifying, understanding, and analyzing critical infrastructure interdependencies. IEEE Control Syst. Mag. **21**, 11–25 (2001). https://doi.org/10.1109/37.960131
3. Vespignani, A.: Complex networks: the fragility of interdependency. Nature **464**, 984–985 (2010). https://doi.org/10.1038/464984a
4. Rehak, D., Senovsky, P., Hromada, M., Lovecek, T., Novotny, P.: Cascading impact assessment in a critical infrastructure system. Int. J. Crit. Infrastruct. Prot. **22**, 125–138 (2018). https://doi.org/10.1016/j.ijcip.2018.06.004
5. Li, H., Rosenwald, G.W., Jung, J., Liu, C.-C.: Strategic power infrastructure defense. Proc. IEEE **93**(5), 918–933 (2005). https://doi.org/10.1109/JPROC.2005.847260
6. Katay, M.E.: Electric power industry as critical infrastructure. Network World, 6 September 2010. https://www.networkworld.com/article/2217677/data-center/electric-power-industry-as-critical-infrastructure.html

7. Liu, K., Wang, M., Zhu, W., Wu, J., Yan, X.: Vulnerability analysis of an urban gas pipeline network considering pipeline-road dependency. Int. J. Crit. Infrastruct. Prot. **22**, 125–138 (2018). https://doi.org/10.1016/j.ijcip.2018.08.008
8. Kurian, M., McCarney, P. (eds.): Peri-urban Water and Sanitation Services. Policy, Planning and Method, p. 300. Springer, New York (2010). https://doi.org/10.1107/978-90-481-9425-4_11.
9. Stergiopoulos, G., Kotzanikolaou, P., Theocharidou, M., Lykou, G., Gritzalis, D.: Time-based critical infrastructure dependency analysis for large-scale and cross-sectoral failures. Int. J. Crit. Infrast. Prot. **12**, 46–60 (2016). https://doi.org/10.1016/j.ijcip.2015.12.002
10. Cavdaregla, B., Hammel, E., Mitchell, J.E., Sharkey, T.C., Wallace, W.A.: Integrating restoration and scheduling decisions for disrupted interdependent infrastructure systems. Ann. Oper. Res. **203**, 279–294 (2013). https://doi.org/10.1007/S10479-011-0959-3
11. Nepal, R., Jamasb, T.: Security of European electricity systems: conceptualizing the assessment criteria and core indicators. Int. J. Crit. Infrastruct. Prot. **b**(3–4), 182–196 (2013). https://doi.org/10.1016/j.i.cip.2013.07.001
12. Larsen, E.R., Osorio, S., van Ackere, A.: A framework to evaluate security of supply in the electricity sector. Renew. Sustain. Energy Rev. **79**, 646–655 (2017). https://doi.org/10.1016/j.rser.2017.05.085
13. Rechak, D., Senovsky, P., Hromada, M., Lovecek, T.: Complex approach to assessing resilience of criterial infrastructure elements. Int. J. Crit. Infrastruct. Prot. **25**(2), 125–138 (2019). https://doi.org/10.1016/i.ijcip.2019.03.003
14. Eusqeld, I., Nan, C., Dietz, S.: "System–of–systems" approach for interdependent critical infrastructures. Reliab. Eng. Syst. Saf. **96**(6), 679–686 (2011). https://doi.org/10.1016/j.ress.2010.12.010
15. He, X., Cha, E.J.: Modeling the damage and recovery of interdependent critical infrastructure systems from natural hazards. Reliab. Eng. Syst. Saf. **177**, 162–175 (2018). https://doi.org/10.1016/j.ress.2018.04.029
16. Gvishiani, A.D., Roberts, F.S., Sheremet, I.A.: On the assessment of sustainability of distributed sociotechnical systems to natural disasters. Russ. J. Earth Sci. **18**, ES4004 (2018). https://doi.org/10.2205/2018ES000627
17. Sheremet, I.A.: Multiset analysis of consequences of natural disasters impacts on large-scale industrial systems. Data Sci. J. **17**(4), 1–17. https://doi.org/10.5334/dsj-2018-004
18. Sheremet, I.: Multiset-based assessment of resilience of sociotechnological systems to natural hazards. In: Tiefenbacher, J. (ed.) Natural Hazards - Risks, Exposure, Response, and Resilience. IntechOpen (2019). https://doi.org/10.5772/intechopen.83508, https://www.intechopen.com/online-first/multiset-based-assessment-of-resilience-of-sociotechnological-systems-to-natural-hazards
19. Sheremet, I.: Multiset-based knowledge representation for the assessment and optimization of large-scale sociotechnical systems. In: Vizureanu, P. (ed.) Enhanced Expert Systems. IntechOpen, London (2019). https://doi.org/10.5772/intechopen.81698 https://www.intechopen.com/books/enhanced-expert-systems/multiset-based-knowledge-representation-for-the-assessment-and-optimization-of-large-scale-sociotech
20. Sheremet, I.: Unitary multiset grammars and metagrammars algorithmics and applications. In: Vizureanu, P. (ed.) Enhanced Expert Systems. IntechOpen, London (2019). https://doi.org/10.5772/intechopen.82713 https://www.intechopen.com/books/enhanced-expert-systems/unitary-multiset-grammars-an-metagrammars-algorithmics-and-application
21. Sheremet, I.A.: Recursive Multisets and their Applications, p. 292. Nauka, Moscow (2010). (in Russian)
22. Sheremet, I.A.: Recursive Multisets and their Applications, p. 249. NG Verlag, Berlin (2011)
23. Petrovskiy, A.B.: Spaces of Sets and Multisets, p. 248. URSS, Moscow (2003). (in Russia)

24. Petrovskiy, A.B.: Theory of Measured Sets and Multisets, p. 360. Science, Moscow (2018). (in Russia)
25. Date, C.I.: An Introduction to Database Systems, 8th edn., p. 247. Pearson, London (2012)
26. Darwen, H.: An Introduction to Relational Database Theory, p. 239. bookboon.com, London (2012)
27. Chomsky, N.: Syntactic Structures, p. 118. The Hague: Mouton de Gruyter (2002)
28. Apt, K.: Principles of Constraint Programming, p. 420. Cambridge University Press, Cambridge (2003)
29. Bratko, I.: Prolog Programming for Artificial Intelligence, p. 696. Wesley, New York (2012)
30. Hillier, S.F., Lieberman, G.J.: Introduction to Operations Research, p. 696. McGraw Hill, Boston (2014)
31. Taha, H.A.: Operations Research: An Introduction, p. 838. Pearson, London (2016)
32. Marx, K.: Capital. A Critique of Political Economy, vol. 1, p. 549. www.marxists.org
33. Bjerkholt, O., Kurz, H.D.: Introduction: the history of input–output analysis, Leontief's path and alternative tracks. Econ. Syst. Res. 18(4), 391–333 (2006)

Chapter 3
Vulnerability Assessment of Digitized Socio-technological Systems via Entropy

Hossein Hassani[1], Nadejda Komendantova[2]([⊠]), and Stephan Unger[3]

[1] Research Institute for Energy Management and Planning (RIEMP), University of Tehran, No. 9, Ghods St., Enghelab St., Tehran, Iran
[2] International Institute for Applied Systems Analysis (IIASA), Advanced Systems Analysis program, Schlossplatz 1, 2361 Laxenburg, Austria
komendan@iiasa.ac.at
[3] Department of Economics and Business, Saint Anselm College, Saint Anselm Drive 100, Manchester, NH, USA
sunger@anselm.edu

Abstract. This article tackles the complexity of assessing the vulnerability of digitized socio-technological systems by application of Entropy weight method. We present the application of a powerful and universal mathematical tool to data-driven applied systems analysis by bridging the socio-technological gap between organizational structures and system development. As information entropy can be significantly reduced, the assessment of the weaknesses in the structure of a socio-technological system improves proportionally to the reduction in information redundancies and losses, as well as to the improvement in information accuracy and efficiency.

Keywords: Applied systems analysis · Socio-technological systems · Entropy measurement · Digitalization

1 Introduction

The increasing digitalization of the world requires a re-evaluation of existing work systems which are in many cases still reliant on old-fashioned frameworks. These systems are often having a hard time adopting to the fast pace of digitalization because they necessitate the incorporation of new measures, cultural changes, and adaption of business models and structures. In most cases the problem that arises through the implementation of a digital framework is the lack of user acceptance or friendliness of the systems.

The direct influence of computerized systems on the working environment may constrain the workflow, put a burden on existing procedures, or simply grow objection against the implementation, thus lower acceptance. Therefore, a more humanistic approach for workplace adaption is needed in order to make digitalization efforts more efficient, valuable, and sustainable. The system to which this humanistic approach is applied to is called the socio-technological system. Emery et al. (1960) were the first ones to use the

© Springer Nature Switzerland AG 2021
F. S. Roberts and I. A. Sheremet (Eds.): Resilience in the Digital Age, LNCS 12660, pp. 35–44, 2021.
https://doi.org/10.1007/978-3-030-70370-7_3

term "socio-technological" system What they intended to describe was the description of the complex interaction between humans, machines and the environmental aspects of the work system.

1.1 Distinguishing the Existing Literature on Socio-technological Frameworks

Existing literature focuses mostly on the analysis of socio-technological frame- works, design and evaluation of complex organizational systems. Specifically, the work Cherns (1976), Cherns (1987), Clegg (2000), Bjerknes and Bratteteig (1995), De Sitter et al. (1997), Mumford (1983), Mumford 1995), Rasmussen et al. (1994), Vicente (1999), Waterson et al. (2002), Hughes et al. (1992), Beyer and Holtzblatt (1999), Hollnagel and Woods (2005), International Standards Organization (International Standards Organization 2010) are distinguished in the analysis in this paper.

Cherns (1976) and Cherns (1987) defines the socio-technological design of an organization as an outcome, and not as an input, since all contributors to the development of a socio-technological framework in an organization are subject to random decision-making processes. While Cherns lists the core principles needed for designing a socio-technological system including compatibility, minimizing the critical specification, accounting for the socio-technical aspect, multi-functional principle (organism vs. Mechanism), boundary location, information flow, support congruence, design and human values, and incompleteness, Cherns's analysis falls short of concretizing specific, applicable tools to conceptualize a socio-technological framework.

Clegg (2000) offers a revised set of socio-technical principles to guide system design. He distinguishes between meta-principles, content principles, and process principles. However, his study focuses very much on work environment related design and remains mostly on a meta level. Rather, Clegg's study falls short of the possibility of quantification and standardization of the meta-principles he offers in his 19 principles for system design, since "*principles of this kind are not offered as blueprints for strict adherence*"(p.474).

Bjerknes and Bratteteig (1995) analyzes user participation as a strategy for increasing working life democracy. They argue that due to a development from politics to ethics in system development research, a reintroduction of politics should be considered. However, the limitations of their analysis is manifested in the human-centered focus of their work. Even though their work considers the use of computer in an organizational context, the use of politics assumes *ex-ante* debates for which the outcome cannot be described through a standardized process as we propose in this paper.

De Sitter et al. (1997) focus on Integral Organizational Renewal by analyzing the transformation of complex organizational structures with simple jobs to simple organizations with complex jobs. They make use of a ratio depicting the degree of system controllability (Sc), based on Ashby (1952), and present different approaches to make the functional interrelation between internal and external relations introducing parameters such as controllability production structure and quality of work, etc. While the presented measures are a valid approach to quantify specific interrelations of components in a system architecture, they are limited to its data availability extent since these approaches are not general applicable. In contrast to that, we provide a general framework which allows to measure and apply inter-relational system components to describe a holistic system design.

Mumford (1983) and Mumford (1995) applies an ethics questionnaire where the objective is to overcome management problems rather than to introduce new technology. The problem with this approach is that it is very human labor focused and does not consider the generalization and importance of quantitative comparability of workflow processes, whereas our approach takes this into account.

Rasmussen et al. (1994) and Vicente (1999) define the problem space in the conceptualization of a system design using analytical approaches to cognitive task analysis, which is based on a functional or goal-means decomposition. It describes an analysis of the goals and structural constraints inherent in the domain. Alternative goal-means representation techniques focus more directly on representing the functions to be performed by domain practitioners and the methods and control actions available to them for performing these functions. Nevertheless, these functions are limited by the data defining the possible action set, which needs to be quantified. Therefore, the usage of our model described in this article serves as auxiliary tool for the definition of this action space and measures in a generalized way the socio-technological vulnerability of the system components.

Waterson et al. (2002) and Hollnagel and Woods (2005) describe a new method for allocating work between and among humans and machines, while Hughes et al. (1992) explore system design in the domain of air traffic control systems. This constitutes sub-areas of our analysis in this article newly introduced standardized socio-technological vulnerability measure.

Beyer and Holtzblatt (1999) focus on human- centered informatics, which helps capturing important information of key determinants of contextual system designs. This includes system constituents which can serve as input for our entropy weight method to measure the vulnerability of socio- technological systems.

1.2 Bases for the Entropy Weight Method

In light of our observations in Sect. 1.1, the goal of our work is not only the quantification, and thus the measurability of socio-technological implementation and progress, but also to provide a general framework how cross-divisional socio-technological systems can be made comparable by application of the entropy weight method.

We note that Kamissoko et al. (2015) provides a generic framework for complex systems representation for vulnerability analysis. They stress that representation is a crucial step for vulnerability analysis, since many socio-technical systems are endowed of such attributes as dynamism, self-organization, emergency etc. These attributes increase complexity of the systems. Wolf et al. (2008) provides definitions and concepts as well as the means for analyzing different definitions and usages of concepts, such as the use of conditional probabilities in order to measure system vulnerabilities.

System vulnerabilities can only be revealed by identification of system inefficiencies. But when is a system inefficient? A socio-technological system is said to be inefficient when it is components (i.e., managers) do not recognize the social and organizational complexity of the environment in which the systems are deployed. The importance of efficient systems lies in its potential scalability, meaning that once a system runs efficient, its underlying design can be rolled over and expanded to other areas of operation. For all these steps, the fundamental requirement and benchmark is a certain accuracy with which the system output meets the system expectations.

What is important for the measurement of the efficiency, scalability and accuracy of socio-technological systems is the focus on the assessment of the vulnerability of these frameworks, which are nowadays mostly large-scale software-intensive systems. However, it is our position that what existing literature is lacking, is a mathematical approach which is capable of quantifying and assessing these vulnerabilities. We are, to the best of our knowledge, the first ones who present a mathematical tool kit using entropy measurement for assessing the vulnerability of digitized socio-technological systems by expanding the improved entropy weight method, explored by Zhang et al. (2014a).

In our opinion, Zhang et al. (2014b) presented a solid framework for assessing eco-environmental vulnerability. They highlight the importance of being able to assess system weaknesses since it provides guidelines for regional planning as well as the construction and protection of ecological environment. Since their approach covers the quantification of eco-system vulnerabilities, their methodology serves as a useful basis for our hypothesis to generalize the measurement of digitized socio-technological systems.

The reason why the construction and usage of an evaluation index system serves as a sound basis for the assessment of socio-technological systems is the flexibility and general applicability of its layers. Since every layer can be measured on an individual basis via the entropy method, an overall assessment of the whole index system is possible and thus allows to identify vulnerabilities of the system. In our case we are interested in vulnerability of the system after the transformation towards a digitized system.

2 Features of the Entropy-Weight Method

In this paper, we apply the notion of information entropy measurement to the assessment of sub-systems' entropy amongst each other. This includes characteristics of human workforce, workplace environment and IT systems. A complex IT system is in this framework meant to be a system that includes *"one or more networked, software- intensive systems that is used to support the work of different types of stakeholder in one or more organizations. In general, we assume that these systems are'systems of systems' involving databases, middle ware and personal applications such as MS Excel."* (Baxter and Sommerville (2011a)).

In order to be able to evaluate the socio-technological vulnerabilities of digitized systems, we first need to define the key characteristics of socio technological systems. According to Badham et al. (2000), there are five key characteristics of open socio-technological systems:

• Systems should have interdependent parts.
• Systems should adapt to and pursue goals in external environments.
• Systems have an internal environment comprising separate but interdependent technical and social subsystems
• Systems have equifinality. In other words, systems goals can be achieved by more than one means. This implies that there are design choices to be made during system development.

• System performance relies on the joint organization of the technical and social subsystems. Focusing on one of these systems to the exclusion of the other is likely to lead to degraded system performance and utility.

The idea of socio-technological thinking is that the implementation of digital systems requires that we account for both social as well as technical factors, which affects the functionality and usage of computer-based systems. The rationale for adopting socio-technical approaches to systems design is that failure to do so can increase the risks that systems will not make their expected contribution to the goals of the organization. (Baxter and Sommerville (2011b).

Systems often meet their technical requirements but are considered to be a failure because they do not deliver the expected support for the real working the organization. The source of the problem is that techno-centric approaches to systems design do not properly consider the complex relationships between the organization, the people enacting business processes and the system that supports these processes. (Norman (1993), Goguen (1999)).

Baxter and Sommerville (2011a) assess the problems of existing approaches to socio-technical systems design such as inconsistent terminology, levels of abstraction, conflicting value systems, and lack of agreed success criteria. These factors bear potential vulnerabilities of the systems which can be, once identified, measured, and optimized using the concept of entropy. Zhang et al. (2014c) apply entropy measurement to the calculation of eco- environmental indices.

2.1 Defining Entropy for System Assessment

In order to assess the entropy of a system we must first define what entropy is. Entropy is a thermodynamic conception, which is used to measure the stage of systemic disorder. It is defined as the information content which can be seen as a negative amount of the logarithm of the probability, an actual pro-motion on the conception of the original thermodynamic entropy. This citation from thermodynamics helps us to explain the entropy for system assessment.

Information entropy reflects the stage of information disorder, which means the smaller the information entropy of ordered information source and the stage of the disordered system, the greater the utility value of information; the larger of the information entropy of ordered information source and the stage of the disordered system, the smaller the utility value of information. Apparently, decision matrix is a carrier of information, which can be evaluated by using information entropy to obtain the stage of order and utility of information system. Therefore, the use of information entropy model to calculate each index essentially means using the utility value of the index information, and the higher the utility value, the more important the evaluation. That model used to calculate each index makes it more objective to screen important indicator and compression evaluation system on the maximum based on the evaluation results without losing accuracy. (Zhang et al. (2014a)).

Due to the close nature of eco-environmental and socio-technological indices, we can apply the same definition and methodology to the identification, quantification, and assessment of the vulnerability of socio-technological systems.

The application of an extended entropy weight method to business applications such as socio-technological systems is novel. Therefore, we present the general methodology of Zhang et al. (2014b) who applied the concept of entropy measurement to eco-environmental vulnerability assessment, and leave it up to the reader, resp. User to apply certain data sets, depending on his specific needs. For an empirical eco-environmental vulnerability assessment example we refer to Zhang et al. (2014c), while we suggest here in this paper a socio-technological approach for multi-level sub-indices of different areas of IT-related business concepts.

In the next section, we present a sample construction of a possible evaluation index system for IT-related business processes. Then we set up a general framework for the application of an applied entropy weight measurement to multi-level socio- technological frameworks. After presenting the extension, we conclude.

2.2   Construction of Evaluation Index System

Each company or organization consists of several divisions, where each division pursues different goals. We assume that these goals are ought to be achieved more efficient through the transformation of an existing systems towards a digitized system. The implementation of such a digitized system requires several phases and layers of technological adaption towards the work environment and the affected users. Each of these phases or layers is subject to vulnerabilities regarding certain factors which can be measured via entropy method. In order to measure the entropy of the socio-technological system we first need to construct the evaluation index system.

This system we propose consists of quantifiable indices which we consider as being affected by the implementation of a digitized system. All related areas in the business divisions can be referred to through the measurement and listing of impact factors. Such indices can be comprised of e.g.:

• User acceptance measurement: User error counting, measurement of usage time, user survey, etc.
• Workplace compatibility: User dwelling capacity, memory storage requirements, system accessibility, etc.
• System compatibility: Error message counting, additional resources spent, daily business operations usability in percentage, etc.
• Financial impact: Incentive measurement for workforce, business division results, headcount improvement, etc.
• Performance/Productivity measurement: KPI evaluation, measurement of re- quired working hours on specific tasks, number of completed tasks/time unit, etc.

Once the index system has been generated, it is possible to measure the entropy of this system. We apply a general entropy weight method in the next chapter to this socio-technological system.

3 Application of Entropy Weight Method

In order to calculate the entropy of a whole socio-technological system we first need
to identify the internal and external environment of the system. Each environment constitutes an index which is comprised of sub-indices, where each sub-index defines the
characteristics of the main index.

For example, the internal environment involves operations, where each operation
can again be divided into several sub-operations which represent the characteristics of
the upper node index. Sub-operations can involve workplace-, IT-, or staff characteristics, etc. as well as performance-, financial-, or soft-statistics, etc. This tree structure
allows a flexible representation of all characteristics defining the socio- technological
environment.

After gathering all necessary inputs, the data will not be comparable because of size
or scale incompatibility or invariance. Therefore, it is necessary to standardize the data.
The standardized index value xij can be calculated via the Z-score:

$$x_{ij} = \frac{X_{ij-\bar{\mu}}}{\sigma_i} \tag{1}$$

where x_{ij} represents the standardized data from the ith index and the jth..., X_{ij} the original
data, while μ_i and σ_i are the mean and standard deviation of the ith index.

In order to ensure consistency during index aggregation, we transform all indices to
positive values using coordinate transformation method:

$$x_{ij}^t = x_{ij} + A \tag{2}$$

where x_{ij}^t is the standard value after the translation, $x_{ij}^t > 0$, and A represents the transla-
tional amplitude $A > |min(x_{ij})|$. The closer the value of A to $|min(x_{ij})|$, the more significant
the assessment result. The index weights are calculated by:

$$p_{ij} = \frac{x_{ij}'}{\sum_{j=1}^n x_{ij}'} \tag{3}$$

where p_{ij} is the specific gravity value for each x_{ij}^t. The index entropy is calculated by:

$$e_i = -k \sum P_{ij}\ln(P_{ij}), k = \frac{1}{\ln(n)} \tag{4}$$

where e_i the ith entropy, k is a positive value, and $k = 1/ln(n)$ is selected to ensure that
$0 \le e_i \le 1$. To solve the difference of the coefficients among various indicators, g_i,
a smaller entropy coefficient indicates a greater difference among the indicators and a
more important index. Therefore, we calculate g_i by:

$$g_i = 1 - e_i \tag{5}$$

The comprehensive index V_j to assess the socio-technological vulnerability of a
certain jth business division is calculated by:

$$V_j = \sum_{i=1}^m w_i P_{ij} \sum_{k=1}^n w_k P_{kj} \tag{6}$$

where w_i the weight of the ith positive indicator:

$$w_i = \frac{g_i}{\sum_{j=1}^{m} g_i} \tag{7}$$

Here, P_{ij} is the standard value of the ith positive indicator, w_k is the weight of the kth contrarian's indicator, and P_{kj} is the standardized value of the kth contrarian's indicator.

The measurement of the entropy of the socio-technological system reveals which index exhibits most vulnerability with respect to its digitization implementation.

Since a small entropy is preferred, as it reflects a higher order than a system of larger entropy, we can identify not only the index with the highest entropy, but also contributing factors for distortion and thus conduct improvement measures.

In Fig. 1, we illustrate the entropy index calculation process by standardizing and homogenizing different sub-indices given certain business divisions.

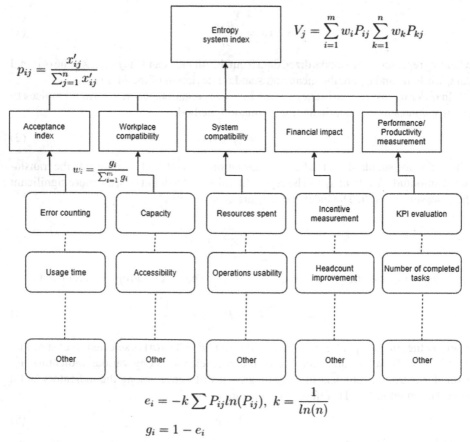

Fig. 1. Example: Index construction for vulnerability identification after system transformation to a digitized system in certain business divisions.

The example highlighted here refers to the digitalization process certain business division within an organization. All sub-indices, such as the acceptance index, can be calculated by compiling the necessary input data such as user error counting, average usage time for certain work processes, etc.

By determination of the weights, the entropy of each index, and thus the overall system entropy can be calculated. Each sub-index entropy displays the relative deviation of its mean, therefore vulnerability of the overall system can be identified by the sub-index with the highest entropy. The limitations of the entropy measurement approach are given through the distorting political decision-making processes involved in the setup of the indicators used for the error or performance measurements.

4 Conclusion

This article investigates the possibility of finding a way to measure the vulnerability of digitized socio-technological systems via entropy. Modern technology requires companies to transform their business models and processes towards digitized systems which are capable of real-time processing, execution, and evaluation. The increased efficiency and accuracy for business processes is significant.

However, the transformation to digitized systems often faces socio-technological challenges, such as user acceptance, workplace, or system compatibility. Socio- techno-logical challenges consider problems which occur at the interface of human and machine. Since it is essential that both factors are compatible, it is important to identify and measure potential vulnerabilities of the system. Other issues that might occur in a work-IT interconnection process are increased time spent on system usage due to increased complexity or user-unfriendliness, quality or quantity of newly performed tasks, and even financial impacts on workforce and headcounts.

In order to be able to measure the vulnerability of socio-technological systems, we take the entropy weight method as proposed by Zhang et al. (2014a), show how the construction of business-IT related evaluation index systems works, and apply the entropy measurement method to the socio-technological framework.

The application field of the entropy method in socio-technological frameworks is very broad since all IT-relevant social factors can be measured and quantified through indexation and thus reduce information redundancies and losses, while im- proving information accuracy and efficiency.

We suggest that future work can deal with the concrete assessment and numerical implementation of the key variables in IT-related social business frameworks and evaluate, resp. Conduct empirical tests in order to analyze the effect of the identification and fixing of vulnerabilities on socio-technological frameworks and business performance measures.

References

Ashby, W.R.: Design for a Brain. Chapman and Hall, London (1952)

Badham, R., Clegg, C., Wall, T.: Socio-technical theory. In: Karwowski, W. (ed.) Handbook of Ergonomics. John Wiley, New York, NY (2000)

Baxter, G., Sommerville, I.: Socio-technical systems: from design methods to systems engineering. Interact. Comput. **23**(1), 4–17 (2011). https://doi.org/10.1016/j.intcom.2010.07.003

Baxter, G., Sommerville, I.: Socio-technical systems: from design methods to systems engineering. Interact. Comput. **23**(1), 10 (2011). https://doi.org/10.1016/j.intcom.2010.07.003

Beyer, H., Holtzblatt, K.: Contextual design. Interactions **6**(1), 32–42 (1999)

Bjerknes, G., Bratteteig, T.: User participation and democracy: a discussion of Scandinavian research on system development. Scandinavian J. Inf. Syst. **7**(1), 73–98 (1995)

Cherns, A.: Principles of socio-technical design. Hum. Relat. **29**(8), 783–792 (1976)

Cherns, A.: Principles of socio-technical design revisited. Hum. Relat. **40**(3), 153–162 (1987)

Clegg, C.: Sociotechnical principles for system design. Appl. Ergon. **31**, 463–477 (2000)

De Sitter, L.U., Den Hertog, J.F., Dankbaar, B.: From complex organizations with simple jobs to simple organizations with complex jobs. Hum. Relat. **50**(5), 497–534 (1997)

Emery, F.E., Trist, E.L.: Socio-technical systems. In: Churchman, C.W., Verhulst, M. (eds.) Management Science Models and Techniques. Pergamon, vol. 2, pp. 83–97. Oxford, UK (1960)

Goguen, J.: Tossing algebraic flowers down the great divide. In: Calude, C.S. (ed.) People and Ideas in Theoretical Computer Science, pp. 93–129. Springer, Berlin, Germany (1999)

Hollnagel, E., Woods, D.D.: Joint Cognitive Systems: Foundations of Cognitive Systems Engineering. CRC Press, Boca Raton, FL (2005)

Hughes, J.A., Randall, D., Shapiro, D.: Faltering from ethnography to design. In: Proceedings of CSCW '1992. ACM Press, New York, NY, pp. 115–122 (1992)

International Standards Organization: Ergonomics of Human-System Inter- action - Part 210: Human-centred Design for Interactive Systems. ISO, Geneva, Switzerland (2010)

Kamissoko, D., Peres, F., Zarate, P., Gourc, D.: Complex system representation for vulnerability analysis. IFAC-Papers OnLine **48**(3), 948–953 (2015)

Mumford, E.: Designing human systems for new technology - The ETHICS Method (1983). <https://www.enid.eu-net.com/C1book1.htm>

Mumford, E.: Effective Systems Design and Requirements Analysis: The ETHICS Method. Macmillan Press, Basingstoke, UK (1995)

Norman, D.A.: Things that make us Smart: Defending Human Attributes in the Age of the Machine. Addison-Wesley, Boston, MA (1993)

Rasmussen, J., Pejtersen, A.-M., Goodstein, L.P.: Cognitive Systems Engineering. Wiley, Chichester, UK (1994)

Vicente, K.: Cognitive Work Analysis. LEA, Mahwah, NJ (1999)

Waterson, P.E., Older Gray, M.T., Clegg, C.W.: A sociotechnical method for designing work systems. Hum. Factors **44**(3), 376–391 (2002)

Wolf, S., Lincke, D., Hinkel, J., Ionescu, C., Bisaro, S.: A formal frame- work of vulnerability final deliverable to the ADAM project. FAVAIA Working Paper, May 2008

Zhang, X., Wang, C., Li, E., Xu, C.: Assessment model of eco-environmental vulnerability based on improved entropy weight method. Hindawi Publishing Corporation. Sci. World J. **2014**, Article ID 797814, 7, 15 July 2014

Zhang, X., Wang, C., Li, E., Xu, C.: Assessment model of ecoenvironmental vulnerability based on improved entropy weight method. Hindawi Publishing Corporation. Sci. World J. **2014**, Article ID 797814, 2, 15 July 2014

Zhang, X., Wang, C., Li, E., Xu, C.: Assessment model of ecoenvironmental vulnerability based on improved entropy weight method. Hindawi Publishing Corporation. Sci. World J. **2014**, Article ID 797814, 3, 15 July 2014

Chapter 4
Two-Stage Nonsmooth Stochastic Optimization and Iterative Stochastic Quasigradient Procedure for Robust Estimation, Machine Learning and Decision Making

Tatiana Ermolieva[(⊠)], Yuri Ermoliev, Michael Obersteiner, and Elena Rovenskaya

International Institute for Applied Systems Analysis, Laxenburg, Austria
ermol@iiasa.ac.at

Abstract. Uncertainties, risks, and disequilibrium are pervasive characteristics of modern socio-economic, technological, and environmental systems involving interactions between humans, economics, technology and nature. The systems are characterized by interdependencies, discontinuities, endogenous risks and thresholds, requiring nonsmooth quantile-based performance indicators, goals and constraints for their analysis and planning. The paper discusses the need for the two-stage stochastic optimization and the stochastic quasigradient (SQG) procedures to manage such systems. The two-stage optimization enables designing a robust portfolio of interdependent precautionary strategic and adaptive operational decisions making the systems robust with respect to potential uncertainty and risks. The SQG iterative algorithms define a "searching" process, which resembles a sequential adaptive learning and improvement of decisions from data and simulations, i.e. the so-called Adaptive Monte Carlo optimization. The SQG methods are applicable in cases when traditional stochastic approximation, gradient or stochastic gradient methods do not work, in particular, to general two-stage problems with implicitly defined goals and constraints functions, nonsmooth and possibly discontinuous performance indicators, risk and uncertainties shaped by decision of various agents. Stylized models from statistics, machine learning, robust decision making are presented to illustrate the two-stage (strategic-adaptive) modeling concept and the SQG procedures. The stylized models are parts of larger integrated assessment models developed at IIASA, e.g. Global Biosphere Management model (GLOBIOM) and Integrated Catastrophe Risk Management model (ICRIM).

Keywords: Uncertainties · Endogenous risks · Thresholds · Quantile-based performance indicators · Nonsmooth two-stage STO · SQG algorithms

© Springer Nature Switzerland AG 2021
F. S. Roberts and I. A. Sheremet (Eds.): Resilience in the Digital Age, LNCS 12660, pp. 45–74, 2021.
https://doi.org/10.1007/978-3-030-70370-7_4

1   Introduction

Uncertainties, risks, thresholds, and disequilibrium are pervasive characteristics of modern socio-economic and environmental systems involving interactions between humans, economics, technology and nature. Interdependencies among the systems resemble a complex network connected through demand–supply relations. Disruption of this network or systemic imbalances may induce systemic risks affecting food, energy, water, and environmental (FEWE) security at different scales with possible global spill-overs. Technological innovations increase uncertainty and risk as each new change introduces new interdependencies and perturbs existing knowledge of systems' structure and dynamics, limitations and constraints, e.g. as a result of deregulations and distributed (variable renewable) energy sources [6,7]. At the same time, many existing systems are too complex and interdependent to allow for precise measurement of the parameters and the state of the system, e.g. environmental or land use systems [45,54,69,72].

Ensuring robust and sustainable performance of the systems in the face of uncertainty and risks is equivalent to equipping them with measures that prepare them in advance and facilitate their proper adaptive responses to changing conditions. These anticipative and adaptive measures reduce the chances of critical imbalances and exceedances of vital thresholds, which could otherwise lead to systemic failures. For example, regional planners may think of long-term investments into new technologies, grain and water storage capacities, irrigation and land use diversifications, insurance, investments, savings, performance of medical check-ups. The decisions can be characterized as long-term anticipative (ex-ante "here-and-now", i.e. before exact scenario of uncertainty becomes known) and short-term adaptive (ex-post "wait-and-see", i.e. after learning additional information). The long-term anticipative (strategic) decisions are independent from the uncertainty scenario. They can be rather expensive and hardly reversible, e.g. land conversion or investments into new technologies [4]. The short-term measures are scenario-specific adaptive actions that are made to adjust the strategic decisions after receiving additional knowledge or observations of the system's parameters.

A portfolio of *robust* interdependent ex-ante and ex-post strategies can be designed by using two-stage stochastic optimization (STO) incorporating both types of decisions. The SQG methods overcome challenges associated with various imbalances, thresholds, and quantile-based safety constraints, typical for nonsmooth and often discontinuous and nonconvex systems ([30–32,37] and references therein). The SQG methods are developed to solve general purpose optimization problems, characterized by implicitly given (nested) nonsmooth and possibly discontinuous goals and constraints, analytically intractable endogenous probability distributions, i.e. in all those cases when traditional solution techniques such as stochastic approximation, gradient or stochastic gradient descent methods are not applicable. The robustness is characterized by the explicit representation of the feasible decisions, potential threats, and adequate quantile-based performance functions and constraints.

Section 2 introduces the two-stage STO and the SQG procedures. The SQG methods can be defined as a "searching" process and we can think of this search as *adaptive machine learning and improvement*" of decisions from data and simulations, i.e. the so-called *Adaptive Monte Carlo* optimization [25–27,33,35]. Various problems of statistics, big data analysis, artificial intelligence (AI), and decision-making under uncertainty can be formulated or can be reduced to the two-stage STO and solved with SQG methods. For example, these are problems that involve minimization or maximization of an objective or a goal function when randomness is present in model's data and parameters, e.g. observations, costs, prices, crop yields, heavy precipitation and drought events, return periods of natural disasters, etc. The methods are essential for agricultural production planning under weather variability and market risks (e.g. robust crop and management diversification), assets allocation and investment portfolio management under financial risks, land use management and investments prioritization for biodiversity preservation, managing security of critical infrastructure, energy technologies investment planning, and for many other areas. Specific applications include: deriving optimal parameters of a statistical model (parametric or nonparametric) for a given dataset; training a machine learning model that maps an input to an output based on examples of input-output pair through minimizing/maximizing a "goodness-of-fit" criteria; deciding on optimal dynamic investments allocation into new technologies (irrigation, energy, agricultural, water management) to minimize costs or/and maximize profits accounting for various norms and constraints; deciding when to release water from a multipurpose reservoir for hydroelectricpower generation, agricultural and industrial production, household requirements, environmental constraints, flood protection; defining insurance coverage and premiums to minimize risk of bankruptcy of insurers and risk of overpaiments of individuals. Randomness enters the problems in several ways: through stochastic (exogenous or endogenous) costs and prices, stochastic resource availability (e.g. water, land, biomass) constraints, random occurrence of exogenous natural disasters depleting resources and assets, stochastic endogenous events (systemic risks) induced by decisions of various agents. Stochastic variables can be characterized by means of a probability distribution (parametric or nonparametric) function or can be represented by probabilistic scenarios.

Probability distributions of stochastic parameters are often non-normal, heavy tailed and even multimodal. In this case, such criteria as *Mean-Variance*, *Ordinary Least Square (OLS)* or *Root Mean Squared Error (RMSE)* are not applicable as they account for the first two moments, i.e. mean and variance, which characterize normal distributions (Sect. 2.1, "Least square regression"). The criteria are not robust, i.e. they are sensitive to outliers, which can significantly distort the results (for the detailed discussions of robustness in statistics and decision-making see [28,29]). By focusing on the mean and variance, the information about the tails of the underlying distributions can be lost. In statistics and machine learning, the OLS and RMSE estimates can be misleading, and the effects can be different for different subsets of data sample.

For general, possibly multimodal, probability distributions it is more natural to use the *median* or other *quantile-based* criteria instead of the mathematical expectation (Sect. 2.1, "Quantile-based regression"). The problem of nonsmooth quantile-based optimization including regression analysis is closely related to the Value-at-Risk (VaR) and Conditional Value-at-Risk minimization (CVaR). It can be formulated as a problem of a two-stage STO with implicit discontinuous chance (probabilistic or quantile-based) constraints used for robust decision-making under uncertainty and risks ([5,6,17,19,21,25,28,38,46,47,51, 52,56,57,59,61], and references therein). For nonsmooth, possibly discontinuous and nonconvex problems, including quantile-based regression and neural networks training, the convergence of the SQG methods is proven in [35–37,43,49].

Sections 3.1–3.4 present stylized two-stage strategic-adaptive STO models for robust decision-making, which can easily become a part of more complex (stochastic) models such as GLOBIOM [13,19,55], MESSAGE [50–52,57], ICRIM [17,26,27,33,34,38] developed at IIASA. The models explore different types of goals and constraints functions, e.g. nonsmooth probabilistic or chance constraints, enabling robust FEWE security management (see also [28,29]). For example, in Sect. 3.1 ("Two-stage pollution reduction model, mitigation versus adaptation: VaR and CVaR risk measure") it is shown that the strategic anticipative decisions manage only a part of the risk, whereas the other part is managed by connected with them properly designed adaptive ex-post decisions. Therefore, the two-stage approach allows to take strategic decisions and leaves sufficient flexibility for their adaptive adjustments to minimize the risks of irreversibility and lock-in situations [4,19].

Section 3.1 ("Managing agricultural risks via irrigation: strategic versus adaptive decisions") further illustrates the interplays between the risk averse (first-stage anticipative) and the risk prone (second-stage adaptive) components of decisions. The model in Sect. 3.3 ("Two-stage production planning under uncertainty: storage versus imports") is useful for the modeling and management of a robust NEXUS between agricultural and energy production, water allocation, and in other problems associated with "hitting" uncertain targets, e.g. regarding food, energy and water demand, pollution level. This model has been used as a part of GLOBIOM model to analyze the emergence of systemic risks which are implicitly characterized by the complex network interdepedencies among land use systems including costs, demand-supply (im)balances, market prices, technologies, security targets, risks and risk measures, and feasible decisions of various agents. The model in Sect. 3.4 ("Stochastic facility allocation problem") generalizes examples of Sects. 3.1–3.3. It addresses a problem of spatial facilities (production, processing, housing, healthcare, food services) allocation when demand and supply are stochastic variables with possible implicit and endogenous character of underlying probability distributions.

Large-scale detailed sectorial models (e.g. GLOBIOM, MESSAGE, GAINS) exist, and they are used to plan the developments in respective sectors. The problem is how to link these models for truly integrative FEWE security analysis and management within joint resource constraints. Reprogramming models into a single code is a tedious task, which is often not feasible because the models and the corresponding data belong to different teams or agents. Section 3.5 discusses an SQG-based procedure for linking the individual models in a decentralized fashion via a central planner (central "hub") without requiring the exact information about models' structure and data, i.e. in the conditions of asymmetric information and uncertainty. The sequential SQG solution procedure organizes an iterative computerized negotiation between sectorial (food, water, energy, environmental) systems (models) representing *Intelligent Agents (IA)*. The convergence of the procedure to the socially optimal solution is based on the results of non-differentiable optimization providing a new type of *machine learning algorithms* [37,41,43]. The linkage problem can be viewed as a general endogenous *reinforced learning* problem of how software agents (models) take decisions in order to maximize the "cumulative reward". Similar computerized negotiation processes between distributed models (agents) have been developed for the design of robust carbon trading markets (e.g. [22,23] and references therein) and for water quotas allocation (e.g. [44]).

Section 4 presents complex *dynamic STO and SQG-based models* developed at IIASA for *energy-efficient technology investments* [6,7] and for *integrated catastrophic risk management* [25–27,38] and references therein). Similar principles of the dynamic two-stage STO models have been used in Global Biosphere Management Model (GLOBIOM) for strategic-operational land and water resources management for FEWE security under systemic risks [19,20], in the energy systems planning MESSAGE model [51,52,57], for robust operation of water reservoir under stochastic inflows [11,59], for restructuring and modernization of heavy industry [61]. Section 5 concludes and highlights main advantages and directions for further implementation of the two-stage STO and the SQG solution procedures, in the context of currently emerging large-scale problems of robust statistical estimation, machine learning, and decision making. Annex discusses some properties of the SQG solution procedures.

2   Endogenous Risks, Two-Stage STO and SQG

Various problems of statistics and decision making under uncertainty can be formulated or can be reduced to the following STO model: find x minimizing (maximizing) the expectation functional:

$$F(x) = Ef(x,\omega) = \int f(x,\omega)P(d\omega), \tag{1}$$

$$x \in X, \tag{2}$$

where the set of feasible decisions X can be a set of scalar quantities, a set of vectors or a set of abstract elements, e.g., a set of probability density functions. In general, the set X can be described by using similar to (1) expectation functionals $F_i(x) = Ef_i(x,\omega) = \int f_i(x,\omega)P(d\omega) \leq 0$, $i = 1, 2, ..., m$, defining the constraints. The vector of stochastic parameters ω, $\omega \in \Omega$, is characterized by a probability measure or probability distribution $P(d\omega)$ (or $P(x, d\omega)$ if the probability distribution depends on x).

Stochastic ω can reflect stochastic costs, prices, returns, crop yields, extreme losses due to natural disasters, resource availability, etc. The stochasticity can be characterized by a probability distribution function or by a set of probabilistic scenarios derived based on expert opinions or generated by a stochastic generator of extreme events [2]. The goal of the STO problem (1–2) is to find a solution x by simultaneously accounting for all realizations of uncertain parameters. The choice of the random function $f(x, \omega)$ depends on the problem under investigation. For example, it can define total producer costs and consumer expenditures, pollution abatement costs, catastrophe-induced losses, etc. Nonsmooth and possibly discontinuous functions $f(x, \omega)$ arise in problems involving threshold constraints, safety requirements, security norms, i.e. in all those cases when the exceedance of a critical vital threshold can lead to very costly and possibly irreversible, consequences. The main goal is then to find such x that allows to avoid the threshold exceedances for all or for a prescribed quantile of ω scenarios. More detailed discussion of these problems can be found in Sect. 3.1–3.4.

The main complexity of STO model (1–2) is that exact evaluation of $F(x)$ is practically impossible. This may be due to various reasons: probability measure $P(d\omega)$ is unknown or only partially known, random function $f(x, \omega)$ is analytically intractable, or the evaluation of $F(x)$ is analytically intractable despite well-defined $f(x, \omega)$ and P, or the distribution of ω depends on solution x, i.e. $P(x, d\omega)$. Often, for fixed x only observations of $f(x, \omega)$ are available, e.g. generated by Monte Carlo simulations of stochastic scenario generators based on historical observations, expert opinions, bio-physical models, models of extreme events (see e.g. [2,38]).

In many problems, when it is not possible to find a solution x that is feasible ($x \in X$) and minimizes the objective function (1–2) for all (or nearly all) ω, it is practical to use a *two-stage* STO model. In the *two-stage* STO problems, the structure of the sampling function $f(x, \omega)$ depends on two types of decisions (x, y), $f(x, \omega) = g(x, y, \omega)$, where y depends on x and ω: *the ex-ante (strategic risk averse, anticipative) decisions $x \in R^n$ of the first-stage are made on the basis of a priory information about random uncertain variables ω. The second-stage ex-post (risk prone, adaptive) decisions $y \in R^r$ are chosen after making an additional observation on ω, after "learning" additional information about* ω. For known ω and x, decisions $y = y(x, \omega)$ are evaluated by some functions $g_i(x, y, \omega), i = 0, 1, ..., m$ which define the constraints

$$g_i(x, y, \omega) \leq 0, i = 1, ..., m, \tag{3}$$

and the objective function $g_0(x, y, \omega)$. The ex-ante decisions x, which are chosen before the observation of ω, cannot properly anticipate ω and, hence, cannot satisfy (3) exactly. Combining them with the ex-post decisions $y(x, \omega)$ allow to fulfill (3) after revealing information on ω. They minimize $g_0(x, y, \omega)$ for given x, ω subject to (3) and some additional constraints $y \in Y$ such as $y \geq 0$. Let us denote the feasible set of this standard deterministic problem as $Y(x, \omega)$

and an optimal solution as $y(x, \omega)$. In various important applications $y(x, \omega)$ is easily calculated, and its existence can be ensured by introducing some auxiliary variables.

The function $g_0(x, y, \omega)$ reflects a trade-off between choosing some options x "now" and postponing other options y "after" full information on ω becomes available. Therefore, in the two-stage models the random objective function $f(x, \omega) = g_0(x, y(x, \omega), \omega)$ is a rather general implicitly defined nonsmooth function even for linear in (x, y) functions $g_i(x, y, \omega), i = 0, 1, ..., m$.

In many problems, in particular when the probability distribution of uncertainty ω depends on solutions x, general purpose SQG methods designed for solving general optimization problems (including problems with nonsmooth, discontinuous, and nonconvex functions [30–32] are applicable for minimizing the two-stage STO model (1–3). In fact, as the following sections show, there are fundamental obstacles in using other methods than the SQG methods even for STO problems with one linear function. The *stochastic quasi-gradient* (SQG) is a *stochastic vector*, which mathematical expectation close (in a certain sense) to the gradient, subgradient or generalized gradient of the function.

The SQG methods do not require exact calculation of objective functions, constraints, and gradients. They incorporate basic ideas of standard optimization methods, random search procedures, stochastic approximation and statistical estimation. The SQG methods are applicable to both deterministic and stochastic minimax (SMM) problems. SMM problems, which are similar to the two-stage stochastic programing, have nested nonsmooth sample (random) objective functions. There are at least three broad applications areas for SQG methods:

- Deterministic problems for which the calculation of descent directions is difficult (large-scale, nonsmooth, distributed, nested, and nonstationary optimization models).
- Multiextremal problems where it is important to bypass locally optimal solutions.
- Problems involving uncertainties or/and difficulties in the evaluation of functions and their subgradients (stochastic, spatial, and dynamic optimization problems with multidimensional nested integrals, simulation and other analytically intractable models).

The SQG methods require only modest computer resources per iteration and reach with reasonable speed the vicinity of optimal solutions, with an accuracy that is sufficient for many applications (for detailed proofs see [37, 43]). The SQG methods can be defined as a "searching" process. We can think of this "search" as "adaptive machine learning", when at each iteration the solution is updated with respect to newly arriving data, information, or simulations. The SQG methods have been used in operations research, robust decision-making, multi-agent systems, control theory, simulation-based optimization, statistics, machine learning, data processing, game theory, optimal water management and quotas allocation, integrated catastrophic risks management, systemic risks and food-water-energy-environmental security management (see e.g. [29–32, 35, 38, 44, 47]).

2.1   STO and SQG Procedures for Statistical Estimation and Machine Learning

Statistics (statistical decision theory) deals with situations in which the model of uncertainty and the optimal solution are defined by unknown sampling model P. The main issue is to recover P by using available samples of observations drawn randomly according to P. In other words, the desirable optimal solution $x = x^*$ is associated with P (or its parameters), the performance of x^* can be observed from available random data on its performance. Consider some important statistical estimation problems which can be formulated as STO model (1–2). Essential assumption is that P does not depend on x.

Least Square Regression. Assume that a random function $u(v)$ for each element v from a set V corresponds a random element $u(v)$ of the set U, where $V \subset R^l$, $U \subset R^1$. Let P be a joint probability measure defined on pairs $\omega = (u, v)$. The regression function is defined as the conditional mathematical expectation $r(v) = E(u|v) = \int uP(U|v)$. It is easy to see that $r(v)$ minimizes the functional

$$F(x) = E\left(u(v) - x\right)^2, \tag{4}$$

where $Eu^2(v) < \infty$. It follows from the fact that

$$\min_{x(v)} F(x(v)) = E \min_x E\left[(u(v) - x)^2|v\right], \quad \frac{d}{dx} E\left[(u(v) - x)^2|v\right] = -2(E(u|v) - x) = 0.$$

The estimation of $r(v)$ is usually considered in *the set of functions given in a parametric form* $\{r(x, v), x \in X\}$. In this case, the criterion $F(x(v)) = E\left(u(v) - x\right)^2$ can be rewritten as

$$F(x) = E(u(v) - r(x, v))^2 = E(r(v) - r(x, v))^2 + E(u(v) - r(x, v))^2,$$

i.e., the minimum of $F(x)$ is attained at the function $r(x, v)$ which is close to $r(v)$ in the metric $L_2(P)$ defined as $\sqrt{E(r(v) - r(x, v))^2}$.

Quantile-Based Regression. The *conditional expectation* $r(v)$ provides a satisfactory representation of stochastic dependencies $u(v)$ when they are well approximated by two first moments, e.g., for normal distributions. For general (possibly, multimodal) distributions it is more natural to use the median or other quantiles, instead of the expectation. Let us define the quantile regression function $r_\rho(v)$ at level ρ as the maximal value x satisfying equation $P(u(v) \geq x|v) = \rho(v)$, where $0 < \rho(v) < 1$, i.e. the probability that $u(v)$ is greater or equal than y is equal to $\rho(v)$ given observations v. In various risk management studies, the estimate $r_\rho(v)$ defines the Value-at-Risk ([28, 65] evaluating the level of downside risk in the in- and out-of-sample analysis of extreme events, production and market risks, etc. The function $r_\rho(v)$ minimizes the functional

$$F(x) = E(\rho(v)x + \max\{0, u(v) - x\}). \tag{5}$$

This is due to the following. First of all, we have

$$\min_x F(x) = E \min_x E \left[\rho(v)x + \max\{0, u(v) - x|v\} \right].$$

Assume that probability measure (probability distribution function) $P(d\omega)$ has a continuous density function $p(\omega)$, $P(d\omega) = p(\omega)d\omega$. Then from the optimality condition for internal stochastic minimax problem it follows that optimal solution x satisfies the equation

$$\rho(v) - \int_x^\infty P(d\omega|v) = 0, \tag{6}$$

i.e., indeed, it satisfies condition $P(u(v) \geq y|v) = \rho(v)$. The optimal value of the functional F at $r_\rho(v)$ is a Conditional Value at Risk (CVaR) at the level of $\rho(v)$.

Let us note that the minimization of a more general at the first glance functional

$$F(x) = E(a(v)x + \max\left\{\alpha(v)(u(v) - x), \beta(v)(x - u(v))\right\})$$

is reduced to the minimization of (5) with the percentile level $\rho(v)$ defined as $\rho(v) = (a + \beta)(\alpha + \beta)^{-1}$, where a is any parameter (for example, costs, profits, returns), α and β can be associated with penalties for over- and under-estimation (similar to the unit surplus and unit shortage cost in Sect. 3.3). The median corresponds to the case when $a \equiv 0$, $\alpha = \beta$. The existence of optimal solution requires $a < \alpha$. The estimation of quantiles $r_\rho(v)$ can be considered by a parametric set of functions $\{r_\rho(x, v), x \in X\}$. In this case, the criterion (5) is rewritten as

$$F(x) = E \left[\rho(v)r(x, v) + \max\left\{0, u(x) - r(x, v)\right\} \right]$$

or equivalently $F(x) = E \max \left[\alpha(v) (u(v) - r(x, v)), \beta(v) (r(x, v) - u(v)) \right]$, for $\alpha(v) > 0$, $\beta(v) > 0$, $\rho(v) = \alpha(v)/(\alpha(v) + \beta(v))$.

If $r(\cdot, v)$ is a linear function for all $v \in V$, then $F(x)$ can be minimized by linear programming methods. For a general form of $r(\cdot, v)$ functions, the solutions can be attained by the SQG methods. In problems of robust decision-making under uncertainty, the probability distribution $P(d\omega)$ can be a complex analytically intractable nested function of decisions, and percentile level $\rho(v)$ can be defined by the structure of the whole model including various costs α and β. The relation between the quantile-based estimation and the two-stage optimization is further clarified in Sects. 3.1–3.4. Calculation of the SQG for various problems is outlined in Annex (SQG calculation).

Machine Learning. In the big data era, vast amount of information are generated every day. Thus, efficient optimization tools are needed to solve the resultant large-scale machine learning problems. Machine learning is based on the principles of statistical learning theory (see e.g. [70,71]). Machine learning is being used in various areas related to patters and image recognition, forecasting markets behavior, etc. The type of the machine learning model (a perceptron, a network of neurons, a decision tree, a random forest, a linear or a logistic regression, Support Vector Machine, and other models) does not affect the general machine learning principles.

Numerical optimization has played an important role in the evolution of machine learning. For example, the gradient decent procedures (GD), the stochastic gradient decent (SGD) and their modifications and extensions (stochastic average gradient (SAG), stochastic dual coordinate ascent (SDCA), Nesterov's accelerated gradient (NAG), stochastic variance reduced gradient (SVRG) and other) have been widely viewed as solution approaches to large-scale machine learning problems [60,66,68]. Many of the algorithms rely on earlier results of Robins and Monro [62], Nesterov [58], Polyak and Judinsky [63] for smooth optimization.

However, many big data and machine learning problems have to deal with nonsmooth quantile-based loss, activation, and regularization functions. In neural networks training, multiple layers and nonsmooth activation functions defined in terms of absolute value, maximum or minimum operations, further complicate the problem. Graphs of nonsmooth functions may have abrupt bends and even discontinuities requiring the development and application of subdifferential and stochastic quasigradient calculus [9,30,32,39,40,43,64]. In these cases, the SQG methods of nonsmooth STO are concerned with extensions of the gradients and stochastic gradients to generalized directional derivatives, subgradients and stochastic quasigradients. The convergence of the SQG methods are proven in rather general cases [37,41,43]. In particular, for highly nonconvex models such as deep neural networks, the SQG methods allow to bypass local solutions. In cases of nonstationary data, the SQGs allow for sequential updating, revision, and adaptation of parameters to the changing environment, possibly, based on offline adaptive simulations.

Let us briefly discuss the application of the SQG method to a neural network learning problem. In general, it can be any machine learning problem where parameters of the prediction model (linear and logistic regression, classification and decision trees, Support Vector Machines) are estimated through minimization of the so-called "loss function" (or "goodness-of-fit") minimising the forecast error. In order to learn a neural network, it is necessary to define the net structure and *train* the net (i.e. estimate the parameters/weights of the network model) on the available set of examples (training set) for which the solution of the problem is known, i.e. on the available input-output data. The input-output data can come from direct or indirect observations, expert opinion, or as input-output of more complex (e.g. socio-economic, bio-physical, environmental) models. The training task is formulated as the task of minimizing a loss function (empirical risk), which measures the forecast error of the model. The root mean squared error (RMSE) (see also Sect. 2.1) predicts only an average response, but not necessarily potential extreme outcomes. Dealing with extreme events/scenarios, e.g. crop yield shocks, production and market risks, catastrophe structural losses, it is more appropriate to use a quantile-based loss (QL) function (similar to Sect. 2.1). Depending on a practical problem, the QL permits

one to distinguish values which are higher or lower than the specified quantile of
the data in the training set and impose different penalty costs for the positive
and negative deviations from the quantile. Formally, the training of a neural net
is equivalent to the minimization of the loss function $F(x)$ with respect to the
parameters x:

$$F(x) = \sum_{i=1}^{N} F(i, x), \tag{7}$$

where the $F(i, x)$ are (nested) neuron-type functions and N is the size of the
training set. Each function $F(i, x)$ corresponds to one training object. At each
step $k = 0, 1, ...$, an object $i = i(k)$ is picked up at random with probability
$\mu(i) > 0$ among N alternatives. Starting from the initial parameter x^0, the
vector x^k of parameters x is adjusted in the direction opposite to the stochastic
(sub)gradient

$$\xi(k) = 1/\mu(i(k))F_x(i(k), x^k) \tag{8}$$

of the function $F(i, x)$, $i = i(x)$. It is easy to see that $E[\xi(k)|x^k] = F_x(x^k)$,
i.e. it is an SQG. The index $i(k)$ changes from iteration to iteration in order to
cover more or less uniformly the set of indices $1, ..., N$. Calculation of $\xi(k)$, and in
particular, $F_x(i(k), x^k)$ for different training cases $i = i(k)$, including nonsmooth
and nonconvex functions F and discrete event systems is discussed in [30–32].

The trained neural network (NN) models can be used as *reduced form generators (meta-models) of stochastic scenarios* or as *submodels* of more complex models. For example, an NN-based generator of crop yield scenarios can be trained
using historical data on weather parameters and crop yields results of a bio-
physical EPIC model, for historical and projected yields, different combinations
of SSP-RCP scenarios, at the resolution of 1 sq. km grid [10, 13, 67]. Quantile-
based loss function allows to capture extreme crop yield scenarios arising due to
biological thresholds in plants growth as a function of various factors. Crop yield
distributions are negatively skewed or even multimodal because of biological constraints that limit plant growth in response to various, often cumulative combinations of weather parameters (precipitation, temperature, pressure), which
have complex temporal and spatial patters. Apart from climate and weather
uncertainty, yields depend on soil conditions and land use management practice.
To capture the main characteristics, various approaches to model crop yield
probability distributions including parametric and nonparametric kernel-based
percentile regression and neural networks techniques, have been tested to determine, in some sense, the best model. Preliminary results show that training a
one-layer neural network produces a better "goodness-of-fit" result (lower forecast error) than training a linear and a logistic regression model on the same
set of training data. However, if the number of input parameters and network
layers increases, the learning process may take too long or even may not be
accomplished at all. As an alternative to neural networks, linear and logistic
regression, nonparametric regression models deserve further exploration.

3   Two-Stage STO and SQG Procedures for Robust decision Making

Uncertainty, thresholds, nonsmoothness, and potential abrupt changes are inherent in many socio-economic, technological and environmental systems. In order to make these systems more robust they can be equipped with the two basic types of measures: the long term anticipative (forward looking, ex-ante) settings or policies (production or technological portfolio, resource allocation, policy directives, engineering design, pre-disaster planning, etc.); and adaptive short-term adaptive adjustments (marketing, reservoir withdrawals, adaptive control, post-disaster adaptation, etc.) adopted after learning additional information ("by-doing", researches, observations). Let us consider stylized stochastic models illustrating that according to the two-stage modeling approach, in general, only a part of the risk is managed by ex-ante strategic scenario-independent anticipative decisions whereas the other part is managed by connected with them properly designed ex-post adaptive decisions adjusting the strategic decisions in each uncertainty scenario. The models show that strong interdependencies among ex-ante and ex-post decisions induce endogenous risk aversion and allows to minimize the risk of irreversibility and sunk costs typically emerging in a scenario-dependent deterministic modeling. These models are in a sense snapshots of more complex stochastic integrated assessment models.

3.1   Two-Stage Pollution Reduction Model, Mitigation Versus adaptation: VaR and CVaR Risk Measure

A stylized pollution (or emission) reduction model can be formulated as follows: let x denotes an amount of pollution reduction and let a random variable β denotes an uncertain critical level of required pollution reduction. Ex-ante pollution reductions $x \geq 0$ with costs cx may underestimate β, i.e. $x < \beta$. To meet the target, adaptation measure y are taken so that the total pollution reduction fulfills the requirement $x + y \geq \beta$. A linear total adaptation cost is dy, where y is an ex-post adaptation when the information about the uncertain β becomes available. Let us assume that $c < d$. The two-stage model is formulated as the minimization of expected total cost $cx + dEy$ subject to the constraint $x + y \geq \beta$. This problem is equivalent to the minimization of function $F(x) = cx + E\min\{dy|x + y \geq \beta\}$ or $F(x) = cx + dE\max\{0, \beta - x\}$, which is a simple stochastic minimax problem. Indicator $E\max\{0, \beta - x\}$ defines the downside risk of not sufficient reduction measures ($\beta > x$) and d is a price (environmental cost) for unit pollution. Optimality conditions ([35,36], pp. 107, 416) for these types of problems show that the optimal ex-ante solution is the critical quantile $x^* = \beta_p$ satisfying the safety constraint

$$Pr[x \geq \beta] \geq p \tag{9}$$

for $p = 1 - c/d$ assuming the distribution of β has a density. It is interesting to notice that if $c/d < 1$, then $x^* > 0$ (i.e., it calls for coexistence of *ex-ante* and *ex-post* decisions). The optimal second-stage solution $y^*(x, \beta)$ is defined as $y^*(x, \beta) = \max\{0, \beta - x^*\}$. Equation (9) means that the level of pollution reduction will be greater than the critical level β at a given probability (acceptable level) p. The constraint (9) is known as chance constraint. This is a remarkable result: highly non-linear and even often discontinuous safety (or chance) constraint (9) is derived from an explicit introduction of ex-post second stage decisions y. In other words, although the two-stage model is linear in variables x and y, the strong risk aversion is induced among ex-ante decisions characterized by the critical quantile β_p. Only the "slice" β_p of the risk is managed ex-ante, whereas the rest $y^* = \beta - \beta_p$ is adapted ex-post.

The probabilistic safety constraint (9) defines the VaR at the level of p. It is easy to see that the optimal value $F(x^*) = dE\beta I(\beta > x^*)$, where $I(\cdot)$ is the indicator function. This is the expected shortfall or Conditional Value-at-Risk (CVaR) risk measure. The chance constraints of the type (9) are important for the regulation of stability in the insurance industry (insolvency constraints); the safety regulation of nuclear reactors requires $p = 10^{-7}$ (i.e., a major failure occurs on average only once in 10^{-7} years). Critical infrastructure resilience also relies on the concept of probabilistic or chance constraints.

In more realistic models, β is defined as a rather complex process dependent on scenarios and policies of future global energy system, land use changes, demographic dynamics, etc., generated by integrated assessment models such as MESSAGE, GLOBIOM, RAINS (for general discussion of various scenarios design see [48]. In these cases, it is practically impossible to derive the distribution of β analytically. Instead, only random scenarios of $\beta, \beta^0, \beta^1, \beta^2, \ldots$, can be generated providing sufficient information for SQG methods to design a new type adaptive machine learning of robust policies defined by the convergent with probability 1 discontinuous stochastic process (10). $F(x)$ is a convex and nonsmooth function, its SQG is $\xi = \xi(x, \beta) = c - d$ for $\beta < x$; and $\xi = c$ otherwise. Therefore, the SQG projection method for $k = 0, 1, \ldots$ is defined as the following:

$$x^{k+1} = \max\{0, x^k - \rho_k \xi(x^k, \beta^k)\}, \tag{10}$$

where ρ_k is a positive stepsize (for details on properties and calculation of ρ_k see [35, 37], "Stochastic quasigradient methods").

3.2 Managing Agricultural Risks via Irrigation: Strategic Versus adaptive Decisions

This example illustrates the nonsmooth character of the objective function (1) (i.e. $F(x) = Ef(x, \omega)$), which prohibits the use of the standard stochastic approximation procedures and requires the SQG methods. The example further illustrates the interplays between the risk averse (first-stage strategic) and the risk prone (second-stage adaptive) components of decisions.

Assume that the agricultural performance of a region can be improved by irrigation. If the river water level is characterized by its average value, the decision to use irrigation is trivial and depends, in particular, on whether the profit per hectare of irrigated area d_1 is greater than the profit d_3 from a hectare without use of irrigation. The stochastic variation of the river water level creates essential difficulties. In situations of low water levels, the land prepared in advance can only be partially supplemented with additional water, resulting in a profit d_2 per hectare in the remainder of such land. Besides this, the situation may also be affected by variations in water prices: it is easy to imagine a scenario when in a dry season the use of irrigation water may become unprofitable although irrigation is profitable under average conditions.

Suppose Q is the level of available water; q is the amount of water required for irrigation of a hectare. Denote by $x \leq a$ the area which must be prepared in advance for irrigation (ex-ante strategic decision), where a is the total irrigable acreage. There may be two types of risks: in situations when $Q < xq$ (water under supply) there is the risk to forego the profit per hectare of land that irrigates. In the case $Q > xq$ (water oversupply) there is the risk to forego the profit per hectare of land not prepared in advance for irrigation. These risks depend on the choice of ex-post adaptive decisions $y = (y_1, y_2, y_3)$ where y_1 is the use of irrigated land, y_2 is the use of land that was prepared for irrigated cultivation but cannot be irrigated, y_3 is the use of land that was not prepared for irrigation.

Let $\omega = (Q, d_1, d_2, d_3)$ and c be the cost per hectare of irrigated land. Ex-ante and ex-post decisions x, y_1, y_2, y_3 are connected by the equations $y_1 + y_2 \leq x$, $0 \leq x \leq a$, $y_1 + y_2 + y_3 \leq a$, $\frac{Q}{q} \geq y_1$, $y_1 \geq 0$, $y_2 \geq 0$, $y_3 \geq 0$. The decision vector $y(x, \omega)$ maximizes the profit $d_1 y_1 + d_2 y_2 + d_3 y_3$ subject to these constraints. The sample objective function can be defined as $f(x, \omega) = -r(x, \omega)$, where $r(\cdot)$ is the revenue function $r(x, \omega) = -cx + d_1 y_1(x, \omega) + d_2 y_2(x, \omega) + d_3 y_3(x, \omega)$.

This function has complex nonsmooth character because $y_i(x, \omega), i = 1, 2, 3$, are discontinuous functions. Thus if, by a chance, $Q > xq$ and $d_1 \geq d_2$, then $y_1(x, \omega) = x$, $y_2(x, \omega) = 0$, $y_3(x, \omega) = a - x$. But if $Q > xq$ and $d_1 < d_2$, then $y_1(x, \omega) = 0$, $y_2(x, \omega) = x$, $y_3(x, \omega) = a - x$. In the case $Q \leq xq$, $d_1 \geq d_2$, the value $y_1(x, \omega) = \frac{Q}{q}$, $y_2(x, \omega) = \frac{x-Q}{q}$, $y_3(x, \omega) = a - \frac{x}{q}$.

3.3 Two-Stage Production Planning Under Uncertainty: Storage Versus Imports

The model is useful for the modeling and management of a robust NEXUS between agricultural and energy production, water allocation, and in other problems associated with "hitting" an uncertain future target. It has been used as a part of stochastic and dynamic partial equilibrium Global Biosphere Management Model GLOBIOM [19,20,55] to analyze the emergence of systemic risks, which are implicitly characterized by the whole structure of land use systems including exogenous threats, costs, demand-supply (im)balances, market prices, technologies, security targets, risk measures, and feasible decisions of agents. In [12,19,20] it is shown that properly designed robust grain and water storages (strategic decisions) and instantaneous adaptive market adjustments hedge consumption and production risks, stabilize trade, and fulfill FEWE security requirements at lower costs.

The model of this section illustrates typical difficulties in dealing with optimization of continuously differentiable expectation functions $F(x)$ when sample functions $f(x, \omega)$ are nonsmooth. As long as there is uncertainty about future demand, prices, input-output coefficients, available resources, etc., the choice of a production level $\bar{x} \geq x \geq 0$ for foreseeable stochastic demand ω is a "hit-or-miss" type decision problem. The cost $f(x, \omega)$ associated with overestimation and underestimation of ω is, in the simplest case, a random piecewise linear function $f(x, \omega) = \max \{\alpha (x - \omega), \beta (\omega - x)\}$, where α is the unit surplus cost (associated with storage costs) and β is the unit shortage cost (associated with import costs, which under certain conditions can be also interpreted as borrowing). The problem is to find the level x that is "optimal", in a sense, for all foreseeable demands ω rather than a function $x \to x(\omega)$ specifying the optimal production level in every possible "scenario" ω. The expected cost criterion leads to the minimization of the following function:

$$F(x) = E \max \{\alpha(x - \omega), \beta(\omega - x)\} \tag{11}$$

subject to $\bar{x} \geq x \geq 0$ for a given upper bound $\bar{x}$. This stochastic minimax problem is also reformulated as a two-stage stochastic programming.

Function $F(x)$ is convex, therefore the SQG algorithm can be defined as the following discontinous adaptive machine learning process:

$$x^{k+1} = \min \{\max \{0, x^k - \rho_k \xi(k)\}, \bar{x}\}, \\ k = 0, 1, ..., \tag{12}$$

where $\xi(k) = \alpha$, if the current level of production x^k exceeds the observed demand ω^k $(x^k \geq \omega^k)$ and $\xi(k) = -\beta$ otherwise, ρ_k is a positive stepsize.

The SQG method (12) can be viewed as an adaptive machine learning process which is able to learn the optimal production level through sequential adjustments of its current levels $x^0, x^1, ...$ to observable (or simulated) demands $\omega^0, \omega^1, ...$ Let us note that the optimal solution of (11) and more general SMM problems [32] defines quantile type characteristics of solutions, e.g., CVaR risk measures. For example, if the distribution of ω has a density, $\alpha > 0$, $\beta > 0$, then the optimal solution x minimizing (11) is the quantile defined as $Pr[\omega \leq x] = \beta/(\alpha + \beta)$.

Therefore, the process (12) is a convergent with probability 1 sequential estimation procedure. Problem (11) illustrates the essential difference between so-called scenario analysis aiming at the straightforward calculation of $x(\omega)$ for various ω and the STO optimization approach: instead of producing trivial optimal "bang-bang" solutions $x(\omega) = \omega$ for each scenario ω (a Pareto optimal solution w.r.t. potential ω), an STO model as (11) produces one solution that is optimal ("robust") against all possible ω.

3.4   Stochastic Facility Allocation Problem

This model [35, 36] generalizes examples in Sects. 3.1–3.3 and illustrates the possible implicit and endogenous character of underlying probability distributions.

Assume that customers living in a district i choose their destination j at random with probability P_{ij} related to the cost of travel between (i,j) and (or) other factors. Let ε_{ij} be a random number of customers traveling from i to j, $\sum_{j=1}^{n} \varepsilon_{ij} = a_i$, $i = 1, ..., m$, where a_i defines the total number of customers leaving from i. The total number of customers attracted by j is τ_j, $\tau_j = \sum_{i=1}^{m} \varepsilon_{ij}$, $j = 1, ..., n$. The actual number τ_j of customers attracted by j may not be equal to x_j. The random cost connected with overestimating or underestimating of the demand τ_j in district j may be a convex function $\alpha_j(x_j - \tau_j)$ for $x_j \geq \tau_j$ or $\beta_j(\tau_j - x_j)$ for $x_j < \tau_j$. The problem is to determine the size x_j that minimizes the expected cost

$$F(x) = \sum_{j=1}^{n} E \max \left\{ \alpha_j(x_j - \tau_j), \beta_j(\tau_j - x_j) \right\}$$

where $\bar{x}_j \geq x \geq 0$. The SQG procedure for solving this problem is similar to (10) and (12).

3.5 Iterative SQG-Based Algorithm for Distributed Models Linkage Under Asymmetric Information

Sections 3.1–3.4 illustrate application of the SQG methods in various types of sectorial models. More detailed sectorial and regional models are being used to anticipate and plan desirable developments of respective sectors and regions. However, solutions that are optimal for a sub-system may turn out to be infeasible for the entire system. For example, major power grid blackouts in India [1] were reported to have happened due to intensive water use (pumping) by individual farmers using subsidized, and often free, electricity and water for agriculture, thus generating infeasible electricity demands. Another example is the US, where in 2007 droughts simultaneously increased the water demand in agriculture and industry, as well as usage by households and for cooling nuclear and coal-fired plants. This unanticipated and uncoordinated water demand increase forced government to shut down some power reactors (e.g., the Browns Ferry facility in August 2007) and curtail operations at others. Therefore, there is a need to link the detailed distributed (independent) models for the analysis of truly integrative solutions for FEWE security. The SQG solution procedures have been used for linking distributed sectorial and regional models in case studies of food-energy-water-environmental NEXUS management in regional and global case studies [14, 15, 18, 53, 56]. The convergence of iterative SQG procedure to the social optimum has been proven by Ermoliev [15, 16] for deterministic and stochastic cases. Let us briefly describe the challenges associated with the linkage problem, which is a not continuously differentiable problem of systems optimization. In Artificial Intelligence (AI), the linkage problem corresponds to the so-called problem of reinforced learning.

The distributed models act as "agents" that communicate with each other via a "central hub" (a regulator or a planner). In this way, they continue to be separate models, and different modeling teams do not need to exchange full information about their models – instead, they only need to harmonize the inputs and outputs that are part of the joint resource constraints. In other words, in this approach the agents operate under asymmetric information. Brief description of the algorithm is as follows. Consider K sectors/regions utilizing some common resources. Let $x^{(k)}$ be the vector of decision variables in sector/region k and assume that each sector/region aims to choose such $x^{(k)}$ to maximize its objective function (net profits) of the form

$$\left\langle c^{(k)}, x^{(k)} \right\rangle \rightarrow max, \tag{13}$$

subject to constraints

$$x^{(k)} \geq 0, \tag{14}$$

$$A^{(k)} x^{(k)} \leq b^{(k)}, \tag{15}$$

$$B^{(k)} x^{(k)} \leq y^{(k)}, \tag{16}$$

where $\left\langle c^{(k)}, x^{(k)} \right\rangle$, $k = 1, 2, ..., K$, denotes the scalar product of vectors $c^{(k)}$ and $x^{(k)}$, $\left\langle c^{(k)}, x^{(k)} \right\rangle = \sum_j c_j^{(k)} x_j^{(k)}$. Here, net unit profits $c^{(k)}$ and matrices $A^{(k)}$ and $B^{(k)}$ define the marginal contribution of each solution component into the total demand, resource use, and environmental impact, and vectors $b^{(k)}$ and $c^{(k)}$ determine the constraints, which are themselves known only to sector/region k. We distinguish between the constraints that are specific to sector/region k expressed by (15) and the constraints that are part of a common inter-sectorial/inter-regional constraint with sectorial/regional quotas $y^{(k)}$ expressed by (16). The sectorial/regional quotas are not fixed, but rather the following joint constraint on the common resources holds:

$$\sum_{k=1}^{K} D^{(k)} y^{(k)} \leq d, \, y^{(k)} \geq 0 \quad , \tag{17}$$

where matrices $D^{(k)}$ define the marginal contribution of each sectorial/regional quota into a joint constraint described by vector $d \geq 0$ that is known to all sectors/regions. Thus, each sector/region k maximizes its objective function (13) by choosing $x^{(k)}$ and $y^{(k)}$ from the feasible set defined by (14), (15), and (16). Consider an arbitrary feasible solution $y^s = (y^{s(1)}, \ldots, y^{s(K)})$ for iteration $s = 1, 2, \ldots$ of the algorithm. For given quotas $y^s = (y^{s(1)}, \ldots, y^{s(K)})$, independently and in parallel, computers of sectors/regions solve primal models (13)–(16) and obtain primal solutions $x^{s(k)} = x^{s(k)}(y^s)$ together with the corresponding shadow prices of resources, that is, solutions $(u^{s(k)}, v^{s(k)})$ of the dual problems

$$\left\langle b^{(k)}, u^{(k)} \right\rangle + \left\langle y^{(k)}, v^{(k)} \right\rangle \rightarrow min, \tag{18}$$

$$A^{(k)} u^{(k)} + B^{(k)} v^{(k)} \geq w_k c^{(k)}, \tag{19}$$

$$u^{(k)} \geq 0, v^{(k)} \geq 0, \tag{20}$$

$k = 1, 2, ...$, where vectors $v^{s(k)}$ are the driving force of algorithm (21). The next approximation of quotas $y^{s+1} = (y^{s+1(1)}, ..., y^{s+1(K)})$ is derived by the computer of the central hub by shifting y^s in the direction of vector $v^s = (v^{s(1)}, ..., v^{s(K)})$, that is, optimal dual variables (shadow prices) corresponding to constraints (19). Hence, we have iterative procedure defining, in a sense, the artificial "intellect" of the designed solution system:

$$y^{s+1} = \pi_Y(y^s + \rho_s v^s), \quad s = 1, 2, ..., \tag{21}$$

where ρ_s is an iteration-dependent multiplier, which is a method's parameter, and $\pi_Y(\cdot)$ is the orthogonal projection operator onto set Y. Vector v^s defines subgradient of the continuously non-differentiable function $F(x)$. The convergence of solutions y^s to an optimal solution of the linkage problem (13–17) as $s \to \infty$ is analyzed in [15, 16].

Thus, the "resource quotas" for each sector/region and each resource are recalculated by sectors/regions independently by shifting their current approximation y^s in the direction defined by the corresponding sectorial/regional dual variables from the primal sectorial optimization problem. The linkage process avoids a "hard linking" of the models in a single code. This also preserves the original models in their initial state for other possible linkages. Using detailed sectorial/regional models instead of their aggregated simplified versions also allows for taking into account critically important local details, which are usually hidden within aggregate data. Similar principles for distributed models' linkage have been also used for the design of a computerized distributed robust emission trading market system [22, 23] and for a cost-efficient and environmentally safe water quotas allocation [44].

4   Stochastic Dynamic Systems

More complex models of stochastic dynamic systems can be formulated utilizing two-stage STO and SQG methodologies. Stochastic dynamic systems are usually defined by implicitly given sample performance functions $f_i(x, \omega)$. The decision vector x represents a sequence of decisions (control actions) $x(t)$ over a given time horizon $t = 0, ..., T$: $x = (x(0), ..., x(T-1))$. In addition to x, there may also be a group of state variables $z = (z(0), ..., z(T))$ that record the state of the system. The variables x, z are connected through a system of equations:

$$z(t+1) = g(t, z(t), x(t), \omega),$$
$$t = 0, ..., T-1, z(0) = z^0. \tag{22}$$

Objective and constraints functions are defined as expectations of some sample performance functions $h_i(z, x, \omega)$, $i = 0, 1, ..., m$.

Due to (22), variables z are implicit functions of (x, ω), i.e. $z = z(x, \omega)$. Therefore, h_i are also implicit functions of (x, ω): $f_i(x, \omega) = h_i(z(x, \omega), x, \omega)$, $i = 0, 1, ..., m$, and the resulting stochastic dynamic optimization problem can be viewed as a stochastic optimization problem of the type (1–2) with implicitly given sample performance functions $f_i(x, \omega)$. A way to solve this problem is to use the SQG methods. In particular (22) requires the calculation of only two "trajectories" (or "realizations") $z(t)$, $t = 0, 1, ..., T$ at each step of SQG procedures. If functions $g(\cdot, \omega)$, $h_i(\cdot, \omega)$ have well-defined analytical structure and the probability measure P does not depend on x, then subgradients $f_{ix}(x^k, \omega)$ are calculated (for fixed ω) using analytical formulas from nonsmooth analysis [35, 42, 43]. Similar, but case-specific, stochastic dynamic models have been developed in [6, 7, 11, 59, 61, 72].

4.1 Strategic Dynamic Stochastic Model for Energy Efficient Technology Investments Under Uncertainty and Systemic Risks

Industries and companies recognize that increasing efficiency of energy use and/or implementing alternative methods of production and operation with energy conservation/saving technologies may increase profits and energy security. On the other hand, introduction of deregulations and highly variable renewable energy sources introduces higher risks in interdependent energy supply-demand networks. Recent global deregulation of energy sectors and new efficiency targets in Europe mean that stakeholders are more exposed to energy and financial market risks, which can be further exacerbated by extreme weather events. However, stakeholders also gain the opportunity to play a more active role in energy security and managing demand and risk. Yet, this flexibility can lead to new systemic risks and potentially irreversible problems if the decisions are inappropriate for the situation that occurs. In the face of these emerging uncertainties and risks, IIASA researchers have developed a strategic Decision Support System (DSS) for energy efficient technology investments [6, 7] and references therein). This system can help design decisions that are robust, ensuring stable system performance no matter what the future may bring.

Here we summarize the two-stage strategic-operational dynamic stochastic model for energy-efficient technology investments planning. The model identifies robust ex-ante (type of technology) and ex-post (dispatching, control, etc.) decisions for optimal energy capacity expansion and operation policies. It should be emphasized that the "stages" of the two-stage problem do not refer to two time periods (units). The x, y vectors may represent sequences of actions $x(t), y(t)$ over a given time horizon $x = (x(0), x(1), ..., x(t), ...)$, $y = (y(0), y(1), ..y(t), ...)$, and in addition to the x, y decision variables, a group of variables $z = (z(0), z(1), ..., z(t), ...)$ can record the state of the system at times $t = 0, 1, ...$ The variables x, y, z, ω are often connected through a system of equations: $z(t+1) = z(t) + h(t, z(t), x(t), y(t), \omega), t = 0, 1, ..., T - 1$. The essential new feature of such a dynamic two-stage stochastic programming problem is that the variables z are implicit functions of x, y, ω in addition to the already rather complex implicit structure of $y(x, \omega)$. This often makes impossible the use of deterministic optimization techniques and the recursive equations of dynamic programming.

Consider a typical problem of optimal technological investments under uncertainty. Let $x_i(t)$ be new capacity made available for electricity producing technology i at time t and $z_i(t)$ be the total capacity of i at time t. Obviously $z_i(t) = z_i(t-1) + x_i(t) - x_i(t - L_i)$, where L_i is the life-time of technology i. If $d_j(t)$ is different possible demand modes (levels) j, at time $t = 0, 1, ..., T$; $y_{ij}(t)$ is capacity of i (effectively) used at time t in mode j, then $\sum_j y_{ij}(t) \leq z_i(t)$ and $\sum_i y_{ij}(t) = d_j(t)$. The evaluation of the future equipment cost, in particular fuel costs, total demand can be considered truly random, i.e. elements forming ω are $d_j(t), q_i(t)$. Let $c_i(t)$ be the unit investment cost for i at time t and $q_{ij}(t)$ be the unit production cost. The random objective function is the sum of investment and production costs: $f(x, \omega) = \sum_{i,t} c_i(t) z_i(t) + E \min \sum_{i,j,t} q_{ij}(t) y_{ij}(t)$. Nonnegative variables $z_i(t)$ are uniquely defined by variables $x(t)$, i.e. $f(x, \omega)$ is an implicit function of x. The general scheme for calculation of SQG is the following. Assume for simplicity $x_i(1 - L_i) = ... = x_i(0) = 0$. Let at step k we have arrived at an approximate ex-ante variables $x_i^k(t), t = 0, 1, ..., T$. Observe then the independent ω^k composed of $d_j^k(t), q_i^k(t)$; calculate $z_i^k(t)$ and ex-post variables $y_{ij}^k(t)$. Let $\lambda_i^k(t)$ be the dual variables for constraints $\sum_j y_{ij}(t) \leq z_i(t)$. Let us note, that the demand constraints can always be fulfilled for each demand level by introducing a fictitious unlimited energy source with high operating cost. An SQG of $f(x, \omega)$ at $x = x^k$ is defined by using adjoint variables $u_i^k(t)$ (commonly used in the control theory) to dynamic equations for $z_i(t)$. In our case they obey simple equations: $u_i^k(T) = -c_i(T), u_i^k(t) = u_i^k(t+1) - c_i(t) + \lambda_i^k(t)$ for $t = T-1, ..., 1, 0$. The SQG ξ^k consists of components $\xi_i^k(t) = u_i^k(t + L_i) - u_i^k(t)$ for $t = 0, 1, ..., T - L_i$ and $\xi_i^k(t) = -u_i^k(t)$ for $t = T - L_i + 1, ..., T$.

The key methodological advancement of the model is that it has a random planning horizon T defined by a stopping time. The stopping time represents an occurrence of new conditions such as, e.g. an exceedance of a vital threshold due to an extreme event such as a market shock or a natural disaster, emergence of new technologies or policies, fluctuations of energy prices and loads, which can lead to a system's failure. The stopping time defines the discount factors linking the discount-related horizon of evaluations to the "stopping time" horizon [24]. Planning time horizons of the model can also be determined by the possible outcomes of stakeholder discussion. The threshold constraints and the systemic safety requirement (e.g. the threshold can be exceeded only in q percent of extreme events), make the problem to a nonsmooth and, in general, nonconvex STO problem.

4.2 Two-Stage Dynamic Stochastic Model for Integrated Catastrophe Risk Management: Adaptive Monte Carlo Optimization

Nonsmooth and discontinuous processes are typical for systems undergoing structural changes and developments. The concept of nonsmooth abrupt catastrophe change is emphasized in the study of environmental and anthropogenic systems by such notions as critical load, surprise, and time bomb phenomena [3,8]. Catastrophes do not occur on average with average patterns. They occur as "spikes" in space and time that require spatial dynamic models to capture the main sources of risks and vulnerability. The analysis of robust catastrophic risk management decisions ([17, 21, 25, 38] and references therein) is based on a spatially-detailed catastrophe model (e.g. floods, hurricanes, seismic risks, epidemics) and a dynamic STO procedure involving endogenous risk processes of various "agents" such as governments, insurers, and individuals. The STO is based on the SQG methods to sequentially "learn" (from simulations) and "improve" current solution to the newly generated stochastic catastrophe scenario. Therefore, the whole process of "simulation-learning-improvement-simulation-learning-improvement" is called "Adaptive Monte Carlo optimization (AMCO)". In [26, 33, 38] the notion "Adaptive Monte Carlo optimization" is used in a rather broad sense, where improvements of the sampling procedure with respect to the variability of estimates may be only a part of the improvements with respect to other robust decision goals. Let us illustrate the idea of AMCO. Consider a typical simple example of a dynamic stochastic risk process of an insurer [26]. Other agents have similar risk processes.

At time $t = 0, 1, \ldots$ risk reserve of an insurer is characterized as $R(x, t) = M(t) + xt - S(t)$, $t = 0, 1, \ldots$, where $M(t)$ is the "normal" part of the reserve, associated with ordinary (noncatastrophic claims); a catastrophic claim occurs at time t with probability p; $S(t) = \sum_{l=1}^{N_t} D_{t_l}$ is the accumulated catastrophic claim from $D_{t_1}, D_{t_2}, \ldots$; N_t is the number of catastrophic claims up to the moment t; xt is the accumulated premium from catastrophic risk. The long term stability can be characterized by the probability of ruin (insolvency) $q(x) = \Pr[R(x, t) \leq 0$ for some $t]$ or $q(x) = E I_{R(x,\tau) \leq 0}$, where $I_{R \leq 0} = 1$ if $R \leq 0$, $I_{R \leq 0} = 0$ otherwise, and τ is the random variable (stopping time): $\tau(x, \omega) =$ first moment t when $R(x, t) \leq 0$; ω is associated with all involved random variables. Assume $d(x)$ is the demand for the insurance generated by the premium x. The problem is to find $x \geq 0$ maximizing a trade-off between profit $xd(x)$ and the risk of ruin, i.e. maximizing $F(x) = d(x) + \gamma E[I_{R(x,\tau) \leq 0}]$, where γ is a substitution coefficient (risk coefficient) between the profit and risks of insolvency. The function $f(x, \omega) = d(x) + \gamma I_{R(x,\tau) \leq 0}$ is an implicit function of x and ω, and it is also a discontinuous function by the nature of indicator function $I_{R \leq 0}$. Assume that the probability $V_t(y) = \Pr[M(t) \leq y]$ is an explicitly known function. In reality, the probability of ruin is a complex nested analytically intractable function dependent on all model's parameters. By taking the conditional expectation for given $D_{t_1}, D_{t_2}, \ldots$, the function $F(x)$ can be written as

$$
\begin{aligned}
F(x) &= d(x) \\
&+ \gamma E \sum_{t=1}^{\infty} p^{N_t} (1 - p)^{t - N_t} \\
&\times V_t \left(\sum_{l=1}^{N_t} D_{t_l} - xt \right).
\end{aligned}
\tag{23}
$$

At step k sample random variable $\varsigma_k \in \{1, 2, \ldots\}$ distributed according to arbitrary $\mu(t)$, $\sum_{t=1}^{\infty} \mu(t) = 1, \mu(t) > 0$, sample $D_{t_l}, l = 1, \ldots, N_{\varsigma_k}$ and take $\xi(k) = d'(x^k) - \gamma p^{N_{\varsigma_k}} (1 - p)^{1 - N_{\varsigma_k}} V'_{\varsigma_k} \left(\sum_{l=1}^{N_{\varsigma_k}} D_{t_l} - x^k \varsigma_k \right) \varsigma_k / \mu(\varsigma_k)$, where d', V'_t are the derivatives of $d(\cdot), V_t(\cdot)$. It is easy to see that $E[\xi(k) | x^k] = F_x(x^k)$.

The stochastic optimization procedure starts with a given initial combination of policy variables. In this case it is only the value of premium x^0. Let us denote

x^k as the value of the premium after k simulations. Step $k + 1$: choose t_k with probability $1/T$ from the set $1, 2, ..., T$, generate $p_k \in [\underline{p}, \overline{p}]$ and the claim $S_{t_k}^k$. Adjust the current value x^k according to the feedback:

$$x^{k+1} = \max\left\{0, x^k + \frac{\rho}{k+1}[Tp(1-p)^{t_k-1}V_{t_k}(S_{t_k}^k - x^k t^k) - \gamma]\right\},$$

where ρ is a positive constant. The value x^k converges to the desired value of premium such that $q(x) = \gamma$. This follows from the fact that the term $Tp(1 - p)^{t_k-1}V_{t_k}(S_{t_k}^k - x^k t^k)$ is an estimate of $q(x)$. In parallel with adjustments of solutions x^k, the AMCO is able to change the sampling procedure itself (importance sampling). A counterintuitive fact is that the estimation of a robust solution x^* and $F(x^*)$ starting from an initial solution x^0 often requires approximately the same (or an even smaller) number of simulations than the estimation of only $F(x^0)$. This is because of two forces. First of all, robust solutions x^* reduce the variability of $F(x)$; therefore, the movement toward $F(x^*)$ according to the SQG methods are themselves a variance-reducing process (see, e.g., numerical calculations in [26]). Secondly, the variance reductions can also be achieved by deliberate switches in the importance sampling. In contrast, $F(x^0)$ may have considerable variability because of the effects of extreme events; therefore, its estimation requires large samples.

4.3   Decision Processes with Rolling Horizon

In the dynamic two-stage problem, the observation of $\omega = (\omega(0), ..., \omega(t), ...)$ takes place only in one step before choosing ex-post decision $y = (y(0), ..., y(t), ...)$. In reality, the observation, learning and the decision making processes may have sequential character. At each step $t = 0, 1, ...$ some uncertainties $\omega(t)$ are revealed followed by ex-post decisions $y(t, x, \omega)$, that are chosen to adapt to new information. The whole decision process looks like a sequence of alternating: decision - observation - decision - .... The dependence of $y(t, x, \omega)$ on x is highly nonlinear, i.e. these functions do not posses, in general, the separability properties necessary to allow the use of the conventional recursive equations of dynamic programming. There are also even more serious obstacles for the use of such recursive equations: tremendous increase of the dimensionality and the computation of mathematical expectations. The dynamic two-stage model provides a powerful approach to dynamic decision making problems under uncertainty. At time $t = 0$ an optimal long term ex-ante strategy $x[0, T - 1]$ is computed by using a priori information about uncertainty within $[0, T - 1]$ time interval (horizon). The decision $x(0)$ from $x[0, T - 1]$ is chosen to be implemented at initial step and the new a priori information is designed for interval $[1, T]$ conditioned on observed $\omega(0)$; new ex-ante strategy $x[1, T]$ is computed and the decision $x(1)$ from $x[1, T]$ is chosen for the implementation at step $t = 1$, and so on. This approach to decision making with rolling horizon avoids the computation of decisions at time t as a function of all previous to t decisions, what reduces enormous computational burden of the recursive dynamic programming equations and multi-stage stochastic programming. The decision path (strategy) $x[t, T+t-1]$ for each $t = 0, 1, \dots$ can be viewed as a strategic plan for coming T time intervals (weeks, months, years) which is "robust" against involving uncertainties. At each $t = 0, 1, \dots$ this plan is revised incorporating new information and new time horizon.

5   Conclusions

This paper discusses the need to use the two-stage STO and the SQG solution procedures for the analysis of systems' dependencies and for the design of robust socio-economic, technological and environmental systems in the presence of uncertainty and risks of various kinds. The systems are characterized by interdependencies and thresholds, requiring nonsmooth quantile-based "goodness-of-fit" indicators, goals and constraints for their robust analysis and planning. The two-stage STO helps to identify a robust portfolio of interdependent anticipative strategic decision preparing the systems in advance and facilitating their proper adaptive actions to changing conditions. The two types of decisions can be characterized as long-term (ex-ante "here-and-now", i.e. before exact scenario of uncertainty becomes known) and short-term adaptive (ex-post "wait-and-see", i.e. after learning additional information).

The SQGs can be defined as a "searching" process, and we can think of this search as "adaptive machine learning" from data or simulations, i.e. Adaptive Monte Carlo optimization. The SQG methods have been developed for solving general optimization problems (including problems with nonsmooth, discontinuous, and nonconvex goal functions, problems involving uncertainties or/and difficulties in the evaluation of functions and their subgradients (stochastic, spatial, and dynamic optimization problems with multidimensional nested integrals, simulation and other analytically intractable models. Thus, SQG methods are used in situations where the structure of the problem does not permit the application of one the many tools of deterministic optimization. Application of STO and SQG methods are illustrated with examples of models developed at IIASA.

In nonsmooth and possibly nonconvex problems of statistical estimation, Big Data analysis and machine learning (due to multiple layers, nonsmooth loss, activation and regularization functions), the SQG methods work better than traditionally applied gradient or stochastic gradient procedures. The convergence of the SQG methods follows from the theory of nonsmooth nonconvex stochastic optimization [35, 37, 43]. For highly nonconvex deep neural networks, the SQG methods allow to bypass local solutions. In cases of nonstationary data, the SQGs allow for sequential revisions and adaptation of parameters to the changing environment, possibly, based on offline adaptive simulations.

Acknowledgements. The authors are thankful to Editor-in-Chief Professor Dr. Fred Roberts, Managing Editors and anonymous referees for detailed comments that allowed us to considerably improve the article.

Annex: Calculation of SQG

Traditional deterministic optimization methods are used for well defined objective and constraint functions, i.e., when it is possible to calculate exactly $F_0(x)$ to be minimized (or maximized) and to verify constraints

$$F_i(x) \leq 0, i = 1{:}m, \tag{24}$$

for each decision vector $x = (x_1, ..., x_n) \in X$, where the set X has a "simple" structure (for example, defined by linear constraints). Usually it is also assumed that gradients or subgradients (for nonsmooth functions) F_{ix} of the functions F_i $i = 0, 1, ..., m$ are easily calculated. *Stochastic Quasigradient (SQG) methods have been developed for solving general optimization problems without exact calculation of F_i, F_{ix}. Thus, SQG methods are used in situations where the structure of the problem does not permit the application of one the many tools of deterministic optimization.* They only require modest computer resources per iteration and reach with reasonable speed the vicinity of optimal solutions, with an accuracy that is sufficient for many applications.

The main idea of the SQG methods is to use statistical (biased and unbiased) estimates of objective and constraints functions and/or their gradients (subgradients). In other words, a sequence of approximate solutions $x^0, x^1, ...$ is constructed by using random variables $\eta_i(k)$, and random vectors $\xi^i(k)$, $i = 0, ..., m$ such that the conditional mathematical expectation for a given "history" B_k (say, $(x^0, ..., x^k)$)

$$E[\eta_i(k)|B_k] = F_i(x^k) + a_i(k), \tag{25}$$

$$E[\xi^i(k)|B_k] = F_{ix}(x^k) + b^i(k), \tag{26}$$

where $a_i(k)$, $b^i(k)$ are "errors" (bias) of the estimates $\eta_i(k)$, $\xi^i(k)$. For the exact convergence of the sequence x^k to optimal solutions $a_i(k)$, $b^i(k)$ must tend (in some sense) to 0 when $k \rightarrow \infty$. Vectors $\xi^i(k)$ are called *stochastic quasigradients*. If $b^i(k) \equiv 0$, then they are also called *stochastic gradients for continuously differentiable $F_i(x)$* and *stochastic subgradients (generalized gradients) for nonsmooth $F_i(x)$*. In what follows, notations $F(x)$, $\eta(k)$, $\xi(k)$ are also used instead of $F_0(x), \eta_0(k), \xi^0(k)$.

Consider the simplest SQG method. Assume that there are no constraints (24), X is a closed bounded (compact) convex set such that the orthogonal projection $\Pi_X(y)$ of a point y on X is easily calculated:

$$\Pi_X(y) = Arg\min\{\|y - x\|^2 : x \in X\},$$

for example, $\Pi_{a \leq x \leq b}(y) = \max\,[a, \min\,\{y, b\}]$.

The SQG projection method is defined iteratively as following

$$x^{k+1} = \Pi_X\left[x^k - \rho_k \xi(k)\right] k = 0, 1, ..., \tag{27}$$

where ρ_k is a positive stepsize, x^0 is an arbitrary initial approximation (guess). Let us consider some important typical examples of SQG calculation.

B.1. Monte Carlo Simulation-Based Optimization. Various practical problems are so complicated that only a Monte Carlo simulation model is available (see e.g. [26]) to indicate how the system might react to any given choice of the decision variable x. We always can view a given simulation run of such a model as the observation of an "environment" ω from a sample space Ω. To simplify matters, let us assume that only a single quantity $f(x\omega)$ summarizes the output of the simulation ω for given x. The problem is then to minimize the expected performance (cost, risk, profit, a "distance" from given goals or a reference point, etc.):

$$F(x) = Ef(x, \omega). \tag{28}$$

This is a typical stochastic optimization problem. Exact values of $F(x)$ are unknown explicitly. Available information at each current solution x^k and simulation run ω is $\eta(k) = f(x^k, \omega)$ satisfying (25) for $a(k) \equiv 0$. The vector $\xi(k)$ can be calculated as in the standard stochastic approximation procedures: At each step k for given x^k simulate random outcomes $f(x^k, \omega^{k0})$, $f(x^k + \Delta_k e^j, \omega^{k,j})$, $j = 1, ..., n$, where $\Delta_k e^j$ is a positive increment in the direction e^j of j-th coordinate axis; calculate

$$\xi(k) = \sum_{j=1}^{n} \Delta_k^{-1} \left[f(x^k + \Delta_k e^j, \omega^{k,j}) - f(x^k, \omega^{k,0}) \right] e^j. \tag{29}$$

Simulations $\omega^{k,0}, \cdots, \omega^{k,n}$ are not necessarily independent: one possibility is to use only one simulation ω^k at each step k: $\omega^{k,0} = ... = \omega^{k,n} = \omega^k$. The variance of such a single run estimate of SQG converges to 0 as $k \to \infty$, whereas for independent simulations it goes to ∞. Since $E\left[\xi(k)|x^k\right] = \sum_{j=1}^{n} \Delta_k^{-1} \left[F(x^k + \Delta_k e^j) - F(x^k) \right] e^j$, then for continuously differentiable $F(\cdot)$:

$$E\left[\xi(k)|x^k\right] = F_x(x^k) + C(k)\Delta_k \tag{30}$$

where $\|C(k)\| < const < \infty$ for all x^k from a bounded set X.

B.2. Optimization by Random Search. Suppose that $F(x)$ can be evaluated exactly but this is time consuming, say, because $F(x)$ is defined on solutions of differential equations or on solutions of other optimization problems. A purely random trial-and-error method (with $x^{k+1} \in X$ drawn at random until that $F(x^{k+1}) < F(x^k)$, and so on) may be time consuming since the probability to "hit" at random even a subspace as large as nonnegative orthant of n-dimensional Euclidean space is 2^{-n}. The traditional finite difference approximation

$$F_x(x^k) \approx \sum_{j=1}^{n} \Delta_k^{-1} \left[F(x^k + \Delta_k e^j) - F(x^k) \right] e^j \tag{31}$$

requires $n + 1$ evaluations of $F(\cdot)$ and this also may be time-consuming. The SQG

$$\xi(k) = 3/2\Delta_k^{-1} \left[F(x^k + \Delta_k \varsigma^k) - F(x^k) \right] \varsigma^k, \tag{32}$$

where ς^k has independent uniformly distributed on $[-1, 1]$ components, requires only two evaluations of $F(x)$ at points x^k and $x^k + \Delta_k \varsigma^k$ independently of the dimensionality n. It is easy to see that vector (32) satisfies (30) for continuously differentiable $F(x)$.

B.3. Finite Difference Approximations of Subgradients. The finite difference approximations (29, 31–32) cannot be used for nondifferentiable functions, e.g., for stochastic two-stage and minimax problems. SQG methods allow to develop simple finite-difference subgradient approximations for general (deterministic and stochastic) nonsmooth optimization problems. The slight randomization of (29, 31–32) by substituting, roughly speaking, the current point x^k by a random point $\overline{x}^k = x^k + \nu^k$, where the random vector ν^k has a density and $\|\nu^k\| \to 0$ with probability 1, ensures their convergence even for locally Lipschitz and discontinuous functions].

Assume that $F(x)$ is a locally integrable (possibly discontinuous) function and the vector ν^k has sufficiently smooth density concentrated in a bounded set. Then

$$\xi(k) = 3/2\Delta_k^{-1} \left[F(\overline{x}^k + \Delta_k \varsigma^k) - F(\overline{x}^k) \right] \varsigma^k, \tag{33}$$

$$\xi(k) = 3/2\Delta_k^{-1} \left[f(\overline{x}^k + \Delta_k \varsigma^k, \omega^{k1}) - f(\overline{x}^k, \omega^{k,0}) \right] \varsigma^k \tag{34}$$

are SQG of $F(k, x) = EF(x + \nu^k)$ or so-called *stochastic mollifier quasigradient* (SMQG) of $F(x)$, which converges (in some sense) to $F(x)$ and for which $F_x(k, x)$ converges to the set of subgradients $F_x(x)$. We have

$$E \left[\xi(k) | x^k \right] = F_x(k, x^k) + C(k)\Delta_k, \tag{35}$$

where $\|C(k)\| < const < \infty$ for all x^k from a bounded set. The analysis of convergence of x^k involves general ideas of nonstationary optimization (see Example 5). The important advantage of this approach is that $F(kx)$ smoothes out rapid oscillations of $F(x)$ and reflects general trend of $F(x)$. In this sense $F(k, x)$ provides a "bird's eye" point of view on the "landscape" $F(x)$ enabling $\{x^k\}$ to bypass inessential local solutions. "Large" enough ν^k force the procedure to concentrate on essential (global) solutions.

B.4. Global Optimization. The simplest way to introduce the "inertia" in the gradient type procedure to bypass some local solutions is to perturb the gradient $F_x(x^k)$ by a random vector ν^k, i.e. to consider $\xi(k) = F_x(x^k) + \nu^k$, $E\nu^k = 0$. A special choice of ν^k corresponds to the simulated annealing. Another approach is to cut off local solutions by sequential convex approximations.

References

1. Abrar, M.: Power cut off and power blackout in India a major threat - an overview. Int. J. Adv. Res. Technol. **5**(7), 8–15 (2016)
2. Amendola, A., Ermolieva, T., Linnerooth-Bayer, J., Mechler, R.: Integrated Catastrophe Risk Modeling: Supporting Policy Processes. Springer, Dordrecht (2013). https://doi.org/10.1007/978-94-007-2226-2

3. Arrow, K.J.: The theory of risk-bearing: small and great risks. J. Risk Uncertain. **12**, 103–111 (1996)

4. Arrow, K.J., Fisher, A.C.: Preservation, uncertainty and irreversibility. Q. J. Econ. **88**, 312–319 (1974)

5. Borodina, O., et al.: Sustainable agriculture, food security, and socio-economic risks in Ukraine. In: Ermoliev, Y., Makowski, M., Marti, K. (eds.) Managing Safety of Heterogeneous Systems. Lecture Notes in Economics and Mathematical Systems, pp. 169–185. Springer, Heidelberg (2012). https://doi.org/10.1007/978-3-642-22884-1_8

6. Cano, E.L., Moguerza, J.M., Ermolieva, T., Yermoliev, Y.: A strategic decision support system framework for energy-efficient technology investments. TOP **25**(2), 249–270 (2016)

7. Cano, E.L., Moguerza, J.M., Ermolieva, T., Ermoliev, Y.: Energy efficiency and risk management in public buildings: strategic model for robust planning. Comput. Manage. Sci. **11**(1–2), 25–44 (2014)

8. Chichilnisky, G., Heal, G.: Global environmental risks. J. Econ. Perspect. **7**(4), 65–86 (1993)

9. Clarke, F.H.: Optimization and Nonsmooth Analysis. Wiley, New York (1983)

10. Ermoliev, Y., Ermolieva, T., Rovenskaya, E., Obersteiner, M., Knopov, P.S., Gorbachuk, V.M.: Robustness, iterative stochastic quasigradient procedures, and adaptive artificial intelligence learning for cat risk management. In: Proceedings of the 5th International Scientific Conference on Computational Intelligence, pp. 61–62. Ministry of Education and Science of Ukraine, Uzgorod (2019)

11. Ermoliev, Y., Ermolieva, T., Kahil, T., Obersteiner, M., Gorbachuk, V., Knopov, P.: Stochastic optimization models for risk-based reservoir management. Cybern. Syst. Anal. **55**(1), 55–64 (2019). https://doi.org/10.1007/s10559-019-00112-z

12. Ermolieva, T., et al.: Addressing climate change adaptation with a stochastic integrated assessment model: analysis of common agricultural policy measures. Financ. Stat. J. 1/2 (2019). https://doi.org/10.24294/fsj.v0i0.913

13. Ermolieva, T., et al.: A strategic decision-support system for strategic robust adaptation to climate change and systemic risks in land use systems: stochastic integrated assessment GLOBIOM model. In: Proceedings of the 1st EU Conference on Modelling for Policy Support, Brussels (2019)

14. Ermoliev, T., Ermolieva, T., Havlik, P., Rovenskaya, E.: Robust food-energy-water-environmental security management: linking distributed sectorial and regional models. In: Proceedings of the 1st EU Conference on Modelling for Policy Support, Brussels (2019)

15. Ermoliev, Y., et al.: Integrated robust management of NEXUS between agricultural, water, energy economic sectors: consistent algorithms for linking distributed models. In: Proceedings of the 6-th International Conference on Mathematical Modeling, Optimization and Information Technologies, Evrica, Kischinev, Moldova, pp. 108–112 (2018)

16. Ermoliev, Y., Ermolieva, T., Havlik, P., Rovenskaya, E.: Linking distributed sectorial models under asymetric information. Eur. J. Oper. Res. (under revisions to EJOR)

17. Ermoliev, Y.M., Robinson, S.M., Rovenskaya, E., Ermolieva, T.: Integrated catastrophic risk management: robust balance between ex-ante and ex-post measures. SIAM News **51**(6), 4 (2018)

18. Ermolieva, T., et al.: Dynamic merge of the global and local models for sustainable land use planning with regard for global projections from GLOBIOM and local technical-economic feasibility and resource constraints. Cybern. Syst. Anal. **53**(2), 176–185 (2017). https://doi.org/10.1007/s10559-017-9917-7

19. Ermolieva, T., et al.: Integrated management of land use systems under systemic risks and security targets: a stochastic Global Biosphere Management Model. J. Agric. Econ. **67**(3), 584–601 (2016)

20. Ermolieva, T.Y., et al.: Systems analysis of robust strategic decisions to plan secure food, energy, and water provision based on the stochastic GLOBIOM model. Cybern. Syst. Anal. **51**(1), 125–133 (2015)

21. Ermolieva, T., Filatova, T., Ermoliev, Y., Obersteiner, M., de Bruijn, K.M., Jeuken, A.: Flood catastrophe model for designing optimal flood insurance program: estimating location-specific premiums in the Netherlands. Risk Anal. **37**(1), 82–98 (2016)

22. Ermoliev, Y., Ermolieva, T., Jonas, M., Obersteiner, M., Wagner, F., Winiwarter, W.: Integrated model for robust emission trading under uncertainties: cost-effectiveness and environmental safety. Technol. Forecast. Soc. Chang. **98**, 234–244 (2015)

23. Ermolieva, T., Ermoliev, Y., Jonas, M., Obersteiner, M., Wagner, F., Winiwarter, W.: Uncertainty, cost-effectiveness and environmental safety of robust carbon trading: integrated approach. Clim. Change **124**(3), 633–646 (2014)

24. Ermoliev, Y., Ermolieva, T., Fischer, G., Makowski, M., Nilsson, S., Obersteiner, M.: Discounting, catastrophic risks management and vulnerability modeling. Math. Comput. Simul. **79**(4), 917–924 (2008)

25. Ermolieva, T., Obersteiner, M.: Abrupt climate change: lessons from integrated catastrophic risks management. World Resour. Rev. **16**, 57–82 (2004)

26. Ermolieva, T.: The design of optimal insurance decisions in the presence of catastrophic risks. IIASA Interim Report IR-97-068 (1997)

27. Ermolieva, T., Ermoliev.Y., Fischer.G, Galambos, I.: The role of financial instruments in integrated catastrophic flood management. Multinational Financ. J. **7**(3–4), 207–230 (2003)

28. Ermoliev, Y., Hordijk, L.: Global changes: facets of robust decisions. In: Marti, K., Ermoliev, Y., Makowski, M., Pflug, G. (eds.) Coping with Uncertainty: Modeling and Policy Issue. Springer, Heidelberg (2003)

29. Ermoliev, Y., von Winterfeldt, D.: Systemic risk and security management. In: Ermoliev, Y., Makowski, M., Marti, K. (eds.) Managing Safety of Heterogeneous Systems. Lecture Notes in Economics and Mathematical Systems, pp. 19–49. Springer, Heidelberg (2012). https://doi.org/10.1007/978-3-642-22884-1_2

30. Ermoliev, Y.: Stochastic quasigradient methods. In: Pardalos, P.M. (ed.) Encyclopedia of Optimization, pp. 3801–3807. Springer, Boston (2009). https://doi.org/10.1007/978-0-387-74759-0_662

31. Ermoliev, Y.: Two-stage stochastic programming: quasigradient method. In: Pardalos, P.M. (ed.) Encyclopedia of Optimization, pp. 3955–3959. Springer, Boston (2009). https://doi.org/10.1007/978-0-387-74759-0

32. Ermoliev, Y.: Stochastic quasigradient methods in minimax problems. In: Floudas, C.A., Pardalos, P.M. (eds.) Encyclopedia of Optimization, pp. 3813–3818. Springer, Boston (2009). https://doi.org/10.1007/978-0-387-74759-0_664

33. Ermoliev, Y.M., Ermolieva, T.Y., MacDonald, G.J., Norkin, V.I.: Stochastic optimization of insurance portfolios for managing exposure to catastrophic risks. Ann. Oper. Res. **99**, 207–225 (2000)

34. Ermoliev, Y.M., Ermolieva, T.Y., MacDonald, G.J., Norkin, V.I.: Insurability of catastrophic risks: the stochastic optimization model. Optimization **47**(3–4), 251–265 (2000)
35. Ermoliev, Y., Wets, RJ-B.: Numerical Techniques for Stochastic Optimization. Springer, Heidelberg (1988)
36. Ermoliev, Y., Leonardi, G.: Some proposals for stochastic facility location models. Math. Model. **3**(5), 407–420 (1982)
37. Ermoliev, Y.: Methods of Stochastic Programming. Nauka, Moscow (1976). (in Russian)
38. Ermolieva, T., Ermoliev, Y.: Catastrophic risk management: flood and seismic risk case studies. In: Wallace, S.W., Ziemba, W.T. (eds.) Applications of Stochastic Programming, SIAM, MPS (2005)
39. Ermoliev, Y., Gaivoronski, A.: Stochastic quasigradient methods for optimization of discrete event systems. Ann. Oper. Res. **39**, 1–39 (1992)
40. Ermoliev, Y., Norkin, V.: On nonsmooth and discontinuous problems of stochastic systems optimization. Eur. J. Oper. Res. **101**(2), 230–243 (1997)
41. Ermoliev, Y., Shor, N.: On minimization of nondifferentiable functions. Kibernetika **3**(1), 101–102 (1967)
42. Ermoliev, Y.M., Shor, N.Z.: Method of a random search for two-stage stochastic programming problems and its generalizations. Kibernetica **1**, 90–92 (1968)
43. Ermoliev, Y.M.: On the method of the generalized stochastic gradients and stochastic quasi-Fjer sequences. Kibernetica **2**, 73–84 (1969). (in Russian). English translation in Cybernetics 5(2), 208–220 (1969)
44. Ermoliev, Y., Michalevich, M., Uteuliev, N.U.: Economic modeling of international water use (The case of the Aral Sea Basin). Cybern. Syst. Anal. **30**(4), 523–527 (1994)
45. Fischer, G., et al.: Integrated modeling framework for assessment and mitigation of nitrogen pollution from agriculture: concept and case study for China. Agric. Ecosyst. Environ. **136**(1–2), 116–124 (2010)
46. Fischer, G., Ermolieva, T., Ermoliev, Y., Sun, L.: Risk-adjusted approaches for planning sustainable agricultural development. Stochast. Environ. Res. Risk Assess. **23**(4), 441–450 (2009)
47. Flam, S.D., Ermoliev, Y.: Investment, uncertainty, and production games. Environ. Dev. Econ. **14**, 51–66 (2009)
48. Fricko, O., et al.: The marker quantification of the Shared Socioeconomic Pathway 2: a middle-of-the-road scenario for the 21st century. Glob. Environ. Change **42**, 251–267 (2017)
49. Gaivoronski, A.: Convergence properties of backpropagation for neural nets via theory of stochastic guasigradient methods: Part 1. Optim. Methods Softw. **4**, 117–134 (1994)
50. Gritsevskyi, A., Ermoliev, Y.: An energy model incorporating technological uncertainty, increasing returns and economic and environmental risks. In: Proceedings of International Association for Energy Economics 1999 European Energy Conference "Technological Progress and the Energy Challenges", Paris, France (1999)
51. Gritsevskii, A., Ermoliev, Y.: Modeling technological change under increasing returns and uncertainty. In: Ermoliev, Y., Makowski, M., Marti, K. (eds.) Managing Safety of Heterogeneous Systems, pp. 109–136. Springer, Heidelberg (2012). https://doi.org/10.1007/978-3-642-22884-1_6
52. Gritsevskyi, A., Nakicenovic, N.: Modeling uncertainty of induced technological change. Energy Pol. **26**, 907–921 (2000)

53. Gao, J., Xu, X., Cao, Y., Ermoliev, Y., Ermolieva, T., Rovenskaya, E.: Optimizing regional food and energy production under limited water availability through integrated modeling. Sustainability **10**(6) (2018). https://doi.org/10.3390/su10061689
54. Gorbachuk, V.M., Ermoliev, Y., Ermolieva, T., Dunajevskij, M.S.: Quantile-based regression for the assessment of economic and ecological risks. In: Proceedings of the 5th International scientific conference on Computational Intelligence, 15–20 April 2019, pp. 188–190. Ministry of Education and Science of Ukraine, Uzgorod (2019)
55. Havlik, P., et al.: Global land-use implications of first and second generation biofuel targets. Energy Policy **39**, 5690–5702 (2011)
56. Kyryzyuk, S., Ermolieva, T., Ermoliev, Y.: Planning sustainable agroproduction for food security under risks. Econ. Agric. **9**, 145–151 (2011)
57. Messner, S., Golodnikov, A., Gritsevskyi, A.: A stochastic version of the dynamic linear programming model MESSAGE III. Energy **21**(9), 775–784 (1996)
58. Nesterov, Y.: Introductory Lectures on Convex Optimization, vol. 87. Springer, Boston (2004). https://doi.org/10.1007/978-1-4419-8853-9
59. Ortiz-Partida, J.P., et al.: A two-stage stochastic optimization for robust operation of multipurpose reservoirs. Water Resour. Manage. **33**(11), 3815–3830 (2019). https://doi.org/10.1007/s11269-019-02337-1
60. Reddi, S.J., Hefny, A., Sra, S., Poczos, B., Smola, A.J.: On variance reduction in stochastic gradient descent and its asynchronous variants. In: Advances in Neural Information Processing Systems, pp. 2647–2655 (2015)
61. Ren, M., Xu, X., Ermolieva, T., Cao, G.-Y., Yermoliev, Y.: The optimal technological development path to reduce pollution and restructure iron and steel industry for sustainable transition. Int. J. Sci. Eng. Invest. **7**(73), 100–105 (2018)
62. Robbins, H., Monro, S.: A stochastic approximation method. Ann. Math. Stat. **22**, 400–407 (1951)
63. Polyak, B.T., Juditsky, A.B.: Acceleration of stochastic approximation by averaging. SIAM J. Control Optim. **30**(4), 838–855 (1992)
64. Rockafeller, T.: The Theory of Subgradient and Its Application to Problems of Optimization: Convex and Nonconvex Functions. Helderman Verlag, Berlin (1981)
65. Rockafellar, R.T., Uryasev, S.: Optimization of conditional value-at-risk. J. Risk **2**, 21–41 (2000)
66. Roux, N.L., Schmidt, M., Bach, F.R.: A stochastic gradient method with an exponential convergence rate for finite training sets. In: Advances in Neural Information Processing Systems, pp. 2663–2671 (2012)
67. Rovenskaya, E., et al.: Artificial intelligence and machine learning for systems analysis of the 21st century. IIASA Working Paper. Laxenburg, Austria: WP-19-010 (2019)
68. Shalev-Shwartz, S., Zhang, T.: Stochastic dual coordinate ascent methods for regularized loss minimization. J. Mach. Learn. Res. **14**(1), 567–599 (2013)
69. Strokal, M., et al.: Cost-effective management of coastal eutrophication: a case study for the Yangtze river basin. Resour. Conserv. Recycling **154** (2020). https://doi.org/10.1016/j.resconrec.2019.104635
70. Vapnik, V.: The Nature of Statistical Learning Theory. Springer, New York (1995). https://doi.org/10.1007/978-1-4757-2440-0. ISBN 0-387-98-780-0
71. Vapnik, V.: Statistical Learning Theory (1998). ISBN 0-471-03003-1
72. Wildemeersch, M., Ermolieva, T., Ermoliev, T., Obersteiner, M.: An integrated environmental-economic model for robust pollution control under uncertainty. In: Proceedings of The 1st EU Conference on Modelling for Policy Support, Brussels, 26–27 November 2019 (2019)

Chapter 5
Robotics as an Enabler of Resiliency to Disasters: Promises and Pitfalls

Rui Wang, Daniel Nakhimovich, Fred S. Roberts, and Kostas E. Bekris$^{(\boxtimes)}$

Rutgers University, New Brunswick, NJ, USA
kostas.bekris@cs.rutgers.edu

Abstract. The Covid-19 pandemic is a reminder that modern society is still susceptible to multiple types of natural or man-made disasters, which motivates the need to improve resiliency through technological advancement. This article focuses on robotics and the role it can play towards providing resiliency to disasters. The progress in this domain brings the promise of effectively deploying robots in response to life-threatening disasters, which includes highly unstructured setups and hazardous spaces inaccessible or harmful to humans. This article discusses the maturity of robotics technology and explores the needed advances that will allow robots to become more capable and robust in disaster response measures. It also explores how robots can help in making human and natural environments preemptively more resilient without compromising long-term prospects for economic development. Despite its promise, there are also concerns that arise from the deployment of robots. Those discussed relate to safety considerations, privacy infringement, cyber-security, and financial aspects, such as the cost of development and maintenance as well as impact on employment.

Keywords: Resiliency · Disasters · Robotics

1 Introduction

Human society and activities are often severely disrupted due to high-impact disasters. For instance, the Covid-19 pandemic has significantly affected human daily lives and brought up destabilizing threats to many societal aspects and the economy at a global scale. There is a long list of other disasters in the 21st century that impacted human life, such as terrorist attacks (e.g., the 9/11 events in New York City), earthquakes and tsunamis (e.g., the Indian Ocean tsunami of 2004 and the Haitian Earthquake of 2010, the Japanese Fukushima Daiichi Nuclear Disaster of 2011), as well as recent years of multiple high-impact hurricanes, forest fires and extreme heat waves or droughts. Each of these disasters has caused casualties, infrastructure destruction and significant economic loss [13]. Two billion people were estimated to have been affected by disasters from 2008 to 2017 [15].

© Springer Nature Switzerland AG 2021
F. S. Roberts and I. A. Sheremet (Eds.): Resilience in the Digital Age, LNCS 12660, pp. 75–101, 2021.
https://doi.org/10.1007/978-3-030-70370-7_5

Given the scale of this impact, there is a continuing need for improving the resiliency of human society against disasters, where technology can play a critical role. Here resiliency refers both to preemptive measures and post-disaster responses. As a long-term strategy towards preventing or reducing the probability of a disaster from happening, technology can help fortify infrastructure, supply chains and the natural environment. Similarly, early detection and warning mechanisms, evacuation management tools and efficient deployment of response resources can help with resilience when a disaster can be foreseen. Once a disaster has occurred, appropriate response and containment measures can help a system to recover quickly and minimize losses in the aftermath. Activities that provide resilience range from immediate medical care to long-term clean-up efforts.

Robotics can play a critical role across this spectrum of disaster resilience activities, given significant advancements over the last few decades through more robust mechanisms, faster computational power, improved sensors, access to more data and more efficient algorithms. Today, robots are deployed primarily in industrial and logistics environments, such as assembly lines and warehouses. They are also used in military and space exploration applications, and have some limited presence in domestic and public facility environments, such as homes and hospitals. The annual global sales of robots hit 16.5 billion dollars in 2018 with a historical maximum of 422,000 units installed globally, 55% of which corresponded to service robots for professional use (logistics, inspection and maintenance, medical, agriculture, etc.) [97]. The role of robots in managing public health and infectious diseases was highlighted by the Covid-19 pandemic [122].

This paper examines the ability of robotics to provide persistent resiliency against high-impact disasters both through preemptive measures for fortification and preparation as well as for post-disaster response activities. It focuses on identifying what aspects of robotics technology are mature enough to be already deployable for resiliency. This effort also identifies robotics domains where further investment is needed in order to achieve more comprehensive and robust disaster resilience, without compromising long-term prospects for economic development. This work also examines the challenges and undesirable side-effects that arise from the deployment of robotics technology in this context, together with ideas on potential mitigation efforts of the undesirable side-effects.

1.1   Past/Present Robotic Deployments

Robotics has already seen use in responding to and preventing disasters. Perhaps one of the first uses was by the military to diffuse or safely detonate mines (Fig. 1 (b)). Various robots with unique mobility features - such as snake-bots (Fig. 1 (a)) - have been used for search and rescue in the aftermath of geological disasters and extreme storms. Firefighting robots have also been demonstrated (Fig. 1 (c)). Although their potential for impact in this domain is significant, robots have been rather limited in their scope and reliability when pushed to the limits.

(a)   (b)   (c)   (d)

Fig. 1. (From Left to Right) (a) A snake-like robot developed by NASA (Image Source: [81] ⊛)). Similar designs are deployed for search and rescue after earthquakes. (b) iRobot's PackBot most commonly used to detect and diffuse improvised explosive devices (Image Source: [23] ⊛)). (c) A POK Jupiter firefighting robot (Image Source: [94] ⊜⊙⊙)·). (d) An aquatic robot deployed under a ship to inspect it (Image Source: [34] ⊛)).

For instance, in March of 2011 when a tsunami hit Japan's Fukushima-Daiichi nuclear plant, robots were deployed to assess damage and attempt cleanup/repair. Unfortunately, many of the robots did not accomplish their designated tasks due to the challenges of navigating a highly unstructured environment and performing complex manipulation [36]. For similar reasons, there has not been wide deployment of firefighting robots or search and rescue robots to help move debris in addition to navigating through it. Fortunately, recent developments in robotics could push the deployments of robots into a larger variety of environments in order to deal with more disasters.

1.2 Examples of Robotics Technology

Robotics encompasses a large variety of systems, which can potentially be deployed to provide resiliency against a wide variety of disasters.

Autonomous Ground Vehicles (AGV). AGVs, such as autonomous vehicles, have advanced and are able to self-localize and navigate in structured spaces with minimal human intervention and increasingly in dynamic and unstructured spaces [41,69,95]. Despite this progress, there is still significant effort required for wide, safe deployments.

Unmanned Aerial Vehicles (UAV). Aerial robots, such as drones and unmanned helicopters, are capable of autonomously flying and hovering in the air. This allows them to quickly reach areas, which are inaccessible to ground vehicles [19,84,91].

Autonomous Underwater Vehicles (AUV). Marine robots, such as automated submarines, are capable of navigating in the water and exploring underwater environments. They are increasingly deployed to monitor the quality of the ocean or search for debris [39,126].

Robotic Manipulators. Robotic arms and hands are built for tasks that require manipulating objects, such as picking and placing, reorienting, pushing, changing the form of an object or rearranging multiple objects [61,64].

They have many industrial applications, such as bin picking [40,42] and part-assembly [2,56]. These robots typically have many degrees of freedom (DOF) and are often mounted on a fixed base to ensure high precision.

Mobile Manipulators. An extension of the above category, where mobile robots carry manipulators, they combine the advantages of mobility from AGVs/UAVs/AUVs and the manipulation ability of robotic arms and hands. This type of robot is needed for tasks that involve both navigation and manipulation, such as debris removal [27,120].

Humanoid Robots. Humanoid robots are designed to have a human-like form that allows them to be easily deployed in spaces made for people. They can perform bi-pedal locomotion over non-flat terrains [3,54], coordinate two arms for manipulation, and more naturally interact with people [59,117].

Other Bio-inspired Robots. Other types of bio-inspired robots, such as snake-like robots, are inspired by non-human biological systems [32]. Mimicking their counterparts, they usually have the appropriate size, form and agility for solving tasks in natural environments [71]. They can also form large collectives, such as robot swarms [72,90].

1.3   Fundamental Challenges for Robotics Technology

Across all of these types of robots, there is a sequence of fundamental robotics problems that need to be addressed in order to endow the corresponding systems with the ability to solve real-world tasks.

Robot Mechanisms and Design. This area encompasses mechanisms and actuators that can: (i) generate sufficiently high and precise forces and torques without significant energy expenditure, (ii) withstand punishing impacts, (iii) be safe for interaction with people, and (iv) be adaptive to different domains. A well-designed robot must withstand the adversity of its environment, such as that of a nuclear plant [83,98] or of the deep ocean [105].

Sensing and Computer Vision. Robots need to perceive and understand their surroundings, e.g., autonomous cars need to detect pedestrians and other vehicles typically through visual sensors [65,74,102,106]. Non-visual sensors, such as tactile or proprioception sensors, can also provide useful data about the robot's environment or its own state.

Simultaneous Localization and Mapping (SLAM). SLAM is a key technique in robot navigation where robots are exploring unknown environments or where the robot's location is critical in solving a task. SLAM techniques are linked to the underlying sensing technology used, such as monocular vision or LiDAR [31]. SLAM in dynamic environments [124] or for multi-robot systems [129] can be more challenging but is needed in many applications.

Telerobotics. Though full autonomy is desirable, telerobotics, i.e., the remote operation or semi-autonomous control of robots, is sufficient and often easier to achieve for many tasks but introduces its own cognitive load challenges. Telepresence [115] and telemedicine [62] are example high-demand tasks that relate to disaster events [29].

Motion Control and Planning. An autonomous robot has to determine how to navigate, locomote in or manipulate its environment. Intelligent planning involves often safe obstacle avoidance [87,114] and determining feasible [67] and optimized [58,99] sequences of actions [51,103] to solve a target task. Control involves the safe and effective execution of the corresponding actions as a fast, online response to sensory input.

Learning. Robots can improve their performance given prior experience and data. Machine learning approaches can be used to improve components of a robot, such as perception or planning, or for end-to-end learning of navigation [121] and manipulation behaviors [63], and transfer learning to bridge the simulation to reality gap (sim2real) [38].

Multi-robot Systems. Many applications require more than one robot [21,75]. Coordinating teams of robots poses non-trivial challenges both in terms of efficiency [125] and safety [24], such as ensuring the robots avoid collisions among themselves while fulfilling the tasks more effectively as more resources are used.

Human-robot Interaction (HRI). Robots need to interact with people in tasks such as emergency evacuation [127] or collaborative assembly [44]. In addition, robots need to be able to understand human task specification. Similarly, people should not feel threatened and surprised by robots' actions [60].

2 Robotics as an Enabler of Resiliency

Robotics technology can help in resiliency against disasters in two distinct ways: (1) via taking measures for averting disasters or preparing a system to better deal with them once they occur (**preemptive measures**) and (2) via responding to disasters and minimizing their impact through technological resiliency (**post-disaster responses**). Figure 2 indicates the 9 Technology Readiness Levels

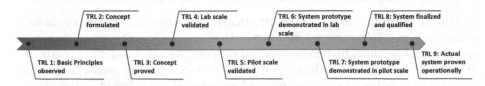

Fig. 2. The Technology Readiness Level (TRL) arrow above indicates the 9 levels of technology readiness. The higher the number, the more mature the technology is. Red phases are early stages of the technology (TRL 1–3); orange phases are transitional stages where the technology is validated conceptually and in small scale (TRL 4–6), and green phases are operational stages where the technology is validated in the industry, and is ready to be used in real applications (TRL 7–9). (Color figure online)

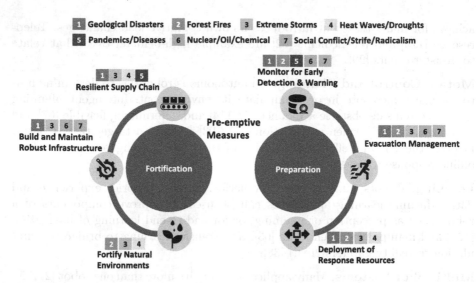

Fig. 3. Robotics can enable the above "preemptive measures" for resiliency. This paper splits preemptive measures into two categories: (1) Fortification and (2) Preparation (dark blue circles), each with its own sub-categories (grey circles). The number-indexed icons with associated colors indicate types of disasters. They appear next to preemptive measures that are more relevant to them. (Color figure online)

according to NASA [12], which provide a metric for estimating the maturity of technology. This paper adopts this metric in the context of evaluating robotics technology to enable resiliency against disasters. For each category below, the paper provides our TRL scores as the evaluation at the end of each discussion.

2.1   Robotics for Preemptive Measures

This paper summarizes in Fig. 3 the resiliency activities related to preemptive measures, which reduce the chance of accidents or machine failures and help with disaster preparation. Preemptive measures are further categorized into those long-term "Fortification" measures and short-term "Preparation" measures.

Resilient Supply Chain (Fortification). An important factor to make a community less vulnerable to disasters is to ensure an operational manufacturing and logistics chain to deliver essential supplies (e.g., first-aid, food, medicine, disinfectants, etc.). The sudden occurrence of a disaster can create a shortage of essential supplies in the proximity of an affected area. Robot manipulators can be used both in production and distribution of supplies, especially those not typically produced in high quantities in ordinary times. For instance, during the Covid-19 pandemic there was a need to convert factory floors towards producing simple hygiene and protection products. Britain's Wales-based Royal Mint produced plastic visors, one every 10 s, to meet the public need, and Minnesota-based Protolabs moved to making parts for Covid-19 test kits using 3D printing;

they were able to produce over 10,000 parts on short notice [79]. Automation technology is needed that allows production lines to be adapted on demand to such drastic changes in supply needs. Given the increasing demand for 3D fabrication, further research is needed in the area of robotic spatial extrusion, an alternative to traditional layer-based 3D printing [46].

On the distribution side of supply chain, automated warehouses have become increasingly popular as they reduce dependence on manual labor [1,7]. Various types of robots can perform diverse tasks including picking, moving, and sorting. This often requires the use of multiple AGVs in the same workspace [50], such as robots that lift shelves of goods and transfer them to human pickers without colliding with each other [47]. In addition, increasing focus in the area of object rearrangement [100] is yielding more efficient methods of performing packing tasks, such as preparing packages for delivery.

TRL 7–9: Robotics technology for manufacturing and distribution of supplies is becoming increasingly mature. 3D printing is increasingly used in production, but maturity varies on materials - e.g. 9 for plastics but 7 for metals. Effective adaptability to changing demand requires additional investment.

Build and Maintain Robust Infrastructure (Fortification). Robots, such as drones and ground vehicles, can be deployed to monitor the health of critical infrastructure. Such surveillance tasks, together with frequent maintenance, that can also be partly automated through robotics, could drastically reduce failures in factories, power-plants, oil rigs or civic infrastructure. Building more secure and safe new facilities is also highly desirable. Nevertheless, constructing such high-profile facilities is both costly and time-consuming. Part of the cost involves manual labor and associated safety measures during construction as well as the requirements for high precision. Leveraging automation could reduce the associated costs as well as injury risks for workers that may arise from interaction with manually controlled heavy machinery (drills, excavators, and cranes). Mobile manipulators can be envisioned as construction and maintenance robots, which navigate sites as well as lift and assemble heavy materials. One approach to handling these heavy load tasks is to utilize the existing machinery and connect it to a computer with advanced software. Companies like Built Robotics [4] integrate artificial intelligence (AI) systems into off-the-shelf equipment, making them operate autonomously. While the prospect of deploying fully autonomous construction robots on a large scale is a future vision, telerobotics [108] and exoskeletons can be deployed more heavily to ensure high efficiency and to lower the risk of injuries.

TRL 4–6: for teleoperation and surveillance tasks; 1–3: for autonomy and construction/maintenance.

Fortify Natural Environments (Fortification). It is important to consider when and where to alter the natural environment in order to reduce the possibility of a disaster. For example, clearing away trees from power lines can reduce the chance of a power outage before a storm. Similarly, clearing out buffer zones in forests can reduce the spread of disastrous fires. Fortifying a water supply network can help agriculture to better manage resources in the case of a drought. While these tasks are routinely performed by humans today, they are both risky and expensive to perform at a large scale. There has been limited use of robots in these domains, however, given the difficulty of deploying robots in such highly unstructured setups. At the same time, there are research efforts on robots that interact with the natural environment without much human intervention. For example, European researchers are working on a mobile manipulator called TrimBot [104] which can trim vegetation. The underlying technology focusing on gardening is an example of how robots can be deployed in forestry-fortification tasks. There are many challenges, however, in hardening such technology; these lie in the integration of several key components: computer vision to understand complex natural environments, 3D mapping techniques for navigation, and manipulation to remove dead plants, trim dry leaves, and plant new trees. So far, forest fire prevention humanoid robots are limited to the design phase [33].

TRL 1–3: for nature fortifying robots.

Monitor for Early Detection and Warning (Preparation). Early detection and monitoring can be effective for minimizing losses in many disasters. For instance, knowing early that a fire started and is growing can speed up evacuation and counter-measures before the disaster gets out of hand. In addition, predicting the duration and magnitude of potential disasters can better inform as to if and where further attention is needed. Furthermore, the detection of warning signals including "behavior pattern recognition" [88] is critical to combat terrorist attacks. Thanks to advances in machine learning and data mining, predictive models of disasters can be obtained through the analysis of data from previous events. Collecting data, however, could be burdensome and even impossible in disaster-prone areas which are not naturally accessible. In these cases, robots can help to both gather data and provide immediate alert of potential disasters through real-time monitoring. Liquid Robotics launched an autonomous Wave Glider robot, a marine robot outfitted with a hydrophone, time-lapse camera, and satellite uplink to communicate with a sensor package on the ocean floor [66]. It looks for changes in water pressure and magnetic fields that indicate whether a tsunami has formed. The concept of fire-detecting robots is also on the horizon as Insight Robotics is developing an early wildfire detection system that combines a high-precision, pan-tilt robot with thermal imaging sensors and advanced vision technology [8]. Given its ability to collect temperature data, it is now being considered for measuring body temperature in the mass screening of fever candidates. It can reduce human labor and lower the risk of testing staff being exposed to infected people in the Covid-19 pandemic.

TRL 4–6: Some of the technologies are currently at the level of minimum viable products (MVP).

Evacuation Management (Preparation). Some unfortunate tragedies due to disasters occur during the evacuation process. For example, in response to the possibility of hurricane Rita hitting Texas in 2005, over 100 people died during the evacuation because heavy traffic caused people to get stuck in traffic jams during a heat wave [11]. Better communicating and guiding an evacuation can help people be more resilient in escaping disasters that are not preventable. There are two main areas where robotics can help: one is deployment of more intelligent or driver-less vehicles (AGVs) and the other is effective means of human-robot interaction during emergencies.

Introducing driverless cars is predicted to significantly lower chaos caused by panic during an evacuation [28]. Automated cars are emotionless when facing dense crowding and traffic disturbances, and are capable of taking more responsive actions while maintaining high accuracy. Before reaching the wide-spread adoption of autonomous vehicles, drones and other types of mobile robots can be used to communicate information to human drivers. Inside buildings, evacuees tend to follow the crowd to find an exit, which can cause gridlock and potentially trampling. Recent work [82] proposes effective evacuation strategies for humanoid robots to positively take advantage of and influence "follow the crowd" behavior. The idea is to assign mobile shepherding robots that lead evacuees to a particular exit and stationary handoff robots that use gestures or verbal commands to direct the evacuees to another robot. This type of human-robot and robot-robot interaction shows promise in improving effectiveness of future evacuations.

TRL 4–6: for autonomous driving technology; 1–3: for evacuation-guiding robots.

Deployment of Response Resources (Preparation). Managing response resources in disaster-prone regions ahead of time is an effective way to alleviate the negative impact of a disaster. This can be achieved by building better transport networks for both people and supplies. Robots are able to distribute response resources both in a shorter period of time and more rationally than humans can. In the event of a drought, for instance, aerial robots and UAVs like drones can take prompt action and deliver water to where it is most needed. In general, due to high precision, such robots could be used to more efficiently water crops [5]. In fact, in drought-stricken California, farmers are using drones as drip systems that save them 40–50% on the water that they previously used [6]. The water savings by these intelligent systems help farmers survive through heat waves and droughts. A future direction to take would be to improve the sensing and vision of the drones (e.g., using infrared cameras) to analyze the coloration of plants and accurately identify the regions in lack of water.

TRL 7: Although drones are viable, there is room for improvement in terms of sensing and vision.

2.2   Robotics for Post-disaster Response

This paper summarizes in Fig. 4 the resiliency activities related to post-disaster responses, which minimize loss of life and reduce the recovery time, i.e., time required to rebuild damaged infrastructure and biotopes after a disaster has taken place. Post-disaster responses are further categorized into those responses focused on "Infrastructure and Nature" and "People".

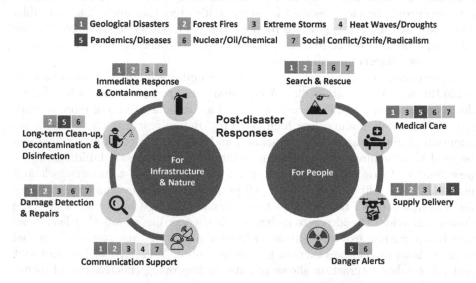

Fig. 4. Robotics can enable the above "post-disaster" responses for resiliency. This paper splits post-disaster measures into two categories: (1) For People and (2) For Infrastructure and Nature (dark blue circles), each with its own sub-categories (grey circles). The number-indexed icons with associated colors indicate types of disasters. They appear next to preemptive measures that are more relevant to them. (Color figure online)

Search and Rescue (People). Timely search and rescue work is essential for victims in geological disasters, nuclear/chemical accidents, and terrorist attacks. A major challenge in search and rescue work arises from navigating adverse and dangerous environments. Rescue teams could face debris from fallen buildings after earthquakes, dense vegetation in forests, and high levels of radiation in contaminated nuclear plants. Robots have the advantage of being less vulnerable and more expendable but they are generally less mobile. Researchers are pushing robot mobility by exploring different mechanisms of motion. For instance, bio-inspired spider-like and snake-like robots are being developed to search and rescue people trapped in the places which are hard for rescue teams to see or reach. In addition to mechanical design advances, rescue robots perform SLAM to effectively localize themselves [113] and multi-robot coordination [73]. Future emphasis will be put on coordinating robots to maximize search coverage. For instance, drones can be dispatched to survey large areas such as entire cities or forests [128].

TRL 5–7: UAVs are currently more mobile but limited by sensor range and bio-inspired robots are still in relatively early stages of control.

Medical Care (People). Fast and effective medical care can save lives in the aftermath of a disaster and can help prevent bio-disasters. A common challenge for the medical community during disasters is the sudden influx of patients. Perhaps more lacking than space and equipment are the medical staff themselves. Telerobotics could be used by offsite staff to quickly look at and possibly treat patients before a doctor becomes available onsite. There are telepresence robots on the market already such as the Double telepresence robot [76]. Even for diagnosis, though, such robots currently lack maneuverability of cameras and any bio-medical imaging sensors. Care is also needed for protecting medical staff from infectious diseases. Teleoperated robots lower the risk of medical worker infection by limiting their exposure. Furthermore, robots that could sanitize rooms and medical equipment regularly without the need of an operator could speed up pre/post patient prep. Already during the Ebola epidemic, germ zapping robots were deployed in hospitals to decontaminate a room by blasting ultraviolet light into it [78]. For such robots, designing optimal coverage paths is an ongoing focus of research [45,57].

TRL 6–7: Telerobotics are advanced but not yet proven in mission critical settings.

Supply Delivery (People). First-aid essentials for earthquake victims, food for people left stranded by storms, fire extinguishers for rangers fighting forests fires, and high-quality masks for medical staff fighting viruses are in desperate need. Such situations pose challenges of limited accessibility to remote or isolated regions and high demand exceeding the capacity for timely delivery. After the outbreak of Covid-19, the demand for doorstep delivery dramatically increased while couriers tried to minimize risk of exposure. Intelligent delivery systems can be used to deliver goods to the door without human involvement. Logistics company DoorDash has started providing food delivery with minimal human interaction by using Starship Technologies' ground robots [109]. UAVs have also been notably explored by Amazon for more general package delivery [85]. UAVs have the added benefit of avoiding traffic but are limited by the weight of goods they can carry. An interesting direction is to design an efficient truck-drone or truck-robot system where the truck aims for long-distance delivery [92] and then the drone/mobile robots arm for last-mile delivery [101] to meet high demand.

TRL 6: Fundamental technology is mature but policies for public operation need further research/testing.

Danger Alerts (People). Besides rescuing or curing those who fall victim to a disaster, it is also critical to prevent those who survive from falling victim to the aftermath and lasting effects. For instance, to prevent disaster escalation, warning signs and protective barriers can deter or prevent people from further danger. Workers setting up such barriers might expose themselves to the hazardous environment and the affected region or facility might be too large to cover all entry points. Robots can tackle unfavorable working conditions and their behavior is reproducible, thus allowing for more scalable solutions. Small mobile robots with sensors can be dispatched on site to guard certain areas [43], detecting and warning people from approaching danger. Humanoid robots for this task would be more effective at getting peoples' attention [123] but UAVs would be more practical for covering larger areas quickly.

TRL 3: How robots interact with people and alert to surrounding dangers still requires fundamental human-robot interaction (HRI) research.

Immediate Response and Containment (Infrastructure and Nature). Immediate actions are needed to reduce the damage from/to the environment and infrastructure after a disaster. Robots are good at immediate response and containment due to durable hardware and fast computational ability. For instance, high-speed helicopters can pour heavy water or sand buckets over fires which are beyond the reach of firefighters. Moreover, a fleet of UAVs that periodically survey a forest to detect wildfires could respond instantly to a smaller fire whereas people typically won't notice until much later [20]. Similar style automation could be used for snow clearance vehicles [68]. The quickened response to clearing snow could greatly improve traffic flow during the winter and minimize road closures.

TRL 7: Semi-automated machines that are deployed in large scale but full autonomy is a work-in-progress.

Long-term Clean Up, Decontamination and Disinfection (Infrastructure and Nature). Though quick action can minimize problems before they get worse, if a disaster does get out of control (such as a forest fire or a nuclear/oil/chemical accident) it can leave behind an unfavorable environment which needs long-term efforts to clean up. As robots are less vulnerable to adverse conditions, they are increasingly used for this type of work. However, disaster cleanup requires specialized mobile manipulators depending on the scenario. For instance, STR-1 robots have been placed on the roof of nuclear plants to clean up destroyed reactors and debris, which mitigated the aftermath of the nuclear leak of the Chernobyl reactor containment walls [55]. Timely clean-up efforts are also important for oil spills as water can spread toxins quickly depending on currents and winds. MIT has been developing a fleet of marine robots called Seaswarm [107] which are designed to clean up oil spills quickly and relatively cheaply. In terms of virus disinfection, remote-controlled ground robots are also used in China to disinfect neighborhoods daily amid the Covid-19 outbreak to ensure a safer environment for residents [48]. The future focus is more on whether they can be in full autonomy and make decisions without human intervention.

TRL 6–9: Special purpose cleaning robots have been deployed but their effectiveness and level of autonomy vary.

Damage Detection and Repairs (Infrastructure and Nature). Quick detection of damage to infrastructure can prevent further destruction in a potential aftershock. Such detection needs high accuracy and undisturbed reasoning, which are the advantages of robots over humans. In addition to navigation challenges, robots performing detection tasks are faced with perception and vision challenges in actually identifying/sensing issues. During the nuclear leak in Fukushima, Japan, the Japanese investigation team dispatched a robot manipulator equipped with dedicate sensors and gauges to identify the main source of the nuclear leak and detect if the danger had been eliminated [25]. There is also active research on designing mobile robots equipped with 2D laser scanners [119] to detect road surface damage; this is especially important after an earthquake or a volcanic eruption occurs. Monitoring technology can also be used to detect weak links in heavy machinery, factories, and power grids. One such technique is motion amplification, currently deployed by RDI Technologies, which helps detect faulty machine behavior by visually exaggerating small vibrations through image processing [10]. It remains a challenge on the mechanism design of such robots so that they can be placed into small regions without the risk of damaging the equipment on the robots.

TRL 7–8: Machines are pretty good at identifying damage or possible weak points but distributing them efficiently to survey infrastructure has plenty of room for improvement.

Communication Support (Infrastructure and Nature). When a disaster such as a geological disaster or a forest fire occurs in a remote area, the ability to maintain communication is very important in order to properly respond to the disaster and keep people safe. One key task is to gather accurate disaster information on site for leaders to make wise decisions. Due to limited human access to those regions, ground vehicles (AGVs) and aerial robots (UAVs) can be used to coordinate with each other to gather information [77,84]. Robots can not only get disaster information on site for the needs of rescue teams, but also successfully gather those for the needs of victims on site. This requires that robots have excellent sensing and analytical tools to locate victims [93], so as to provide guidance for rescue. The deployment of these robots requires many advanced techniques including SLAM [110].

Another important task is to provide backup for existing human communication channels (e.g. phone and internet). If a storm knocks out power in a region and is expected to become even more dangerous, people might not realize the need to evacuate before it is too late. Deploying drones to either provide temporary wireless networks [70] or even dropping warning pamphlets at peoples' doorsteps could prevent people from getting trapped in such situations. Furthermore, the same temporary communication networks could be used for search and rescue teams [86] to improve reliability of government facilities so as to provide extra security in case of a national security incident.

TRL 6: SLAM techniques have been broadly used. However, multi-robot interaction is still challenging especially as the number of robots increases and when centralized communication is not available.

2.3 Summary of Robotics Technology for Resiliency Activities

Table 1 summarizes which robotics technology (column 1) applies to which resiliency activities discussed in Sects. 2.1 and 2.2 (column 2) and the types

Table 1. The table summarizes which robotics technology (column 1) applies to which resilience activities (column 2) and the types of robots involved (column 3) in using the robot technology for the resilience activities.

Robotics Technology	For Resiliency Activities	Types of Robots
Additive Manufacturing	Resilient Supply Chain	Robotic Manipulators
Logistics Robots	Resilient Supply Chain Supply Delivery	Autonomous Ground Vehicles (AGV) Unmanned Aerial Vehicles (UAV) Robotic Manipulators
Construction/Infrastructure Robotics	Build and Maintain Robust Infrastructure Immediate Response and Containment	Mobile Manipulators Unmanned Aerial Vehicles (UAV)
Forestry Robotics	Fortify Natural Environments	Mobile Manipulators
Data Collection and Hazard Detection	Monitor for Early Detection and Warning Danger Alerts Damage Detection and Repairs	Autonomous Ground Vehicles (AGV) Autonomous Underwater Vehicles (AUV)
Driverless Cars	Evacuation Management Deployment of Response Resources	Autonomous Ground Vehicles (AGV)
Human-robot Coordination	Evacuation Management Danger Alerts	Humanoid Robot
Drones	Deployment of Response Resources Search and Rescue Supply Delivery Communication Support	Unmanned Aerial Vehicles (UAV)
Rescue Robots	Search and Rescue Communication Support	Autonomous Ground Vehicles (AGV) Bio-inspired Robots
Medical Robots	Medical Care	Robotic Manipulators Humanoid Robots Bio-inspired Robots
Disinfectant Robots	Medical Care Immediate Response and Containment Long-term Clean up, Decontamination and Disinfection	Autonomous Ground Vehicles (AGV) Autonomous Underwater Vehicles (AUV) Mobile Manipulators

of robots introduced in Sect. 1.1 involved (column 3). There are many types of robotics technologies, at varying levels of maturity, that can aid in both preemptive measures and post-disaster responses to strengthen resiliency against disasters. Broadly speaking, the robotics technologies that rely on simpler movement modalities (autonomous vehicles, warehouse robots, drones) are more mature and even deployed towards some of the useful resiliency activities. Such technologies would gain more benefit from better sensor hardware/software and distributed communication methods. The less mature robotics technologies are predominantly those that deal with more complex movement modalities (bio-inspired movement, unstructured environments), dexterous manipulation tasks (assembly, rearrangement), and human interaction. Such technologies still need fundamental research and experiments involving new algorithmic and hardware ideas before becoming practical for deployment in disaster resiliency tasks.

When considering strategies for disaster resilience, it is important to know which technologies are available now, which can be pushed to work soon, and which should be developed in the long term for future use. This information alone, however, is not enough to fully make decisions on which resilience actions to take. It is important to also consider the negative consequences that can result from the use of robotics technology whether by intentional abuse or negligent misuse, which is the topic of the next section.

3 Pitfalls of Robotics Deployment for Disaster Resiliency

While robots enable resiliency to disasters, their deployment can also result in side effects if not executed properly. This section brings up such potential undesirable consequences resulting from either intentional or negligent application of robotics technology and suggests general policies and broad guidelines to mitigate the negative impact. The proposed guidelines in this section reflect the opinions of the authors, and not necessarily of any cited works. In fact, we want to stress that as technology itself is developing, careful considera- tion and further socio-technological research is needed to inform prac- tical policies for the deployment of specific types of robotics technol-

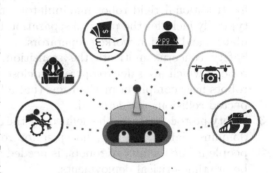

Fig. 5. Potential undesirable consequences from the deployment of robotics technology as a resiliency strategy include but are not lim- ited to (from left to right circles): (1) Safety Concerns; (2) Impact on Employment; (3) Size of Investment; (4) Unbalanced Expectations and Reactions; (5) Privacy Infringement and Cyber Security; (6) Undesirable Uses of the Same Technology.

ogy. Figure 5 summarizes potential undesirable consequences.

Robotics Safety Concerns. Industrial robots are generally precise, powerful and fast. Therefore they are deployed in assembly lines and warehouses to achieve high efficiency and throughput. These good features, however, are also sources of potential danger for humans that are in proximity to or interact with robots. The fast and unpredictable motion of a robot manipulator leaves little time for an operator to respond and thus can cause permanent injury or even death. In 2015, a worker at a Volkswagen plant was grabbed by a robot arm and smashed into a metal plate [37], which is just one of approximately 40 robot-related occupational accidents reported since 1988 [9]. Such accidents may even happen more frequently during a disaster where supply chains and autonomous delivery are in high demand. Workers and robot operators are asked to take longer shifts to meet manufacturing and distribution demand. Fatigue increases the risks of unsafe robot operation, and can delay human reaction to malfunctioning robots. Furthermore, the number of robotic failure modes in more unstructured setups, such as in natural environments or for post-disaster responses, can be significantly higher, and human supervision is needed. In the domain of surgical robots where robots are expected to perform super-accurate minimal invasive surgeries, a study reported that at least 144 deaths and more than 1000 injuries are linked to robotic malfunction during surgery over a 14-year period in the US [14]. If surgical robots are going to see increased use during disasters where doctors are in short supply, technical difficulties and complications need to be addressed.

Mitigation Strategies:

1. Regardless of demand, established safety protocols and warning systems [30] for traditional rigid robot manipulators must be enforced at all times. This typically includes the physical separation between traditional robotic manipulators and human workers/operators.
2. Safety concerns motivate the transition from traditional to collaborative robots, which are safer to operate in close proximity to human workers. Such robots have compliant mechanisms that allow them to safely stop when unexpected collisions are detected.
3. Safety protocols need to be defined for the operation of robots in unstructured domains. Safety training, not just for robot operators, but also for other people in the vicinity of robots, is needed and should not be overlooked even before time-critical deployments.
4. Robot exoskeletons have been increasingly used to provide protection and endurance for workers so as to reduce failure from handling machines. Side effects from body contact with robot exoskeletons, such as excessive pressure or tension, are not well known and should be examined further.
5. Human operators of robots require sufficient breaks and task variety in their daily shift so as to maximize alertness during robot supervision.

Impact on Employment. Technology displacing human laborers has been a constantly re-emerging concern. In the long term, advancement in technology can increase job opportunities, in the short term, however, sudden deployment of technology without concern for people can cause waves of unemployment. It has been argued that about 1.7 million manufacturing jobs world-wide have been lost to robots since 2000 [16]. Tangentially, unemployment can further increase in the event of a disaster; many jobs were lost at the peak of the Covid-19 pandemic [96] as companies were reducing in-person interaction or due to lost revenue. Though such unemployment is mainly due to the pandemic, not robot deployment, arguments can be made that job replacement is likely to continue with the objective of minimizing human contact and saving labor cost. This trend has already spread from manufacturing industry to healthcare; more robots have been used in hospitals to disinfect areas, measure patients' temperatures and deliver medicine. They can do it without getting anyone else (both care providers and the patients) infected [49]. The robots are also increasingly deployed in restaurants and may reshape the industry after the pandemic. At the end of the day, if a machine costs less to maintain than the wages for an "equivalent" number of workers, then companies will be incentivized not to rehire people.

Mitigation Strategies:

1. The machines deployed in factories and warehouses need monitoring and maintenance work. Training existing workers to operate and repair the robots can effectively reduce job loss while increasing safety and resiliency. Though robots can replace human laborers, new human tasks can be defined that involve the operation and coordination of the corresponding tools. Other jobs will arise from the need to understand and explain accidents involving robots.
2. Skilled workers are far more valuable than unskilled workers. Thus, making higher education and vocational training more accessible would reduce unemployment from automation as well as benefit society more broadly [89].
3. More potential administrative jobs are also created as robotic applications introduce new considerations, especially those related to regulatory and safety compliance.

Size of Investment. Despite technology's positive economic benefits, it may require a very significant initial investment to make technology practical. For instance, the rapid advance in computing power and cognitive systems is contingent on significant improvement of materials. To give an example, an American supplier of Applied Materials is experimenting with Cobalt as the alternative to Tungsten and Copper in transistors but is held back by the much higher cost of Cobalt [26]. High cost also lies in software engineering and algorithmic innovations as programmers are in high demand and paid high salaries while research funding focuses on the long term. Systems architecture is similarly costly as cleverer development takes a lot of design, prototyping, and testing time [35]. In terms of disaster resilience, the cost invested in resiliency technology can potentially be significant relative to the losses from an infrequent disaster. Consider the task of recovering black boxes and fuselage/debris [80] after air crashes. Currently such efforts can exceed $35 million in cost. Since airplane crashes happen infrequently there is less immediate need to develop an autonomous black-box recovery system if manual human effort or simpler teleoperation methods already work. Instead, there is motivation to focus research and funding towards developing robotic systems that improve plane manufacture, construction, and operation in order to minimize damage during crashes and to avoid crashes altogether.

Mitigation Strategies:

1. Design robots to be used for multiple purposes. For instance, a robot which can extinguish emergent fires during a disaster can be used as a gardening robot when it doesn't fight fires.

2. Many robots are designed to work for long periods without being powered off. To mitigate the energy cost, natural energy resources such as solar energy could be used. For marine robots, the cost of operation can be minimized by installing equipment that can collect and harness wave and wind energy.
3. Though different robots have different functionality and work in different fields, some of the mechanism design like the joints, controllers and motors can be standardized. Modularizing common robotic components can save cost in design, manufacture, and repair.

Unbalanced Expectations and Reactions. The effectiveness of robotic-related products can be easily exaggerated to obtain overly optimistic expectations from the public in the surge of interest in artificial intelligence. For instance, a lot of resources have been invested in the development and promotion of self-driving cars with the promise of decreasing car accidents and inner-city traffic. Several car companies bragged that self-driving cars will be widely deployed in the year 2020 with Level 5 (a.k.a full) autonomy [22]. Nevertheless, self-driving cars still have yet to overcome some hard challenges, such as sensing accuracy, collision avoidance under dynamically-changing environments, and generalization to different weather conditions [52]. Such overly zealous praise of incremental successes can make people become overly optimistic and careless when the technology is used in atypical situations and behaves unexpectedly. For instance, the Tesla accident in 2015 [118] and Uber accident in 2018 [111] shared one common factor that the driver was inattentive during the period of the accident (either kept hands off the wheel or was on the phone). Such recklessness is not entirely the fault of the driver as they were misled into putting too much trust in an autonomous system which had nowhere near 100% success rate. These incidents spiked public concern and consequently many companies suspended their road testing and recalled their cars. Only 16% of respondents to a recent survey [17] felt comfortable allowing autonomous driving without the option of human control. Unfortunately, this new public distrust is also too extreme. Just because driverless technology isn't good enough yet doesn't mean it can't be developed further. If such public distrust lingers when the technology does become ready it could delay the deployment of disaster resilience techniques - such as using autonomous cars for faster evacuation - and ultimately cost more lives.

Mitigation Strategies:

1. Companies and research organizations should provide more realistic plans and properly inform customers of the exact maturity level of high-tech products so as not to form unreasonable expectations or biases.
2. Users of high-tech products, or drivers for instance, should receive training which involves abnormal situations and operation under emergency scenarios in addition to regular use, to fully understand the applicability of a product.
3. In the case of autonomous cars, some regulations can be considered such as drivers having to take periodic tests (like fire drills) in order to renew a certification for operating driverless cars.

Privacy Infringement and Cyber Security. As highlighted in Sect. 2, drones are an effective resiliency technology for delivering essential supplies or extending short term communication to remote or suddenly inaccessible areas in the event of a disaster. Improper use of drones, however, can result in massive invasion of privacy if used for unsolicited surveillance of private residents (e.g., taking pictures of the outside or possibly inside of someone's place of residence). Correlating such gathered data to a potential customer could lead to targeted advertisement at an unprecedented level; thus, companies are certainly motivated to break privacy if unregulated. Furthermore, drones, whether military or commercial, can be hacked even if they are well regulated.

Mitigation Strategies:

1. Better regulation or law enforcement should be formulated to ensure the safe use of drones [18]. For instance, limiting the range of sensors which commercial drones are allowed to be built with could prevent certain data from being collected in the first place.
2. In addition, recipients of drone deliveries should have the right to obtain the pictures/data taken or collected from the drone during delivery and the ability to ask for their deletion.

In terms of cyber security, an attack on a communication platform facilitating both rescue teams and victims as discussed in Sect. 2 would undermine the disaster responses and even escalate problems. Using state-of-art encryption algorithms is becoming standardized but negligent system design and human gullibility are still common weak points that hackers exploit, which may result in a factory accident, a building collapse and a misleading public transportation system. One prediction is that by 2040 more crimes will be committed by machines than by humans [116].

Mitigation Strategies:

1. Regular scanning and penetration tests should be performed more frequently and used to inform and strictly enforce proper protocols (both in software and for people).
2. One effective way to protect critical machinery such as cars and nuclear reactors from cyber attacks is to have physically inherent safety mechanisms; such as lacking a physical link to a wide area network (WAN).
3. In order to reduce crimes through robots, critical robotic services (e.g., ridesharing, product delivery, military use) should be registered and monitored by a third party.

Undesirable Uses of the Same Technology. Military interests and contracts are a large source of funding for robotics research. It was reported that global spending on military robotics grew from about $2.4 billion in 2000 to $7.5 billion in 2015 and is projected to reach $16.5 billion by 2025. Not coincidentally, 26% of the new robotics companies formed from 2012 are focused on military applications [112], mostly involving autonomous drones. Though military robots are increasingly deployed in the context of national defense and disaster responses, the improper use of such robots can cause significant negative consequences. For instance, if a natural disaster occurs at the border of two countries in conflict, a military robot may mistake victims in need of rescue as potential invaders to defend against. Such misuse could escalate political tension between the two countries and lead to retaliation.

Mitigation Strategies:

1. In addition to mechanical design and control strategies to improve robots' abilities to handle harsh environments, moral responsibilities should also be assigned to intelligent robots. As pointed out in [53], military robots should be designed with some moral framework in mind. For instance, a robot could be designed with the ability to reason about and prevent unwanted behaviors commanded by its operators.
2. To mitigate security concerns, mission critical robots need to be designed with some level of transparency in mind. Some software and hardware components should be publicly available so that external security audits can be frequently conducted and so that any vulnerabilities can be fixed more quickly by a larger invested community.

4 Discussion

Robotics technology has many applications towards strengthening disaster resilience including preventative measures, reactionary measures, and methods to mitigate the impact of the aftermath of disasters. The state-of-art in robotics manipulation and perception needs technological advancement in order to more effectively provide post-disaster resiliency given the unstructured nature of the challenge. Meanwhile many preemptive resiliency measures involving efficient resources in manufacturing or distribution are already seeing real deployment due to advancements in autonomous mobility. Additional capabilities can be achieved across resiliency activities by further exploring human-robot interaction and employing more advanced locomotion modes inspired by animals. There are also potential downsides and concerns to consider in the application of robots in these domains; these include safety, employment, cost, trust imbalance, privacy, abuse, and negligence.

As robotics is an interdisciplinary subject involving research efforts from multiple domains, the deployment of robotics also calls for a convergence of approaches based on science, technology, sociology, and ethics. Improvement through both technological and social means is necessary to ensure effective and proper use of robotics technology.

Acknowledgement. The authors would like to acknowledge the support of the NSF NRT award 2021628 and the NSF HDR TRIPODS 1934924.

References

1. Amazon Robotics. https://www.amazonrobotics.com/#/
2. Assembly Robots. https://www.robots.com/applications/robotic-assembly
3. BostonDynamics: ATLAS. https://www.bostondynamics.com/atlas
4. Built Robotics. https://www.builtrobotics.com/
5. DroneDeploy: Drones in Agriculture, Then and Now. https://medium.com/aerial-acuity/drones-in-agriculture-then-and-now-ebde3df01667
6. Euronews: Farmers use drones to fight drought. https://www.euronews.com/2016/09/12/farmers-use-drones-to-fight-drought
7. GeekPlus Robotics. https://www.geekplus.com/
8. Insight Robotics. https://www.insightrobotics.com/en/
9. Occupational Safety and Health Administration: Robot-related Accident. https://www.osha.gov/
10. RDI Technologies. https://rditechnologies.com/
11. Wiki: Hurricane Rita. https://en.wikipedia.org/wiki/Hurricane_Rita
12. Wiki: Technology readiness level. https://en.wikipedia.org/wiki/Technology_readiness_level
13. World Disasters Timeline. http://www.mapreport.com/disasters.html
14. BBC News: Robotic surgery linked to 144 deaths in the US (2015). https://www.bbc.com/news/technology-33609495
15. Two Billion People Hit by Natural Disasters in the Past Decade (2018). https://www.securitymagazine.com/articles/89535-two-billion-people-hit-by-natural-disasters-in-the-past-decade
16. Robots' to replace up to 20 million factory jobs' by 2030 (2019). https://www.bbc.com/news/business-48760799
17. Self-Driving Cars-facts and Figures (2020). https://www.driverlessguru.com/self-driving-cars-facts-and-figures
18. (ACLU), A.C.L.U.: Protecting privacy from aerial surveillance: Recommendations for government use of drone aircraft (2011). https://www.aclu.org/files/assets/protectingprivacyfromaerialsurveillance.pdf
19. Afghah, F., Razi, A., Chakareski, J., Ashdown, J.: Wildfire monitoring in remote areas using autonomous unmanned aerial vehicles. In: IEEE INFOCOM 2019-IEEE Conference on Computer Communications Workshops (INFOCOM WKSHPS), pp. 835–840. IEEE (2019)
20. Afzaal, H., Zafar, N.A.: Robot-based forest fire detection and extinguishing model. In: 2016 2nd International Conference on Robotics and Artificial Intelligence (ICRAI), pp. 112–117. IEEE (2016)
21. Ahmadi, M., Stone, P.: A multi-robot system for continuous area sweeping tasks. In: Proceedings 2006 IEEE International Conference on Robotics and Automation. ICRA 2006, pp. 1724–1729. IEEE (2006)
22. Anderson, M.: Surprise! 2020 Is Not the Year for Self-Driving Cars (2020). https://spectrum.ieee.org/transportation/self-driving/surprise-2020-is-not-the-year-for-selfdriving-cars
23. Army, T.U.: iRobot PackBot (2009). https://commons.wikimedia.org/wiki/File:Flickr_-_The_U.S._Army_-_iRobot_PackBot.jpg
24. Bao, D.Q., Zelinka, I.: Obstacle avoidance for swarm robot based on self-organizing migrating algorithm. Procedia Comput. Sci. **150**, 425–432 (2019)
25. Becker, R.: Robot squeezes suspected nuclear fuel debris in Fukushima reactor (2019). https://www.theverge.com/2019/2/15/18225233/robot-nuclear-fuel-debris-fukushima-reactor-japan

26. Bhagavatula, S.: Robots are getting expensive (2019). https://medium.com/datadriveninvestor/automation-is-getting-expensive-1a4656b1bd9a

27. Bischoff, R., Huggenberger, U., Prassler, E.: Kuka youbot-a mobile manipulator for research and education. In: 2011 IEEE International Conference on Robotics and Automation, pp. 1–4. IEEE (2011)

28. Bliss, L.: Could Self-Driving Cars Speed Hurricane Evacuations? (2016). https://www.theatlantic.com/technology/archive/2016/10/self-driving-cars-evacuations/504131/

29. Burke, R.V., et al.: Using robotic telecommunications to triage pediatric disaster victims. J. Pediatr. Surg. **47**(1), 221–224 (2012)

30. Burmeister, S., Holz, M.: Warning method and robot system, US Patent 9,908,244, March 6 2018

31. Chen, X., Zhang, H., Lu, H., Xiao, J., Qiu, Q., Li, Y.: Robust slam system based on monocular vision and lidar for robotic urban search and rescue. In: 2017 IEEE International Symposium on Safety, Security and Rescue Robotics (SSRR), pp. 41–47. IEEE (2017)

32. Coyle, S., Majidi, C., LeDuc, P., Hsia, K.J.: Bio-inspired soft robotics: material selection, actuation, and design. Extrem. Mech. Lett. **22**, 51–59 (2018)

33. Crozier, S.: Forest Fire "Clear Cut" Robot (2008). https://www.yankodesign.com/2008/04/24/forest-fire-clear-cut-robot/

34. Customs, U., Protection, B.: CBP Officers deploy underwater robot below a ship (2012). https://commons.wikimedia.org/wiki/File:CBP_Officers_deploy_underwater_robot_below_a_ship_(8405583933).jpg

35. Deierling, K.: The End of Moore's Law and the Return of Cleverness (2019). https://blog.mellanox.com/2019/08/the-end-of-moores-law-and-the-return-of-cleverness

36. D'Monte, L.: 5 Robots That May Rescue You From Natural Disasters (2015). https://www.govtech.com/em/safety/5-Robots-That-May-Rescue-You-From-Natural-Disasters.html

37. Dockterman, E.: Robot Kills Man at Volkswagen Plant (2015). https://time.com/3944181/robot-kills-man-volkswagen-plant/

38. Doersch, C., Zisserman, A.: Sim2real transfer learning for 3D human pose estimation: motion to the rescue. In: Advances in Neural Information Processing Systems, pp. 12949–12961 (2019)

39. Dunbabin, M., Grinham, A., Udy, J.: An autonomous surface vehicle for water quality monitoring. In: Australasian Conference on Robotics and Automation (ACRA), pp. 2–4. Citeseer (2009)

40. Ellekilde, L.P., Petersen, H.G.: Motion planning efficient trajectories for industrial bin-picking. Int. J. Robot. Res. **32**(9–10), 991–1004 (2013)

41. Ess, A., Schindler, K., Leibe, B., Van Gool, L.: Object detection and tracking for autonomous navigation in dynamic environments. Int. J. Robot. Res. **29**(14), 1707–1725 (2010)

42. Fallon, P.J.: Acoustical/optical bin picking system, US Patent 4,985,846, January 15 1991

43. Feng, S.W., Yu, J.: Optimally guarding perimeters and regions with mobile range sensors. arXiv preprint arXiv:2002.08477 (2020)

44. Foster, M.E., By, T., Rickert, M., Knoll, A.: Human-robot dialogue for joint construction tasks. In: Proceedings of the 8th International Conference on Multimodal Interfaces, pp. 68–71 (2006)

45. Galceran, E., Carreras, M.: A survey on coverage path planning for robotics. Robot. Auton. Syst. **61**(12), 1258–1276 (2013)

46. Garrett, C.R., Huang, Y., Lozano-Pérez, T., Mueller, C.T.: Scalable and probabilistically complete planning for robotic spatial extrusion. arXiv preprint arXiv:2002.02360 (2020)
47. Gonzalez, C.: Changing the Future of Warehouses with Amazon Robots (2017). https://www.machinedesign.com/mechanical-motion-systems/article/21835788/changing-the-future-of-warehouses-with-amazon-robots
48. González-Jiménez, H.: Can robots help us overcome the coronavirus health crisis and lockdown? (2020). https://theconversation.com/can-robots-help-us-overcome-the-coronavirus-health-crisis-and-lockdown-134161
49. Gow, G.: COVID-19 and unemployment: the robots are coming (2020). https://www.forbes.com/sites/glenngow/2020/07/07/covid-19-and-unemployment-the-robots-are-coming/?sh=225497141fab
50. Han, S.D., Yu, J.: DDM: fast near-optimal multi-robot path planning using diversified-path and optimal sub-problem solution database heuristics. IEEE Robot. Autom. Lett. **5**(2), 1350–1357 (2020)
51. Hanheide, M., et al.: Robot task planning and explanation in open and uncertain worlds. Artif. Intell. **247**, 119–150 (2017)
52. Hecht, J.: Self-driving vehicles: many challenges remain for autonomous navigation (2020). https://www.laserfocusworld.com/test-measurement/article/14169619/selfdriving-vehicles-many-challenges-remain-for-autonomous-navigation
53. Hellström, T.: On the moral responsibility of military robots. Ethics Inf. Technol. **15**(2), 99–107 (2013)
54. Hereid, A., Cousineau, E.A., Hubicki, C.M., Ames, A.D.: 3D dynamic walking with underactuated humanoid robots: a direct collocation framework for optimizing hybrid zero dynamics. In: 2016 IEEE International Conference on Robotics and Automation (ICRA), pp. 1447–1454. IEEE (2016)
55. Husseini, T.: From Cherno-bots to Iron Man suits: the development of nuclear waste robotics. https://www.power-technology.com/features/cleaning-up-nuclear-waste-robotics/
56. Islam, F., Salzman, O., Agraval, A., Likhachev, M.: Provably constant-time planning and re-planning for real-time grasping objects off a conveyor. arXiv preprint arXiv:2003.08517 (2020)
57. Kapoutsis, A.C., Chatzichristofis, S.A., Kosmatopoulos, E.B.: DARP: divide areas algorithm for optimal multi-robot coverage path planning. J. Intell. Robot. Syst. **86**(3–4), 663–680 (2017)
58. Karaman, S., Frazzoli, E.: Incremental sampling-based algorithms for optimal motion planning. Robot. Sci. Syst. VI **104**(2), 267–274 (2010)
59. Kerzel, M., Strahl, E., Magg, S., Navarro-Guerrero, N., Heinrich, S., Wermter, S.: Nico–neuro-inspired companion: a developmental humanoid robot platform for multimodal interaction. In: 2017 26th IEEE International Symposium on Robot and Human Interactive Communication (RO-MAN), pp. 113–120. IEEE (2017)
60. Khalid, M.A.B., Shome, R., Stone, C.M.K.B.M.: That and there: judging the intent of pointing actions with robotic arms (2019)
61. King, J.E., Haustein, J.A., Srinivasa, S.S., Asfour, T.: Nonprehensile whole arm rearrangement planning on physics manifolds. In: 2015 IEEE International Conference on Robotics and Automation (ICRA), pp. 2508–2515. IEEE (2015)
62. Koceska, N., Koceski, S., Beomonte Zobel, P., Trajkovik, V., Garcia, N.: A telemedicine robot system for assisted and independent living. Sensors **19**(4), 834 (2019)

63. Kroemer, O., Niekum, S., Konidaris, G.: A review of robot learning for manipulation: challenges, representations, and algorithms. arXiv preprint arXiv:1907.03146 (2019)
64. Krontiris, A., Bekris, K.E.: Efficiently solving general rearrangement tasks: a fast extension primitive for an incremental sampling-based planner. In: 2016 IEEE International Conference on Robotics and Automation (ICRA), pp. 3924–3931. IEEE (2016)
65. Kulik, S.D., Shtanko, A.N.: Experiments with neural net object detection system YOLO on small training datasets for intelligent robotics. In: Misyurin, S.Y., Arakelian, V., Avetisyan, A.I. (eds.) Advanced Technologies in Robotics and Intelligent Systems. MMS, vol. 80, pp. 157–162. Springer, Cham (2020). https://doi.org/10.1007/978-3-030-33491-8_19
66. LaMonica, M.: Ocean-faring Robot Cashes in on Offshore Oil and Gas (2013). https://www.technologyreview.com/2013/03/20/253500/ocean-faring-robot-cashes-in-on-offshore-oil-and-gas/
67. Lavalle, S.M.: Sampling-based motion planning (2006)
68. Lavine, K.: Take3: Left Hand Robotics creates snow-clearing robot (Video) (2018). https://www.bizjournals.com/denver/news/2018/01/02/take3-left-hand-robotics-creates-snow-clearing.html
69. Levinson, J., Thrun, S.: Robust vehicle localization in urban environments using probabilistic maps. In: 2010 IEEE International Conference on Robotics and Automation, pp. 4372–4378. IEEE (2010)
70. Li, X., Guo, D., Yin, H., Wei, G.: Drone-assisted public safety wireless broadband network. In: 2015 IEEE Wireless Communications and Networking Conference Workshops (WCNCW), pp. 323–328. IEEE (2015)
71. Lopez-Arreguin, A., Montenegro, S.: Towards bio-inspired robots for underground and surface exploration in planetary environments: an overview and novel developments inspired in sand-swimmers. Heliyon 6(6), e04148 (2020)
72. Lu, Q., Fricke, G.M., Tsuno, T., Moses, M.E.: A bio-inspired transportation network for scalable swarm foraging. In: 2020 IEEE International Conference on Robotics and Automation (ICRA), pp. 6120–6126. IEEE (2020)
73. Luo, C., Espinosa, A.P., Pranantha, D., De Gloria, A.: Multi-robot search and rescue team. In: 2011 IEEE International Symposium on Safety, Security, and Rescue Robotics, pp. 296–301. IEEE (2011)
74. Mandloi, A., Jaisingh, H.R., Hazarika, S.M.: Perception based navigation for autonomous ground vehicles. In: Deka, B., Maji, P., Mitra, S., Bhattacharyya, D.K., Bora, P.K., Pal, S.K. (eds.) PReMI 2019. LNCS, vol. 11942, pp. 369–376. Springer, Cham (2019). https://doi.org/10.1007/978-3-030-34872-4_41
75. Manjanna, S., Li, A.Q., Smith, R.N., Rekleitis, I., Dudek, G.: Heterogeneous multi-robot system for exploration and strategic water sampling. In: 2018 IEEE International Conference on Robotics and Automation (ICRA), pp. 1–8. IEEE (2018)
76. Margaret Rouse, I.W.: Telepresence robot. https://searchenterpriseai.techtarget.com/definition/telepresence-robot
77. Meguro, J.I., Ishikawa, K., Hasizume, T., Takiguchi, J.I., Noda, I., Hatayama, M.: Disaster information collection into geographic information system using rescue robots. In: 2006 IEEE/RSJ International Conference on Intelligent Robots and Systems, pp. 3514–3520. IEEE (2006)
78. Michael Martinez, P.V., Hannah, J.: CNN: germ-zapping robot Gigi sets its sights on Ebola (2014). https://www.cnn.com/2014/10/16/us/germ-zapping-robot-ebola/index.html

79. Miller, N.: How factories change production to quickly fight coronavirus (2020). https://www.bbc.com/worklife/article/20200413-how-factories-change-production-to-quickly-fight-coronavirus

80. Mohney, G.: Long Search for Missing Plane Could Cost 'Hundreds of Millions of Dollars' (2014). https://abcnews.go.com/International/long-search-missing-plane-cost-hundreds-millions-dollars/story?id=22899690

81. NASA: Snakebot (2000). https://www.nasa.gov/centers/ames/news/releases/2000/00images/snakebot/snakebot.html

82. Nayyar, M., Wagner, A.R.: Effective robot evacuation strategies in emergencies. In: 2019 28th IEEE International Conference on Robot and Human Interactive Communication (RO-MAN), pp. 1–6. IEEE (2019)

83. Noha, S.Y., et al.: Design of a 2dofs pantograph leg mechanism for rapid response robot platform in nuclear power plant facilities (2020)

84. Onosato, M., et al.: Disaster information gathering aerial robot systems. In: Rescue Robotics, pp. 33–55. Springer (2009). https://doi.org/10.1007/978-1-84882-474-4_3

85. Palmer, A.: Amazon wins FAA approval for Prime Air drone delivery fleet (2020). https://www.cnbc.com/2020/08/31/amazon-prime-now-drone-delivery-fleet-gets-faa-approval.html

86. Pan, Q., Lowe, D.: Search and rescue robot team RF communication via power cable transmission line-a proposal. In: 2007 International Symposium on Signals, Systems and Electronics, pp. 287–290. IEEE (2007)

87. Panagou, D.: Motion planning and collision avoidance using navigation vector fields. In: 2014 IEEE International Conference on Robotics and Automation (ICRA), pp. 2513–2518. IEEE (2014)

88. Paraskevas, A., Arendell, B.: A strategic framework for terrorism prevention and mitigation in tourism destinations. Tourism Manag. **28**(6), 1560–1573 (2007)

89. Paul, M.: Don't Fear the Robots: Why Automation Doesn't Mean the End of Work (2018). https://rooseveltinstitute.org/publications/dont-fear-the-robots-automation-doesnt-mean-the-end-of-work/

90. Pierson, A., Schwager, M.: Bio-inspired non-cooperative multi-robot herding. In: ICRA, pp. 1843–1849. Citeseer (2015)

91. Quaritsch, M., Kuschnig, R., Hellwagner, H., Rinner, B., Adria, A., Klagenfurt, U.: Fast aerial image acquisition and mosaicking for emergency response operations by collaborative UAVs. In: ISCRAM (2011)

92. Ramirez, V.B.: Waymo Just Started Testing Its Driverless Trucks in Texas (2020). https://singularityhub.com/2020/08/27/waymo-just-started-testing-its-driverless-trucks-in-texas/

93. Reich, J., Sklar, E.: Robot-sensor networks for search and rescue. In: IEEE International Workshop on Safety, Security and Rescue Robotics, vol. 22 (2006)

94. Reise, R.: POK Jupiter firefighting robot (2019). https://commons.wikimedia.org/wiki/File:POK_Jupiter_firefighting_robot_(3).jpg

95. Sadigh, D., Sastry, S., Seshia, S.A., Dragan, A.D.: Planning for autonomous cars that leverage effects on human actions. In: Robotics: Science and Systems, vol. 2. Ann Arbor (2016)

96. Semuels, A.: Millions of Americans Have Lost Jobs in the Pandemic – and Robots and AI are Replacing them Faster than Ever (2020). https://time.com/5876604/machines-jobs-coronavirus

97. Shaw, K.: World Robotics Report: Global Sales of Robots Hit $16.5B in 2018 (2019). https://www.roboticsbusinessreview.com/research/world-robotics-report-global-sales-of-robots-hit-16-5b-in-2018/

98. Shi, S., Wu, H., Song, Y., Handroos, H.: Mechanical design and error prediction of a flexible manipulator system applied in nuclear fusion environment. Ind. Robot: Int. J. **44**(6), 711–719 (2017)
99. Shome, R., Nakhimovich, D., Bekris, K.E.: Pushing the boundaries of asymptotic optimality in integrated task and motion planning. In: The 14th International Workshop on the Algorithmic Foundations of Robotics (2020)
100. Shome, R., et al.: Towards robust product packing with a minimalistic end-effector. In: 2019 International Conference on Robotics and Automation (ICRA), pp. 9007–9013. IEEE (2019)
101. Simoni, M.D., Kutanoglu, E., Claudel, C.G.: Optimization and analysis of a robot-assisted last mile delivery system. Transp. Res. Part E: Logistics Transp. Rev. **142**, 102049 (2020)
102. Ruiz-del Solar, J., Loncomilla, P., Soto, N.: A survey on deep learning methods for robot vision. arXiv preprint arXiv:1803.10862 (2018)
103. Srivastava, S., Fang, E., Riano, L., Chitnis, R., Russell, S., Abbeel, P.: Combined task and motion planning through an extensible planner-independent interface layer. In: 2014 IEEE International Conference on Robotics and Automation (ICRA), pp. 639–646. IEEE (2014)
104. Strisciuglio, N., et al.: Trimbot 2020: an outdoor robot for automatic gardening. In: ISR 2018 50th International Symposium on Robotics, pp. 1–6. VDE (2018)
105. Stuart, H., Wang, S., Khatib, O., Cutkosky, M.R.: The ocean one hands: an adaptive design for robust marine manipulation. Int. J. Robot. Res. **36**(2), 150–166 (2017)
106. Sun, P., et al.: Scalability in perception for autonomous driving: Waymo open dataset. In: Proceedings of the IEEE/CVF Conference on Computer Vision and Pattern Recognition, pp. 2446–2454 (2020)
107. Sutter, J.D.: MIT unveils swimming, oil-cleaning robots (2010). http://edition.cnn.com/2010/TECH/innovation/08/26/mit.oil.robot/index.html
108. Tanimoto, T., Shinohara, K., Yoshinada, H.: Research on effective teleoperation of construction machinery fusing manual and automatic operation. ROBOMECH J. **4**(1), 14 (2017)
109. Team, R.O.M.: Food Delivery Robots Take to the Streets (2019). https://www.robotics.org/blog-article.cfm/Food-Delivery-Robots-Take-to-the-Streets/212
110. Tuna, G., Gulez, K., Gungor, V.C.: Communication related design considerations of WSN-aided multi-robot slam. In: 2011 IEEE International Conference on Mechatronics, pp. 493–498. IEEE (2011)
111. Wakabayashi, D.: Self-Driving Uber Car Kills Pedestrian in Arizona, Where Robots Roam (2018). https://www.nytimes.com/2018/03/19/technology/uber-driverless-fatality.html
112. Walker, J.: Military Robotics Innovation - Comparing the US to Other Major Powers (2019). https://emerj.com/ai-sector-overviews/military-robotics-innovation/
113. Wang, H., Zhang, C., Song, Y., Pang, B.: Master-followed multiple robots cooperation slam adapted to search and rescue environment. Int. J. Control. Autom. Syst. **16**(6), 2593–2608 (2018)
114. Wang, R., Mitash, C., Lu, S., Boehm, D., Bekris, K.E.: Safe and effective picking paths in clutter given discrete distributions of object poses. arXiv preprint arXiv:2008.04465 (2020)
115. Wang, Y., Jordan, C.S., Hanrahan, K., Sanchez, D.S., Pinter, M.: Telepresence robot with a camera boom, US Patent 8,996,165, March 31 2015

116. Winder, D.: Is the future of cyber crime a nightmare scenario (2016). https://www.raconteur.net/is-future-cyber-crime-a-nightmare-scenario/
117. Wood, L.J., Zaraki, A., Walters, M.L., Novanda, O., Robins, B., Dautenhahn, K.: The iterative development of the humanoid robot kaspar: an assistive robot for children with autism. In: International Conference on Social Robotics, pp. 53–63. Springer (2017). https://doi.org/10.1007/978-3-319-70022-9_6
118. Yadron, D., Tynan, D.: Tesla driver dies in first fatal crash while using autopilot mode (2016). https://www.theguardian.com/technology/2016/jun/30/tesla-autopilot-death-self-driving-car-elon-musk
119. Yamada, T., Ito, T., Ohya, A.: Detection of road surface damage using mobile robot equipped with 2D laser scanner. In: Proceedings of the 2013 IEEE/SICE International Symposium on System Integration, pp. 250–256. IEEE (2013)
120. Yamamoto, T., Terada, K., Ochiai, A., Saito, F., Asahara, Y., Murase, K.: Development of human support robot as the research platform of a domestic mobile manipulator. ROBOMECH J. **6**(1), 4 (2019)
121. Yan, C., Xiang, X., Wang, C.: Towards real-time path planning through deep reinforcement learning for a UAV in dynamic environments. J. Intell. Robot. Syst. 1–13 (2019)
122. Yang, G.Z., et al.: Combating Covid-19–the role of robotics in managing public health and infectious diseases (2020)
123. Yatsuda, A., Haramaki, T., Nishino, H.: A robot gesture framework for watching and alerting the elderly. In: International Conference on Network-Based Information Systems, pp. 132–143. Springer (2018). https://doi.org/10.1007/978-3-319-98530-5_12
124. Yu, C., et al.: Ds-slam: A semantic visual slam towards dynamic environments. In: 2018 IEEE/RSJ International Conference on Intelligent Robots and Systems (IROS), pp. 1168–1174. IEEE (2018)
125. Yu, J., LaValle, S.M.: Optimal multirobot path planning on graphs: complete algorithms and effective heuristics. IEEE Trans. Robot. **32**(5), 1163–1177 (2016)
126. Yuh, J., Marani, G., Blidberg, D.R.: Applications of marine robotic vehicles. Intell. Serv. Robot. **4**(4), 221 (2011)
127. Zhang, S., Guo, Y.: Distributed multi-robot evacuation incorporating human behavior. Asian J. Control **17**(1), 34–44 (2015)
128. Zheng, X., Jain, S., Koenig, S., Kempe, D.: Multi-robot forest coverage. In: 2005 IEEE/RSJ International Conference on Intelligent Robots and Systems, pp. 3852–3857. IEEE (2005)
129. Zhou, X.S., Roumeliotis, S.I.: Multi-robot slam with unknown initial correspondence: the robot rendezvous case. In: 2006 IEEE/RSJ International Conference on Intelligent Robots and Systems, pp. 1785–1792. IEEE (2006)

Data Science and Resilience

Chapter 6
Big Data and FAIR Data for Data Science

Alexei Gvishiani[1,2], Michael Dobrovolsky[1]([✉]), and Alena Rybkina[1,2]

[1] Geophysical Center of the Russian Academy of Sciences, Molodezhnaya St. 3,
119296 Moscow, Russia
m.dobrovolsky@gcras.ru
[2] Schmidt Institute of Physics of the Earth of the Russian Academy of Sciences,
Bolshaya Gruzinskaya Street 10-1, 123242 Moscow, Russia

Abstract. The article is devoted to the review of such modern phenomena in the field of data storage and processing as Big Data and FAIR data. For Big Data, you will find an overview of the technologies used to work with them. And for FAIR data, their definition is given, and the current state of their development is described, including the Internet of FAIR Data & Services (IFDS).

Keywords: Big Data · FAIR data · Data science

1 Introduction

Currently, there is a continuous increase in the volume of data collected and processed by organizations from different fields of science and business. The main sources of such data are social networks, Internet of Things (IoT), sensory observation networks, etc. This leads to the need to process truly huge data streams. An important feature of such data is that it is not always presented in a structured form, but rather often is unstructured or partially structured. Data creation also happens at high speeds, quite often in real time or near real time. Such features of modern data generation and processing are a general trend, and such data are called Big Data. Big Data can be characterized as follows: they occupy huge volumes, are presented in a variety of formats, are generated and processed at high speed. It is not possible to work with them using traditional relational databases. At the same time, technologies for storing and processing such data are also constantly evolving, which helps to cope with the growing volumes, diversity, and speed of data flows.

For scientific data, another important trend is the adoption and dissemination of FAIR principles. These principles are the result of a long-term development of data access issues among scientific data providers, data repositories, research funding organizations, scientists themselves, and scientific publishing houses. The purpose of the FAIR Data Principles is to ensure that data are made available and stored in such a way that they can be analyzed and used in combination with other data through the use of common terminology and formats and are reusable through the use of complete and reliable metadata, detailed information about the origin of the data, and explicit data use licenses.

© Springer Nature Switzerland AG 2021
F. S. Roberts and I. A. Sheremet (Eds.): Resilience in the Digital Age, LNCS 12660, pp. 105–117, 2021.
https://doi.org/10.1007/978-3-030-70370-7_6

This article provides an overview of the current situation in these two areas of data handling.

2 Big Data

The term Big Data has recently become extremely popular both in scientific literature and in business literature and press. It can be found in scientific papers, popular scientific journals, business literature, and mass media. Big Data is entering more and more different fields of science and technology. The use of this term has become a kind of fashion and is not always justified.

The term was first introduced in 2008 by analogy with such terms as Big Water, Big Money, Big Oil. On September 3, 2008, Clifford Lynch, editor of the Nature journal, prepared a special issue on 'How can technologies that open up the possibilities for working with large volumes of data affect the future of science?'. The term has since become firmly established in scientific and business literature, first in the United States and then worldwide. Later, Big Data even became an academic discipline in universities around the world. The reason for the rapid adoption of the term is the impressive results that have been achieved in science and business using Big Data, as well as the creation and implementation of technologies to work with Big Data.

If you trace the history of the term even further, you can detect its use already in the 1990s. The popularization of the term at this time is associated with the name John Mashey [1]. When talking about Big Data, it usually involves such data, the amount of which is difficult to store and process with standard programs, such as relational databases [2]. Another important point is that Big Data is often unstructured, which makes it more difficult to work with them [3]. At the same time, it is clear that the size of data itself, which is considered to be big, is constantly changing with time and technology development. Because of these features of Big Data, special methods and technologies are required to process them and extract knowledge from them [4].

Initially, Big Data were described using the so-called 3V: volume, velocity, variety. Later, other characteristics such as variability, validity, value were added to these characteristics, but these additional characteristics refer more to useful information obtained from data than to the Big Data itself [5].

According to one of the more modern definitions 'Big data is where parallel computing tools are needed to handle data' [6]. One of the key features of Big Data is that it is mostly data with low information density. The tasks of Big Data processing are to identify relationships and dependencies among this information and to construct different predictions based on it.

2.1 Defining Big Data

The following features are used to describe Big Data:
Volume. Amount of data. The size of the data determines their value and potential results of their analysis, and whether they can be considered Big Data at all.
Variety. Different types of data used. It can be text or graphic information, audio, video, etc.

Velocity. The speed at which data is generated and processed. Big data is typically generated and processed in real time and generally at higher speeds than small data.
Veracity. This characteristic refers to the extended definition of Big Data and means data quality [7]. The quality of available data directly affects the results of their analysis. Other characteristics of Big Data are [8]:
Exhaustive. Whether the data provide complete coverage of the entire observed system.
Extensional. The ability to easily add or modify data fields.
Scalability. Ability to quickly increase data size.
Value. How you can gain value from your data.
Variability. Changing the values or other data characteristics.

The classic sources of Big Data are Internet of things and social media. Other sources of Big Data include previously unrecorded internal information of organizations, data from medicine and bioinformatics, astronomical observations, Earth sciences data, sensor-based observation networks.

Examples of Big Data sources are continuous observation data from measuring devices, events from radio frequency identifiers, message flows from social networks, meteorological data, data from Earth remote sensing, location data flows of cellular communication networks subscribers, data from audio and video registration devices [8].

Big data analysis methods include:

- data mining: association rule learning, classification, cluster and regression analysis.
- crowdsourcing: the categorization and enrichment of data by a wide range of volunteers;
- data fusion and integration - a set of techniques to combine heterogeneous data from different sources for further analysis. Examples are digital signal processing and natural language processing;
- machine learning, including supervised and unsupervised learning, and ensemble learning;
- artificial neural networks, network analysis, optimization methods including genetic algorithms;
- pattern recognition;
- predictive analytics;
- simulation modeling;
- spatial analysis;
- statistical analysis;
- visualization.

The basic principle of processing Big Data is horizontal scalability. We are talking about distributed data processing on a large number of computing nodes. This principle is included in the definition of Big Data from NIST: 'Big Data consists of extensive datasets primarily in the characteristics of volume, variety, velocity, and/or variability that requires a scalable architecture for efficient storage, manipulation, and analysis' [9]. As the technologies to work with Big Data are usually considered NoSQL, MapReduce,

Hadoop, R. Sometimes to these technologies are also added Business Intelligence and relational database management systems with SQL support.

Technologies for working with Big Data are divided into different layers such as Data Storage Layer, Data Processing Layer, Data Querying Layer, Data Access Layer, and Management Layer.

The most popular Big Data technology is Apache Hadoop. It allows you to avoid low performance and complexity that arise when working with Big Data using traditional technologies. The main advantage of Hadoop is the ability to quickly process large arrays of data using parallel clusters and distributed file system. Unlike traditional technologies, Hadoop does not copy entirely remote data into memory. Instead, Hadoop performs calculations in the place where the data is physically located. This can greatly reduce the communication load on the network and computing nodes [10]. For example, querying terabytes of data on Hadoop can be performed for just a few seconds instead of tens of minutes on traditional systems. In addition, Hadoop provides fault tolerance when performing computations, which is particularly important in a distributed environment. This is ensured by the replication of data between computational nodes.

The main components of the Hadoop platform are Hadoop Distributed File System (HDFS) and the MapReduce framework. The system is also expandable by the capability to add custom modules to address specific tasks and requirements such as capacity, performance, reliability, scalability, and security. There is a large ecosystem of open-source Hadoop custom modules, which plays a significant role in the popularity and spread of the platform. For corporate use, there are commercial Hadoop distributions from several major IT vendors.

Hadoop Data Storage Layer consists of an HDFS file system and an Apache HBase non-relational database.

HDFS [11] is a distributed storage system. It supports hundreds of nodes in the cluster and provides cost-efficient and reliable data storage. The system provides storage of structured and unstructured data in files of huge volume (more than one terabyte). HDFS is not a general-purpose file system. It is designed to perform batch operations with relatively high latency. However, it does not provide a fast search of individual records in files. An important feature of HDFS is its portability to various hardware and software platforms. Performing computations directly where the data is stored reduces the load on the network and improves performance. Fault tolerance is achieved through the replication of data between computational nodes. The architecture of HDFS is 'master-slave' [12]. Big data is stored in a distributed manner using a cluster.

HBase [13] is a distributed non-relational HDFS-based database. Its task is to perform operations with relatively low latency. A column-oriented data model of the key/value type is used. High data update rates and horizontal scaling through distributed clusters are supported. HBase tables allow storing billions of rows and millions of columns. Attributes are grouped into a family of columns stored together. This is a more flexible approach than the row-oriented traditional relational databases where all columns are stored together. The disadvantage of HBase is the lack of support for a structured query language like SQL. Among the Hbase features are: real-time queries, search in the natural language, consistent access to sources of Big Data, linear and modular scalability [14]. It is used in many Big Data systems, such as Facebook Messaging Platform.

There are two solutions for data processing on the Hadoop platform (job scheduling, resource management, and the whole cluster management): MapReduce and YARN. Among them, YARN is more universal.

MapReduce [15] combines a programming model that supports parallel data processing and its implementation. The MapReduce programming model is based on two functions, Map and Reduce.

To be more detailed, the program in the MapReduce model consists of the following steps:

- The Map function divides input data into non-intersecting parts that consist of key-value pairs.
- All key and value pairs are sent to Mapper, which processes them separately using several parallel tasks in the cluster. Each part of the data is assigned a computing node. The results of Mapper's work are intermediate pairs of keys and their values. After that, all intermediate pairs of keys and values are collected and sorted and grouped by keys. The result of such operation is a set of keys, each key having a list of associated values.
- The intermediate output data obtained in this way are processed by the Reduce function. For each key, the Reduce function performs the aggregation operation by values corresponding to that key. The aggregation operation is defined by a predetermined program. Examples of such operations are filtering, summation, sorting, hashing, calculation of the average, or discovery of the maximum. The output of the Reduce function is also a set of keys and their values.
- At the end of the procedure, the output pairs of keys and their values are saved to the output file.

YARN is a more versatile tool than MapReduce. It provides better scalability, parallelism, and resource management. YARN provides operating system functions for Big Data analytical applications. Modern Hadoop architectures include YARN Resource Manager. YARN is based on HDFS. This enables parallel execution of several applications at the same time. YARN supports both batch processing and interactive execution in real time. Application programming interface (API) level compatibility with MapReduce is provided. Therefore, it is enough to recompile MapReduce jobs to run them in YARN.

The Data Querying Layer of the Hadoop ecosystem is represented by such products as Pig, JAQL, and Hive.

Apache Pig [16] is an open-source framework that generates the high-level scripting language Pig Latin. It reduces the complexity of MapReduce by supporting parallel execution of MapReduce tasks and workflows on Hadoop. The Pig interactive environment simplifies the parallel processing of data arrays using HDFS. Pig also provides interaction with external programs such as shell scripts, executable files, and programs in other programming languages. The data model used in Pig is called Map Data (a map is a set of key-value pairs) [17].

Pig Latin is based on the intuitive syntax to support easy development of MapReduce jobs and workflows. It reduces development time with parallelism support [18]. Unlike

SQL, Pig does not require data schema definition and can work with semi-structured and unstructured data.

JAQL [19] is a declarative language on top of Hadoop, providing a query language and processing huge amounts of data. It converts high-level queries into MapReduce jobs. The JAQL task is to query semi-structured data based on JSON (JavaScript Object Notation) format. But it can be used for queries of other data formats as well (for example, XML, comma-separated data (CSV), flat files). JAQL, like Pig, does not require a data schema.

Apache Hive [20] is a data storage system that simplifies the work with Hadoop. Unlike MapReduce, which works with data in files via HDFS, Apache Hive provides data storage in a structured database. The Hive data model is based on tables.

Hive provides an SQL-like language HiveQL [21]. It allows accessing and manipulating data stored in HDFS or HBase. Therefore, Hive is suitable for many business applications. But Hive is not suitable for real time transactions. Like Hadoop, Hive is designed for large-scale processing and can take several minutes to complete even small jobs. Internally, HiveQL transparently converts requests into MapReduce jobs.

Data Access Layer consists of several parts.

Data Ingestion is represented by such solutions as Sqoop, Flume, and Chukwa.

Apache Sqoop [22] is an open-source software that provides a command line interface (CLI) for efficient transfer of large amounts of data between Hadoop and structured data warehouses (relational and NoSQL databases). Sqoop provides speed, fault tolerance, and optimization to reduce the load on external systems. Data is imported using MapReduce or any other high-level language such as Pig, Hive, or JAQL. When importing data from HDFS, the output is a set of files.

Flume [23] is designed to collect, aggregate, and transfer data from external sources to HDFS. It is based on a simple extensible data model to work with large, distributed data sources. Flume provides fault tolerance, customizable reliability mechanism, and disaster recovery service.

Chukwa [24] is a Hadoop-based data collection system. Its task is to monitor large distributed systems. Chukwa uses HDFS for data collection and MapReduce for data analysis. It provides an interface for displaying, monitoring, and analyzing results.

2.2 Data Streaming: Storm and Spark

Storm [25] is a distributed open-source system providing real-time data processing unlike Hadoop, which is designed for batch processing.

Storm can potentially support any incoming data and record data into any output system. It can be used in many cases such as real-time data analysis, online machine learning, continuous computing, and distributed RPC.

Apache Spark [26] is an open-source distributed processing framework. It was created at UC Berkeley AMPLab. Spark is based on an in-memory system to improve performance. As a result, it can run programs hundreds of times faster than Hive and Hadoop. Spark's data model is based on the Resilient Distributed Dataset (RDD) abstraction [27]. RDD is a read-only collection of objects stored in system memory on multiple machines. These objects can be accessed without accessing the disk.

The following components are part of Spark [28]:

- Spark SQL. It combines two abstractions: relational tables and RDD. This allows you to easily combine data queries from external sources in SQL language with complex analytics.
- Spark streaming provides automatic parallelization as well as scalable and fault-tolerant stream processing.
- MLlib is a distributed machine learning system based on Spark. It provides various optimized machine learning algorithms, such as classification, regression, and clustering.

GraphX is a library for working with graphs and performing parallel computations on them. It provides a set of operators and algorithms to perform various manipulations on graphs.

Apache HCatalog [29] provides a table and storage management for Hadoop. Its goal is to provide interoperability between different data processing tools (such as Pig, Hive, and MapReduce). To solve this task, a common data schema and data type mechanisms are provided. HCatalog uses abstract tables for the relational representation of data stored in HDFS. This allows working in tabular format with heterogeneous data formats.

Apache Mahout and R are among the Big Data analytics tools.

Apache Mahout [30] is an open-source library for machine learning. Mahout can work with Hadoop as well as other platforms. It is a set of libraries in Java language, providing scalability and implementation of machine learning algorithms for large data sets. Among the available algorithms, there are algorithms for clustering, classification, collaborative filtering, thematic modeling, dimensionality reduction, text vectorization, and many others. Using Mahout allows you to concentrate your efforts on solving the necessary task of data analysis without the need to implement the necessary algorithms and models of machine learning.

R [31] is a freely distributed programming language for working with statistics and machine learning. It is used by many distributions to work with Big Data as their analytical component. Such distributions include products from Cloudera, Hortonworks, and Oracle.

A significant disadvantage of the R language is its limitation of RAM on one computing node. This makes it uniquely challenging when working with very large data sets. An additional difficulty is that R uses temporary copies of objects instead of references to already existing objects. This leads to the fact that with its use, you can process data that occupy only 10–20% of RAM on a single computational node.

To get around these limitations, several R language packages were developed. These are Rmpi, Snow, and sfCluster packages for explicit paralleling of programs, Multicore, Parallel and Collect, and Foreach packages for implicit paralleling, bigmemory, ff (Fast File Access), mapReduce, hadoopstreaming, and Rhipe packages for direct work with large data. Another solution is the pdDR (Big Data programming in R) project which provides high-level distributed data parallelism.

The advantage of R is the greater number of implemented algorithms and models of statistics and machine learning in comparison with Mahout. But using tools such as Mahout or Spark can provide greater performance when working with Big Data [32].

The control level when working with Big Data is divided into the following parts.

2.3 Coordination and Workflow: Zookeeper, Avro, and Oozie

Zookeeper [33] is an open-source service for coordinating applications and clusters in the Hadoop environment. It provides high performance, data availability, simplified distributed programming, and reliable distributed storage. Zookeeper is based on a distributed client-server architecture. Recently, it has been increasingly used in Hadoop as a high availability solution.

Apache Avro [34] is a framework for modeling, serialization, and remote procedure call execution (RPC). It provides a compact binary data format and supports this format for different programming languages. This allows for efficient data compression and storage on Hadoop nodes.

Apache Oozie [35] is a workflow scheduler system for running and managing jobs in Hadoop clusters. It represents workflow jobs as Directed Acyclical Graphs (DAG). Oozie supports different types of Hadoop jobs and allows you to track their execution.

2.4 System Deployment: Ambari, Whirr, and Hue

Apache Ambari [36] simplifies Hadoop management through an intuitive web interface for initializing, managing, and monitoring Hadoop clusters. To ensure security, Ambari uses the Kerberos authentication protocol and user authentication, authorization, and audit functions.

Apache Whirr [37] simplifies the creation and deployment of clusters in cloud environments through libraries for running cloud services. It can be run locally from the command line as well as within the cloud.

Hue [38] is a web-based application for the Hadoop ecosystem that provides access to its components through a single interface. Its main purpose is to ensure that Hadoop can be used without worrying about its internal complexity. Hue supports all versions of Hadoop and is available in all its major distributions.

The development of technologies to work with Big Data in the form of separate open-source modules contributes to the advancement and widespread use of these technologies, but the disadvantage is that individual modules of different versions, which eventually build the Hadoop platform, may be incompatible with each other. Combining different technologies on one platform also increases security risks, because such combinations of modules are not always properly tested as a whole. Therefore, several IT vendors such as IBM, Cloudera, MapR, and Hortonworks provide their own distributions for work with Big Data. Such distributions should ensure compatibility, security, and performance of a system consisting of a set of individual modules as a whole.

In geosciences, the sources of Big Data are Earth remote sensing (ERS), meteorological observation data, geo-ecological information, seismic exploration data. In recent years, observations from unmanned aerial vehicles [39], data from networks of wireless sensors [40], numerical modeling data [41], as well as crowdsourcing data [42] have been added to the Big Data in the geosciences.

Such technologies as data cubes [43], USGS Earth Explorer online portal [44], Copernicus Sentinel Hub [45], and GEOSS portal [46] are used for data access and analysis in Earth sciences. Data analysis-oriented solutions such as Google Earth Engine [47] and EarthServer [48] effectively provide pre-processing of Big Data.

3 FAIR Data

The principles of FAIR data were first formulated in [49]. These principles are Findability, Accessibility, Interoperability, and Reusability. The goal is to apply these principles not only to the data itself but also to algorithms and formalized workflows that allow data to be created. The application of these principles allows for repeatability and reusability of all stages of the data production process. The FAIR Guiding Principles define modern requirements for the publication of data that allow for the addition, discovery, and reuse of data, both in manual and automated mode. They provide concise and domain-independent general principles applicable to a wide range of scientific tasks related to data and metadata.

The details of the FAIR Guiding Principles are formulated as follows:

To be Findable:
F1. (meta)data are assigned a globally unique and persistent identifier.
F2. Data are described with rich metadata (defined by R1 below).
F3. Metadata clearly and explicitly include the identifier of the data it describes.
F4. (meta)data are registered or indexed in a searchable resource.

To be Accessible:
A1. (meta)data are retrievable by their identifier using a standardized communications protocol.
A1.1 the protocol is open, free, and universally implementable.
A1.2 the protocol allows for an authentication and authorization procedure, where necessary.
A2. Metadata are accessible, even when the data are no longer available.

To be Interoperable:
I1. (meta)data use a formal, accessible, shared, and broadly applicable language for knowledge representation.
I2. (meta)data use vocabularies that follow FAIR principles.
I3. (meta)data include qualified references to other (meta)data.

To be Reusable:
R1. Meta(data) are richly described with a plurality of accurate and relevant attributes.
R1.1. (meta)data are released with a clear and accessible data usage license.
R1.2. (meta)data are associated with detailed provenance.
R1.3. (meta)data meet domain-relevant community standards.

The above FAIR principles are not tied to specific technologies and implementations of these principles and are not a standard of any kind. They provide general guidance for people and organizations involved in publishing and providing access to data to assess the extent to which their technology and methods allow for easy retrieval, storage, and reuse of data. Currently, many repositories for scientific data already implement all or part of the FAIR principles using different technologies.

The GO FAIR [50] initiative was created to implement FAIR principles in various fields of science. It is a bottom-up, self-governing initiative aimed at implementing the FAIR principles by stakeholders in specific areas of scientific research. Implementation networks (INs) are the way to organize stakeholders in GO FAIR initiative. INs operate in three main directions: GO CHANGE, GO TRAIN, and GO BUILD.

The task of GO CHANGE is to develop priorities, strategies, and incentives to implement the principles of FAIR.

The objectives of GO TRAIN are to raise awareness and train qualified specialists in FAIR data.

The objectives of GO BUILD are to create the technical standards, best practices, and infrastructure components required to implement the principles of FAIR data.

Under the leadership of these three communities, the Internet of FAIR Data & Services (IFDS) is gradually developing. The concept of the Internet of FAIR Data and Services (IFDS) is based on maximum freedom of implementation as well as the modern Internet, where there is no single centralized management. It copies the 'hourglass model' with a minimum of strict standards and protocols. This ensures open and common implementation and participation of various stakeholders. A key feature of the planned Internet of FAIR Data and Services is scalable and transparent 'routing' of data, tools, and computing tools to run these tools. For prototyping applications of such Internet of FAIR Data and Services, it is enough to create a minimum set of standards and interaction rules.

Work on the Internet of FAIR Data and Services (IFDS) is already underway in Europe, the United States, China, Brazil, Australia, and Africa. The European contribution to the creation of the Internet of FAIR Data and Services is the creation of a unified European Open Science Cloud (EOSC). EOSC is a virtual environment for researchers to access, store, manage, analyze, and reuse data.

Currently, there are also a number of INs in various fields: AdvancedNano, ASTRON, BiodiFAIRse, Biodiversities, C2CAMP, CBS (Economics), Chemistry, CO-OPERAS, Discovery, Data Stewardship Competence Centers, EcoSoc, FAIR Microbiome, FAIR StRePo, Food Systems, FAIR Funders, GAIA Data, GeRDI, GO Inter, GO NANOFAB, IN-Africa, INOSIE (IN for Open Science in Industrial Research), Marine Data Centres, Materials Cloud, Metabolomics, NOMAD, Personal Health Train, Rare Diseases, Real World Observations in Health, Season Schools, Training Curriculum, Training Frameworks, Vaccine IS, VODAN (Virus Outbreak Data Network).

4 Conclusion

The article provides an overview of the current situation in two areas related to storage, access, and processing of data: Big Data and FAIR data. For Big Data, the modern understanding of this phenomenon is given, the main sources of these data, methods of their processing are listed, and technologies for working with Big Data are described. For FAIR data are given principles of working with data and what tasks these principles are designed to solve.

Acknowledgments. This work was conducted in the framework of budgetary funding of the Geophysical Center of RAS, adopted by the Ministry of Science and Higher Education of the Russian Federation.

References

1. Lohr, S.: The Origins of 'Big Data': An Etymological Detective Story. The New York Times (2013). https://bits.blogs.nytimes.com/2013/02/01/the-origins-of-big-data-an-etymol ogical-detective-story/
2. Snijders, C., Matzat, U., Reips, U.-D.: "Big Data": big gaps of knowledge in the field of internet science. Int. J. Internet Sci. **7**, 1–5 (2012)
3. Dedić, N., Stanier, C.: Towards differentiating business intelligence, big data, data analytics and knowledge discovery. In: Piazolo, F., Geist, V., Brehm, L., Schmidt, R. (eds.) ERP Future 2016. LNBIP, vol. 285, pp. 114–122. Springer, Cham (2017). https://doi.org/10.1007/978-3-319-58801-8_10
4. Hashem, I.A.T., Yaqoob, I., Anuar, N.B., Mokhtar, S., Gani, A., Khan, S.U.: The rise of "big data" on cloud computing: review and open research issues. Inf. Syst. **47**, 98–115 (2015). https://doi.org/10.1016/j.is.2014.07.006
5. Grimes, S.: Big Data: Avoid 'Wanna V' Confusion. InformationWeek (2013). https://www.informationweek.com/big-data/big-data-analytics/big-data-avoid-wanna-v-confusion/d/d-id/1111077
6. Fox, C.: Data Science for Transport. Springer Textbooks in Earth Sciences, Geography and Environment. Springer, Cham (2018). doi: https://doi.org/10.1007/978-3-319-72953-4
7. Onay, C., Öztürk, E.: A review of credit scoring research in the age of Big Data. J. Financ. Regul. Compliance. **26**, 382–405 (2018). https://doi.org/10.1108/JFRC-06-2017-0054
8. Kitchin, R., McArdle, G.: What makes Big Data, Big Data? Exploring the ontological characteristics of 26 datasets. Big Data Soc. **3**(1), 2053951716631130 (2016). https://doi.org/10.1177/2053951716631130
9. NIST Big Data Interoperability Framework, vol. 1, Definitions. Version 3. NIST Special Publication 1500–1r2 (2019). https://doi.org/10.6028/NIST.SP.1500-1r2
10. Usha, D., Aps, J.A.: A survey of Big Data processing in perspective of Hadoop and MapReduce. Int. J. Curr. Eng. Technol. **4**, 602–606 (2014)
11. White, T.: Hadoop: The Definitive Guide. O'Reilly Media Inc., United States (2012)
12. Mall, N.N., Rana, S.: Overview of Big Data and Hadoop. Imperial J. Interdisc. Res. **2**, 1399–1406 (2016)
13. Prasad, B.R., Agarwal, S.: Comparative study of Big Data computing and storage tools: a review. Int. J. Database Theory Appl. **9**, 45–66 (2016)
14. Dimiduk, N., Khurana, A., Ryan, M.H., Stack, M.: HBase in Action. Manning, Shelter Island (2013)
15. Hashem, I.A.T., Anuar, N.B., Gani, A., Yaqoob, I., Xia, F., Khan, S.U.: MapReduce: review and open challenges. Scientometrics **109**(1), 389–422 (2016). https://doi.org/10.1007/s11192-016-1945-y
16. Chen, X., Hu, L., Liu, L., Chang, J., Bone, D.L.: Breaking down Hadoop distributed file systems data analytics tools: apache Hive vs. Apache Pig vs. pivotal HWAQ. In: 2017 IEEE 10th International Conference on Cloud Computing (CLOUD), pp. 794–797. IEEE (2017)
17. Swarna, C., Ansari, Z.: Apache Pig - a data flow framework based on Hadoop Map Reduce. Int. J. Eng. Trends Technol. **50**, 271–275 (2017)
18. Gates, A., Dai, D.: Programming Pig: Dataflow Scripting with Hadoop. O'Reilly Media Inc., United States (2016)
19. Singh, N., Agrawal, S.: A performance analysis of high-level MapReduce query languages in Big Data. In: Proceedings of the International Congress on Information and Communication Technology, pp. 551–558. Springer, Singapore (2016). https://doi.org/10.1007/978-981-10-0767-5_57

20. Camacho-Rodríguez, J., et al.: Apache Hive: From Mapreduce to enterprise-grade Big Data warehousing. In: Proceedings of the 2019 International Conference on Management of Data, pp. 1773–1786 (2019)
21. Pen, H.D., Dsilva, P., Mascarnes, S.: Comparing HiveQL and MapReduce methods to process fact data in a data warehouse. In: 2017 2nd International Conference on Communication Systems, Computing and IT Applications (CSCITA), pp. 201–206. IEEE (2017)
22. Vohra, D.: Using apache sqoop. In: Pro Docker, pp. 151–183. Apress, Berkeley, CA (2016)
23. Lydia, E.L., Swarup, M.B.: Analysis of Big Data through Hadoop ecosystem components like flume mapreduce, pig and hive. Int. J. Comput. Sci. Eng. 5, 21–29 (2016)
24. Mehta, S., Mehta, V.: Hadoop ecosystem: an introduction. IJSR. 5, 557–562 (2016)
25. Jain, A.: Mastering Apache Storm: Real-time Big Data Streaming using Kafka. Packt Publishing Ltd., Hbase and Redis (2017)
26. Zaharia, M., et al.: Apache Spark: a unified engine for Big Data processing. Commun. ACM 59, 56–65 (2016)
27. Jayaratne, M., Alahakoon, D., De Silva, D., Yu, X.: Apache Spark based distributed self-organizing map algorithm for sensor data analysis. In: IECON 2017–43rd Annual Conference of the IEEE Industrial Electronics Society, pp. 8343–8349. IEEE (2017)
28. Luu, H.: Beginning Apache Spark 2: With Resilient Distributed Datasets, Spark Sql, Structured Streaming, and Spark Machine Learning Library. Apress, Berkeley (2018)
29. Vaddeman, B.: HCatalog. In: Beginning Apache Pig, pp. 103–113. Apress, Berkeley, CA (2016). https://doi.org/10.1007/978-1-4842-2337-6_7
30. Lyubimov, D., Palumbo, A.: Apache Mahout: Beyond MapReduce. CreateSpace Independent Publishing Platform, United States (2016)
31. Schmidt, D., Chen, W.C., Matheson, M.A., Ostrouchov, G.: Programming with BIG data in R: scaling analytics from one to thousands of nodes. Big Data Res. 8, 1–1 (2017)
32. Elshawi, R., Sakr, S., Talia, D., Trunfio, P.: Big data systems meet machine learning challenges: towards Big Data science as a service. Big data Res. 14, 1–1 (2018)
33. Haloi, S.: Apache Zookeeper Essentials. Packt Publishing Ltd., United Kingdom (2015)
34. Vohra, D.: Apache Avro. In: Practical Hadoop Ecosystem, pp. 303–323. Apress, Berkeley, CA (2016). https://doi.org/10.1007/978-1-4842-2199-0_7
35. Islam, M.K., Srinivasan, A.: Apache Oozie: The Workflow Scheduler for Hadoop. O'Reilly Media Inc., United States (2015)
36. Wadkar, S., Siddalingaiah, M.: Apache Ambari. In: Pro Apache Hadoop, pp. 399–401. Apress, Berkeley, CA (2014). https://doi.org/10.1007/978-1-4302-4864-4_20
37. Saxena, A., Singh, S., Shakya, C.: Concepts of HBase archetypes in Big Data engineering. In: Roy, S.S., Samui, P., Deo, R., Ntalampiras, S. (eds.) Big Data in Engineering Applications. SBD, vol. 44, pp. 83–111. Springer, Singapore (2018). https://doi.org/10.1007/978-981-10-8476-8_5
38. Sirisha, N., Kiran, K.V.D.: Stock exchange analysis using Hadoop user experience (Hue). In: 2017 International Conference on Intelligent Sustainable Systems (ICISS), pp. 1141–1144. IEEE (2017)
39. Ofli, F., et al.: Combining human computing and machine learning to make sense of big (aerial) data for disaster response. Big Data. 4, 47–59 (2016). https://doi.org/10.1089/big.2014.0064
40. Chen, D., Liu, Z., Wang, L., Dou, M., Chen, J., Li, H.: Natural disaster monitoring with wireless sensor networks: a case study of data-intensive applications upon low-cost scalable systems. Mob. Netw. Appl. 18(5), 651–663 (2013). https://doi.org/10.1007/s11036-013-0456-9
41. MacLachlan, C., et al.: Global seasonal forecast system version 5 (GloSea5): a high-resolution seasonal forecast system. Q. J. R. Meteorol. Soc. 141, 1072–1084 (2015). https://doi.org/10.1002/qj.2396

42. Poblet, M., García-Cuesta, E., Casanovas, P.: Crowdsourcing tools for disaster management: a review of platforms and methods. In: Casanovas, P., Pagallo, U., Palmirani, M., Sartor, G. (eds.) AI Approaches to the Complexity of Legal Systems, pp. 261–274. Springer, Heidelberg (2014)

43. Nativi, S., Mazzetti, P., Craglia, M.: A view-based model of data-cube to support big earth data systems interoperability. Big Earth Data. **1**, 75–99 (2017). https://doi.org/10.1080/209 64471.2017.1404232

44. USGS Earth Explorer online portal. https://earthexplorer.usgs.gov/

45. Copernicus Sentinel Hub. https://scihub.copernicus.eu/

46. GEOSS portal. https://www.geoportal.org/

47. Gorelick, N., Hancher, M., Dixon, M., Ilyushchenko, S., Thau, D., Moore, R.: GoogleEarth engine: planetary-scale geospatial analysis for everyone. Remote Sens. Environ. **202**(Suppl C), 18–27 (2017). https://doi.org/10.1016/j.rse.2017.06.031

48. Baumann, P., et al.: Big Data analytics for earth sciences: the earthserver approach. Int. J. Digit. Earth. **9**, 3–29 (2016). https://doi.org/10.1080/17538947.2014.1003106

49. Wilkinson, M., Dumontier, M., Aalbersberg, I., et al.: The FAIR Guiding Principles for scientific data management and stewardship. Sci. Data. **3**, 160018 (2016). https://doi.org/10.1038/sdata.2016.18

50. GO FAIR initiative. https://www.go-fair.org/

Chapter 7
Data Science and Resilience

Fred S. Roberts(⊠)

DIMACS Center, Rutgers University, Piscataway, NJ 08854, USA
froberts@dimacs.rutgers.edu

Abstract. Our modern digitized socio-technological systems are vulnerable to destructive events such as disease, floods, and terrorist attacks. Data science might help these systems to become more resilient if a variety of challenges described in this paper can be addressed.

Keywords: Resilience · Data science · Disease events · Natural disasters · Terrorism

1 Introduction

Our modern digitized socio-technological systems have enabled dramatic changes in our way of life, but leave us open to destructive events such as diseases, floods, terrorist attacks, and just plain human error. While our systems are vulnerable to such events, the key is how resilient they can become, i.e., how well they are able to recover from disruptions to return to a "normal" state or close to it, and how quickly they can do so. Data science has enabled the digital world of rapid communication, intelligent machines, and instant information. Data science may also hold the key to making our systems more resilient through the availability of massive amounts of data from sensors, satellites, and online activities, allowing us to monitor the state of the power grid, get early warning of emerging diseases, find ways to minimize the effect of flooding, identify looming problems in supply chains, etc. Tools of machine learning can provide early warning of anomalies and alert us that a system may be approaching a critical threshold, thus allowing more time for mitigation that will minimize the effect of disruptions. However, for tools of data science to help us create more resilient systems, we will need to overcome a variety of challenges. It is these challenges we discuss in this paper.

The challenges we present arise in a multitude of applications and the paper will illustrate them to demonstrate the opportunities to enhance resilience. Applications to be discussed include spread of diseases such as COVID-19 and Ebola; natural and man-made disasters such as floods, hurricanes, oil spills, and cyberattacks; counter-terrorism; protecting infrastructure such as the electric power grid and the transportation system; threats to ecosystems, urban systems, food systems, and agriculture; and varied modern challenges arising from climate change, self-driving vehicles, and participatory democracy.

F. S. Roberts and I. A. Sheremet (Eds.): Resilience in the Digital Age, LNCS 12660, pp. 118–138, 2021.
https://doi.org/10.1007/978-3-030-70370-7_7

2 The Fusion Challenge

A key to the data revolution is that massive amounts of data are available from a large number of sources. A key to using data science to enhance resilience is to find effective ways to utilize all those data, to learn from past disruptions, and to get early warning of potential new problems.

Fusion Challenge: Many analysis tasks require the fusion of information from numerous media or sources.

2.1 Urban Health and Climate Change

Many key indicators allow us to monitor the overall health of an urban system. These include the state and spatial distribution of critical infrastructure such as the transportation, electricity, gas, and water systems; the capacity of the healthcare system; the distribution of vulnerable populations (such as those living near flood plains or without air conditioning during a heat wave). Many of these indicators are enhanced in importance by climate change.

Climate change affects our urban areas in a multitude of ways. We can expect more and more severe hurricanes, heat waves, drought, and floods. Sea levels will rise. What can urban areas do to prepare for them and mitigate their effects? Fusing data from many sources, can we predict which subways might be flooded? (During "Super Storm" Sandy in 2012, a massive hurricane, some of the subway tunnels in New York City were flooded. Mathematical models developed at Columbia University had predicted exactly which ones [46, 48]. Could we have taken precautionary measures knowing this?) Many power plants are located in low-lying areas near bodies of water. Can we fuse data from many sources to predict which ones might be flooded with sea level rise and move them in advance of those floods or otherwise protect them from flood damage? Train tracks leading to the heart of downtown areas are also often in low-lying areas prone to floods. Can we figure out which tracks are subject to flooding and raise them in advance? The New York City Climate Change Adaptation Task Force set out to address these kinds of questions and, according to a New York City Panel on Climate Change report in 2010, this objective "will require ongoing and consistent monitoring of a set of climate change indicators. Monitoring of key indicators can help to initiate course corrections in adaptation policies and/or changes in timing of their implementation" [47]. Moreover, according to the most recent such Panel on Climate Change report in 2019, "A centralized, coordinated indicators and monitoring system is essential for a comprehensive, city-wide risk assessment of trends in climate and impacts and course correction toward climate change adaptation and resiliency goals and targets" [76].

There are many parameters that determine the normal healthy state of a complex system, and it is necessary to gather information from numerous sources to monitor the health of such a system and get early warning of departures from the "normal." For example, in predicting floods in urban areas, one needs to consider data from rain gauges, radar, satellite algorithms, computer models of atmospheric processes, and hydrological models. In understanding extreme events that may trigger tidal flooding in urban areas, one needs to monitor sea level rise, flood insurance claims from businesses and individuals, urban growth trends, the capacity to restore power after a flood, and socioeconomic factors. Understanding factors involved in previous floods, and using them to get early warning about new floods, can help us mitigate impacts and recover faster. To give just one example, the Peak over Threshold approach uses multiple events to estimate return periods for such floods [60, 82].

Urban heat is a major issue leading to adverse effects not only on public health but also on the economy. Extreme heat events have been a major topic of concern at the US Centers for Disease Control and Prevention for at least a decade [20]. Such events can result in increased incidence of heat stroke, dehydration, cardiac stress, and respiratory distress. Individuals under stress due to climate may also be more susceptible to infectious diseases. Among the data fusion tools designed to determine urban heat exposure for the population in a city is the Spatial and Temporal Adaptive Reflectance Fusion Model (STARFM), using both ground sensor temperature and satellite readings [39, 41]. Fefferman [36] led a study of how to evacuate the most vulnerable individuals to climate controlled environments during a major heat event in an urban area (Newark, New Jersey, US), aimed at minimizing health effects of such an event. Her goal was to determine where to locate evacuation centers and whom to send to which center. The project required a major effort at fusing data as to location of potential centers, travel routes and times to the centers, population size and demographic distribution per city block, and at-risk groups and their likely levels of healthcare required.

2.2 Animal Health: Biodiversity and Farmyards

Biodiversity is the variability in the plant and animal life in species, total numbers of the species, their habitat, and their distribution. Evidence about the health of ecosystems is often obtained by measuring their biodiversity [73]. Identifying species and individual animals or plants offers insight into the crisis of biodiversity loss on our planet. Modern methods of data science allow for the use of a great deal of data to identify species and, sometimes, even individual animals. Identification of individual animals is important if we are trying to estimate the population of a given species in a given region. But how hard is it to identify an individual lion or elephant, especially if we may only see the animal through a "camera trap" image that may only include part of their body and often with poor illumination? Automated methods for identification of species and of individual animals, built on modern methods of artificial intelligence, enable us to get early warning of disruptions to the population of ecosystems. These methods depend upon the fusion of large amounts of biometric data, such as identification of external body pattern, footprints, scent, acoustics, DNA barcoding, etc. [49]. Biometric techniques have the advantage that they don't require invasive interventions since data can be collected without capture, instrumentation or tagging. The amounts of data can be huge. For example, the project called Snapshot Serengeti, based in Tanzania, has collected millions of camera trap images of lions, leopards, cheetahs, elephants, and other animals [63]. Recordings of animal vocalizations can produce over half a gigabyte of data per hour. Machine learning can be very helpful in classifying animal calls. For example, it has been used to classify and count syllables in an animal's call, and can then be used to distinguish between calls of different species, including types of frogs, birds, etc. [86]. We are far from being able to identify species, let alone individual animals, in the wild. However, new methods of artificial intelligence and machine learning are leading to some successes. For instance, [63] describes the use of "deep convolutional neural networks" to identify and count species in the Snapshot Serengeti dataset of 3.2 million images. Identification is accurate 93.8% of the time.

Identification of individual animals is becoming important for domesticated animals. As the number of farms decreases but the number of cattle on each farm grows, it becomes increasingly important to identify individual animals in an efficient way for health monitoring, adjusting feeding to enhance milk production, tracking food and water consumption, and tracking and registration of cattle. Existing methods such as microchip embedding or ear tagging can be expensive and are subject to forgeries or damage. Identification of individual livestock is also important to contain spread of disease and has become recognized as important by international organizations, e.g., in preventing spread of diseases such as Bovine Spongiform Encephalopathy (BSE). Recent work shows that individual cattle can be identified through a deep learning approach based on "primary muzzle point (nose pattern)" characteristics. This addresses the problem of missing or swapped animals (especially during large movements of cattle) and false insurance claims [52, 53]. Tools of face recognition, computer vision, animal behavior, pain metrics, and other tools are already useful in identifying diseases of many domesticated animals, including sheep, and pigs, and to give early warning of potentially devastating epidemics from diseases such as BSE, a critical factor in keeping modern farms resilient [49, 74].

3 The Decision Support Challenge

Decision science is an old subject that was once the domain of social scientists and economists but is now also the domain of computer scientists and mathematicians who, working with traditional decision scientists, are developing tools of modeling, simulation, algorithmics, uncertainty quantification, and consensus. This new data-driven decision support can allow comparison of a vast array of alternative solutions. While using data to make decisions is not new, data science has led to many different techniques to make better decisions, especially new algorithmic approaches. The new field of algorithmic decision theory aims to exploit algorithmic methods to improve the performance of decision makers (human or automated) [15, 67, 71, 79].

Decision Support Challenge: Today's decision makers have available to them remarkable new technologies, huge amounts of information, and ability to share information at unprecedented speeds and quantities. These tools and resources will enable better decisions if we can surmount concomitant challenges: Data is often incomplete or unreliable or distributed, and involves great uncertainty; many sources of data need to be fused into a good decision, often in a remarkably short time; interoperating/distributed decision makers and decision-making devices need to be coordinated; decisions must be made in dynamic environments based on partial information; there is heightened risk due to extreme consequences of poor decisions; decision makers must understand complex, multidisciplinary problems [71].

3.1 Ebola and COVID-19

The 2014 Ebola outbreak in West Africa should have reminded us that the world is ill-prepared for a severe disease epidemic. When in 2020 the COVID-19 pandemic hit, the world was indeed poorly prepared. The successful fight to contain the Ebola outbreak was helped by application of data analysis and mathematical models to support decision makers. Those models accurately predicted how and where the disease was spreading and how to contain it. The data allowed decision makers to understand things like: how many beds and lab tests would be needed—and where and when to deploy them. Important to the success of the Ebola containment was the sheer and unprecedented magnitude of epidemiological data made available online to researchers and modelers by the World Health Organization and health ministries of the most affected countries. Though modelers had analyzed ongoing epidemics before, such as the 2003 SARS epidemic and 2009 Swine Flu pandemic, they did not have access to such rich sources of data. Data fed into models showed we could stop this outbreak if 70% of Ebola cases could be placed in Ebola treatment units, had effective isolation, and had safe burials [18].

During the COVID-19 pandemic, there has been literally a tsunami of data available within a short time, enabling scientists and policy makers around the world to fit their models and simulations. As models show, faster decisions to shelter in place might have saved a great many lives [66]. However, decision makers have to balance many considerations, which can slow down decisions at potential peril. The more we can develop tools to make effective decisions faster, the better we can ensure resilience in our systems.

3.2 Resilient Supply Chains

During COVID-19, there have been major shortages in items such as ventilators, personal protective equipment and other medical supplies, as well as in consumer goods such as toilet paper and disinfectant wipes and sprays. Our supply chains have been dramatically changed in the digital age, with artificial intelligence allowing both the private sector and the government to minimize inventories due to extremely accurate knowledge of customer demand. However, these AI tools fail when there is an anomalous event. A key to making supply chains more resilient is to develop tools to allow them to identify alternative sources and change priorities in a speedy way [28, 55]. Data science will be critical to support decisions involving changed priorities, alternative suppliers, modified transportation routes or carriers, etc.

3.3 Precision Agriculture

Data science has led to precision agriculture, which allows the farmer to "leverage AI and fine-grain data about the state of crops" to improve yield, helping to make decisions as to when to plant, when to harvest, when to water, when to implement pest control or fertilizer usage, etc. [27]. Thus, using sensors on farm equipment or in the soil can make agricultural practices sustainable and reduce environmental impact through data-driven farming, reducing water and fertilizer use and minimizing the use of pesticides. It can make farms "self-healing" and more resilient. As Daugherty and Wilson [27] observe, "The ultimate goal with precision agriculture is that disparate systems can come together to produce recommendations that farmers can then act on in real time," and of course in the future perhaps even have intelligent machines act on those data without having the farmer in the loop. Being able to modify plans quickly on the basis of data and corresponding models can make agriculture more resilient. However, if watering a field is automated, based on embedded sensors and machine learning, but the crops dry out, entirely new jobs will be needed to recreate what happened in order to improve decision making in the future.

4 The Combinatorial Explosion Challenge

Combinatorial Explosion Challenge: Data science allows comparison of an array of alternative solutions to problems. However, the number of alternatives is often so large that we cannot take all into account in a timely way. We may not even be able to express all possible preferences among alternatives.

4.1 Counterterrorism: Nuclear Detection

Terrorist attacks are a major potential source of disruption to modern societies. One challenge is to minimize the effect of terrorism by doing thorough screening and testing, but designing the most efficient screening protocols can be difficult due to the number of possibilities. Consider inspecting containers at ports for nuclear materials. There are a variety of tests that can be performed on containers, for example determining whether or not the ship's manifest sets off an alarm in an "anomaly detection" program; whether or not the container gives off neutron or Gamma emissions that are above some threshold; whether or not a radiograph image recognition test comes up positive; whether or not an induced fission test comes up positive. One can look at tests sequentially, choosing the next test to perform based on the outcome of the previous test. This kind of sequential diagnosis is common in many fields such as medicine. In container inspection, one can represent the possible tests in a binary decision tree (BDT), where the nodes are tests and we take the right arrow after a given test if the result is positive and left arrow if it is negative. Ultimately, the container is either allowed through or designated for complete unpacking. One seeks a BDT that is optimal in some sense. However, even with five tests, there are 263,515,920 possible BDTs, and the number of possibilities makes it computationally impossible to find an optimal one. Among promising approaches to this problem is specialization of the class of BDTs and development of new search algorithms to move from one tree to better ones [6, 58, 59].

Another example of Combinatorial Explosion also arises from counter-terrorism applications, the problem of comparing the performance of alternative nuclear detection algorithms. The problem is to design experiments to compare algorithm performance, taking into account many relevant factors such as type of special nuclear material being tested, shielding, masking, altitude, humidity, temperature, and speed of vehicle being screened. For each of these factors, there are several possible values, and there are too many combinations to test all of them in experiments. This requires development of tools to design experiments that test together all significant pairs of values [26, 50].

4.2 Testing for Disease: COVID-19

An alternative approach to the container inspection problem is a tool called SNSRTREE [12, 13]. This tool involves a large-scale linear programming model for sequential inspection of containers that allows for mixed strategies, accommodates realistic limitations on budget and testing capacity and time limits, and is computationally more tractable. Recently, research has begun on applying this tool to testing for COVID-19. The goal is to determine how to optimally select from among the available tests for COVID-19 according to the person, their work, the results of any prior tests, and current, dynamic test availability. The goal is to use SNSRTREE to determine the probability that a specific individual is, or is not, "infective." Tests for the COVID-19 infection include self-reports of symptoms, thermometer readings, clinical observations, nasal swab tests, saliva tests, etc. Tests vary as to cost, reliability, and assay time to get a result. To develop optimal testing policies, we first ask for the result of a first test, and depending on that result, we may reach a decision or choose a second test. After a second test, we may reach a decision, or choose a third test, etc. Every such policy has a cost, integrating the expected cost of the tests with the economic and human costs of false positives and false negatives. SNSRTREE finds the entire set of "optimal" testing policies for all possible budgets. Read in one way, it provides least estimated infection at a given cost; read the other way, it provides lowest estimated cost for a given infection control. What makes the modification of SNSRTREE or any other algorithm for application to COVID-19 testing complicated is that infection is a moving (time dependent) target rather than a fixed property; tests may have different assay times and availabilities over time; and test results may not be stochastically independent – all of which add to the combinatorial explosion of possibilities.[1]

4.3 Ecological Monitoring

Still another example of the Combinatorial Explosion Challenge comes from NEON (National Ecological Observatory Network), a project that involves gathering data from 20 sites across the US to get a continent-wide picture of the impacts on natural resources and biodiversity of climate change, land use change, and invasive species. The understanding gained from NEON can contribute to the resilience of the ecosystem in numerous ways. How are those 20 sites chosen? NEON divides the country into 8 million patches. For each patch, the project collects 9 pieces of information about its ecology and climate, clusters the patches, and chooses a representative patch for each cluster. But why limit this to 9 pieces of information when one could easily come up with 100 pieces of information about each patch? The problem is that it would then become combinatorially impossible to do the clustering [23].

---

[1] Thanks to Endre Boros, Dennis Egan, Nina Fefferman, Paul Kantor, and Vladimir Menkov for discussions and the specific ideas in this paragraph.

5   The Real-Time Analytics Challenge

Near-real-time situational awareness (real-time analytics) is becoming increasingly feasible, based on massive amounts of data from simulation and modeling, mobile applications, and sensors. Such data can be too rapid for real-time human consumption or exploration.

Real-Time Analytics Challenge: Some data rates are so large that not all the data can be saved and yet real-time or almost real-time decisions must be made.

5.1   Resilience in the Electric Power Grid

The electric power grid provides an example where real-time analytics can dramatically improve resilience.[2] Today's electric power systems operate under considerable uncertainty. Cascading failures can have dramatic consequences [3]. Algorithmic methods are needed to improve security of the energy system in light of its haphazard construction and dynamically changing character and to find early warning of a changed state, i.e., to rapidly detect anomalies. "Smart grid" data sources enable real-time precision in operations and control previously unobtainable (see e.g., [2, 4, 5, 23, 25, 88]): Time-synchronous phasor data, linked with advanced computation and visualization, will enable advances in state estimation, real-time contingency analysis, and real-time monitoring of dynamic (oscillatory) behaviors in the system; sensing and measurement technologies will support faster and more accurate response, e.g., through remote monitoring; advanced control methods will enable rapid diagnosis and precise solutions appropriate to an "event." Status updates that used to come in every two to four seconds are now approaching ten times a second using new phasor technologies. That rate may be too rapid for a human alone to absorb the presence of an anomaly in time to act upon the information, thereby requiring software agent or algorithmic support.

5.2   Smart Transportation Systems

Traffic management in "smart cities" presents many examples of the Real-time Analytics Challenge.[3] "Intelligent transportation systems" involve integrated fare management, variable road usage charging, and traffic information made available in real time, all requiring fusion of a great deal of information. Real-time traffic management takes account of sensors of all kinds, ability to monitor the actual traffic situation (volumes, speeds, incidents), and the ability to control or influence the flow using that information to reduce traffic congestion, deal with incidents, and provide accurate information to drivers and authorities. Sensor data depends heavily on GPS data that needs to be related to the underlying network by map matching algorithms that are computationally

---

[2] Much of the following discussion is based on a white paper [1] in [23] and a presentation by Gilbert Bindewald of the US Department of Energy to the SIAM Science Policy Committee on October 28, 2009.

[3] Many of the ideas on traffic management here are taken from the talk "Smart Cities – How can Data Mining and Optimization Shape Future Cities," by Francesco Calabrese of IBM Ireland, at the DIMACS/LAMSADE workshop on Smart Cities, Paris, Sept. 2011.

expensive. GPS data is sampled at irregular intervals, possibly with large gaps – which requires advanced analytics to reconstruct GPS trajectories. Also, GPS data is inaccurate, needs "cleaning." Additional complexity arises from the need to combine the "hard" numerical readings of sensors monitoring vehicle movements with the "soft" natural language utterances of drivers and tweets of the public. Understanding human transit demands/needs in real-time involves challenges to help design adaptive urban transportation systems, help citizens navigate the city, detect and predict travel demand, and offer real-time alternative routings in case of problems. The ability to offer such real-time adjustments can make today's smart transportation systems more resilient. For some relevant references, see [8, 40].

5.3 Food Security

The food system has multiple components: producers of food, those who process, ship, or sell food products, and those who shop for food and consume it. At all steps "from farm to fork" there are possible disruptions [83]. Such disruptions include extreme weather events, animal diseases, terrorist attacks, and disease events such as COVID-19, which has both closed down meat packing plants, leading to shortages, and rapidly changed demand, leading to farmers plowing under crops and pouring out milk. Today's sensing and computing capacities allow us to monitor the food system in real time and to take action to maintain security of the food supply. Such monitoring includes observational data (soil conditions, land use) and data on social processes and preferences. Automatic image processing of satellite data [56], information from crop and soil sensors, and real-time reports of changing supply chain conditions, can be used to gain real-time awareness and make changes. Such methods have been used for example to estimate the resilience of the wheat market to potential ruptures in the global transportation system [34]. For more on real-time monitoring of the food system, see [51][4].

5.4 Resilient Ecosystems

Ecosystems are subject to increasing disturbances in the face of global change (climate change, land use change, migration patterns, increasing urbanization, etc.). Resilience of ecosystems allows them to bounce back from perturbations [85]. Is it possible to judge in real-time when an ecosystem is at the brink of suffering a perturbation that would irreversibly disrupt it, i.e., when it is on the edge of collapse [9, 11]? Examples of such dramatic "state changes" in an ecosystem are desertification of certain parts of the earth [21, 33], coral bleaching [10], lake eutrophication [16], major disruption of the atmospheric chemistry as a result of agriculture [38], and the transformation of tropical forests under slash and burn agriculture [54]. One approach is to study satellite images over a long period of time (many years) and use "deep learning" methods to identify ecosystems that are stressed and that might have undergone a shift from a stable state to another. By identifying general characteristics of an ecosystem including climate fluctuations, biogeochemical cycles or vegetation-atmosphere interactions, it may be possible to identify those characteristics that indicate a shift is about to occur.[5]

---

[4] Thanks to Hans Kaper for many of the ideas in this paragraph.

[5] Many of the ideas in this paragraph are due to Paolo D'Odorico and Wayne Getz.

6 The Vulnerabilities Challenge

Modern society is critically dependent upon data from manufacturing and production systems, power and water, transportation, financial transactions, medicine, etc. Vulnerabilities are ever present, enhancing cyberattacks on our infrastructure, causing cascading failures, leading to rapid spread of anomalies and exacerbating the impacts of all kinds of failures. It is the very ability to utilize and benefit from large amounts of data that sometimes creates vulnerabilities.

Vulnerabilities Challenge: How do we identify new vulnerabilities caused by usage of data? How do we develop tools for monitoring and minimizing such vulnerabilities?

6.1 Medical Facilities

Electronic medical records are a case in point. They lead to being able to share data about a person's medical condition rapidly and with a variety of medical personnel. However, these electronic medical records lead to vulnerabilities. Recently several hospitals have had to postpone surgeries after having lost access to electronic medical records in a cyberattack, and had to pay ransom to regain access to these records [61]. During times of uncertainty and confusion, especially disasters, criminals take full advantage. That is particularly true of the COVID-19 pandemic. An FBI release says that criminals are "using COVID-19 as a lure to deploy ransomware ... designed to lock" hospital or public health department computers [35]. There have already been examples of ransomware attacks on hospitals and labs treating COVID-19 patients or working on treatments, vaccines, etc. [37]. Numerous other frauds and scams by criminals during the COVID-19 pandemic also seek to take advantage of the situation. The FBI release describes offers of sham treatments and vaccines, bogus investment opportunities in medical companies, and people impersonating doctors demanding payment for treatment.

6.2 Cybersecurity of Supply Chains

Information and communication devices have enabled rapid information sharing, created the ability to make financial transactions from anywhere, and provided access from the workplace to markets worldwide. However, the very nature of these devices as tools, which use, process and share huge amounts of data rapidly, has led to vulnerabilities. In recent years, there has been a major concern about cyber threats to information and communication devices and processes. A report of the US Department of Homeland Security Cybersecurity and Infrastructure Security Agency (CISA) Information and Communications Technology (ICT) Supply Chain Risk Management (SCRM) Task Force [22] gives a great deal of detail about the importance of and new approaches to supply chain risk assessment in the information and communication technology (ICT) domain, as do reports from the US National Institute of Standards and Technology (NIST) [14] and the US National Counterintelligence and Security Center, Supply Chain Directorate [62]. The CISA report makes it clear that cyber is a key issue. As a supply chain is only as strong as its weakest link, all components of the supply chain have to be engaged in cybersecurity issues, but how to achieve this goal is a major challenge. A disruption in one device connected to the supply chain can cascade through the entire system, and the development of protection against such cascading effects of cyberattacks is of central importance. The maritime transportation system is key to the world's supply chains. See Rose [75] for some work on models of cascading impacts of cyberattacks on the maritime transportation system. Some of those cascading effects on supply chains result from supply substitutions. How can the potential for supply substitutions to lead to cascading failures be minimized? Models such as those of [31, 32] of how to control the cascading impact of power grid disruptions are very relevant here, and could lead to improved resilience of many types of supply chains.

6.3 Autonomous Vehicles

Due to the ready availability of data, there is a huge increase in number of cyber-physical systems. Today's cars are more like computers on wheels. Yet, the very ability to utilize large amounts of data to perform better leads to vulnerabilities. Cyber-physical systems control much of how a car operates. This makes today's cars already semiautonomous, taking decisions away from the driver, and thereby frequently aiding in preventing accidents. But could a criminal or terrorist take control of a car remotely through a cyberattack and use it to cause damage? This seems to be a serious challenge as in-car technology becomes more sophisticated. And it is likely to become even more of a challenge as we develop fully autonomous vehicles. In 2013, Miller (Twitter) and Valasek (IOActive) demonstrated they could take control of a Toyota Prius and a Ford Escape from a laptop [42]. They were able to remotely control the smart steering, braking, displays, acceleration, engine, horn, lights, and so on. As we move to self-driving cars, similar vulnerabilities might exist. This is not just hypothetical. Already in our seaports, trucks and cranes operate in driverless mode, and there have been cyberattacks on cranes in ports [29, 30]. One approach to minimizing the impact of attacks on self-driving cars begins with risk assessment of different kinds of attacks. See [72] for an approach.

6.4 Oil Rigs

The failure of a blowout preventer on an oil rig in the Gulf of Mexico in 2010 led to the devastating Deepwater Horizon oil spill, the largest oil spill in US history. That was not due to a cyberattack. However, there have been cyberattacks on oil rigs. According to security company ThetaRay, a cyberattack on a floating oil rig off the coast of Africa managed to tilt the rig slightly and as a result it was forced to shut down. It took a week to identify and fix the problem [87]. In another drilling rig event, in 2010, a drilling rig being moved at sea from South Korea to South America was infected by malicious software. Its critical control systems could not operate and it took 19 days to fix matters [24, 87]. The cyberattack infected the computers controlling the blowout preventer, the system at fault for the Deepwater Horizon accident. The results could have been disastrous. Oil rigs are critically dependent on GPS for stability, yet hackers have been able to tilt an oil rig, putting it out of commission for days at high cost. Modern GPS, dynamic positioning systems, and other technologies that depend on large amounts of data have made it possible to manipulate oil rigs in efficient ways, yet open them up to attacks and outages [29]. How can we minimize the impact of such attacks? That will be crucial to make oil rigs and other systems more resilient.

7   The Information Sharing Challenge

Secure information sharing is a key to enable organizations and individuals to work together on a wide range of issues. Such information sharing is a critical component of ensuring resilience of systems and networks.

Information Sharing Challenge: Information sharing requires appropriately safeguarding both systems and information; selecting the most trusted information sources; and maintaining secure systems in potentially hostile settings. How can one best accomplish these things?

7.1   The Terror Attacks of September 11, 2001

Failure to detect and prevent the September 11th, 2001 attacks in New York City was, in many ways, a result of an intelligence failure due to lack of information sharing. At the time, there was no coordinated way to "connect the dots." Subsequent analyses, detailed in the Report of the National Commission on Terrorist Attacks Upon the United States, also known as the 9/11 Commission Report [84], resulted in an emphasis on information sharing to facilitate situational awareness and understanding. In addition to the loss of life, the 9/11 attacks had a major economic impact in the US, in particular on the transportation system, from which it took a long time to recover. The hope is that information sharing will prevent successful terrorist attacks or criminal behavior, or at least minimize their impacts, i.e., make the country and its various systems more resilient.

In order to gain situational understanding when there are many organizations or individuals each having some relevant information, one can create an 'information sharing environment' (ISE) - a decentralized, distributed, coordinated milieu that connects existing systems and builds on their capabilities, while protecting individuals' privacy [19]. In the US, for example, "fusion centers" were created to share information among numerous agencies and the private sector following the September 11th attacks. They can have thousands of federal, state and local partners, and utilize information from numerous government agencies and the private sector, to aid in counter-terrorism and anti-crime efforts. Successful creation of an ISE requires implementation of both technical and operational components. Technical components (like interoperability and rules as to who can gain access and how) are necessary, but also fundamental are the human components and procedures that ultimately allow an ISE to succeed. An ISE requires coordination and integration of information-sharing through collaboration and cooperation. However, there have to be shared standards for identification, access, and utilization of information, there have to be policy, procedures, and technical solutions for safeguarding information, and there need to be standards and accountability procedures for the protection of privacy, civil rights, and civil liberties.

7.2 "Participatory Democracy"

Information sharing is coming to be a key component of what some people are calling "participatory democracy." Here, the idea is that participation by all stakeholders, including the public, can lead to better policies for governments. While the concept of participatory democracy goes back to Athenian days [7] it is becoming more and more important in this digital age. The book [70] develops the concept of "e-democracy," which, among other things, includes web-based participation leading to changes in public policy. The underlying assumption is that decisions reached through public participation can lead to more stable societies, smarter cities, etc. Such participatory democracy has been explored in the context of water usage, power supply, health care, and other applications, but it requires the development of methods of sharing information and views, beliefs, and preferences. Tools for reaching good decisions using participatory methods have been explored by various authors, for example [69]. The goal is to develop tools to facilitate stakeholders' participation and achieve collective commitment, which in turn would seem to lead to greater stability and resilience.

7.3 "Super Storm" Sandy

After "Super Storm" Sandy, the massive hurricane that hit New York City in 2012, the port of New York/New Jersey was left dramatically damaged. Yet, it was very resilient and recovered quickly. In a report on the resilience of the port [81], the authors point out that "soft" resilience strategies were vital in its recovery after Hurricane Sandy. Such strategies "include ways to reduce vulnerability and improve response and recovery capability through planning, people, partnerships and policy" and "planning for response and recovery; increasing access to high quality data; and developing a web of bonds, ties and relationships across sectors - that is, building what scholars have called 'social capital' through collaboration." Thus, a stronger social infrastructure (keyed by good information sharing) led to a more resilient port.

7.4 Secure Multi-party Computation

One theoretical approach of note has come to be called "Secure Multiparty Computation" [89], an area aiming at allowing parties to jointly compute something over their inputs while keeping those inputs private. It is a model for "secure information sharing." We have begun to see a new effort in systematizing secure computation to allow decision makers to understand essential strengths and weaknesses of different secure computation solutions (e.g., whether or not they guarantee fairness and their prerequisites regarding correctness, auditability, and compliance) and determine which best applies in a given scenario [68].

8   The Trustworthiness Challenge

Data comes from multiple sources and some are more accurate than others. Multiple information sources often provide inconsistent or conflicting information – whether maliciously, or due to noise. This is especially so in emergency situations where hetero-geneous information streams describe damage, physical needs, information needs, etc. in different locations. To utilize the vast amounts of data available to us in this age of Big Data, we have to understand what sources we can trust. We need precise definitions of factors contributing to trustworthiness: accuracy, completeness, bias. For work along these lines, see for example [64, 65]. Work is also needed to develop claim verification systems, with automated claim verification by finding supporting and opposing evidence.

The Trustworthiness Challenge: How can we develop computational frameworks and other tools that address the problem of trustworthiness in disasters and other situations?

8.1 Trust in Authorities During Disasters

Responses to disasters will work better if people trust those in charge and comply with instructions, thus allowing more rapid and effective response to disasters and making society more resilient. Greenberg [44] argues that there are two factors that determine whether individuals trust organizations, in particular government organizations. One is perception of the competence of the organization and the second is the perception that the organization possesses values and intentions consistent with those of the individual asked to trust it, things like fairness or non-bias or willingness to listen and communicate. In 2013, after Super Storm Sandy, Greenberg [43, 44] investigated the New Jersey public's willingness to support rebuilding of devastated parts of the state. He asked residents if they were willing to contribute to a special fund for rebuilding. "The vast majority were unwilling, and we found that mistrust of the state was a strong predictor of their unwillingness to contribute. Many did not trust state government to use a dedicated fund for the designated purpose" [44]. In the midst of a disaster such as the COVID-19 pandemic, many technologies are being touted as helpful, e.g., for screening, testing, contact tracing, enforcing social distancing, etc. If Greenberg is right, issues of fairness and ethics involving the government agencies that will deploy the technologies will enter just as significantly as issues of technical competence of those agencies and technical performance of the technologies.

8.2 Risk Communication and Human Perception During a Pandemic

COVID-19 reminded us that communications and human behavior are important factors to consider when preparing for and during a disaster, e.g., a pandemic. How does human behavior such as panic hoarding of toilet paper, hand sanitizer, and pasta, which we have seen during the COVID-19 pandemic, arise? To some extent, hoarding is a rational response to being told not to venture out a lot, in which case it makes sense to stock up on a lot of goods when you do [57]. How do communications impact hoarding behavior? Among other things, they can impact our trust in the supply system. In the US, there were some early inconsistencies in such messaging. For example, the Centers for Disease Control and Prevention recommended keeping a 2-week supply of food at hand and the Federal Drug Administration recommended that people should only buy enough for the week ahead [57]. Good risk communication is a key to resilience in the case of a disaster.

One critical element involved in reopening an economy after people are required to stay home at the height of a disease outbreak such as COVID-19 is the availability of healthy and willing workers. It is important to understand the workers' mental models of the risk of infection, and how they frame decisions related to the safety of the workplace. This will involve questions relating to workers' concerns about competence of those laying out guidelines about workplace safety. For relevant research on how workers might make such decisions after disasters, see [77, 78], where the authors studied flu epidemics and an urban biological catastrophe involving anthrax and explored people's decisions about returning to work. Their work demonstrates the importance of risk communication in making the economy more resilient.

8.3 Identity and Access Management

To return to the topic of information sharing discussed in Sect. 7, another critical principle underlying a successful information sharing environment (ISE) is trust. This is both a human and a technical issue. ISEs only work when, over time, participants learn to work together and trust each other. On the technical side, trust can be accomplished through identity credential access management solutions, which are a means for participants to have confidence in the identity of collaborators. "Trustmarks" are digitally-signed assertions by a third party assessor that are shared between parties seeking to share information. The parties treat a third party verification as evidence that the trustmark recipient meets the trust and requirements as set forth in some agreement. For more information on trustmarks, see [45]. For more on the subject that is coming to be called identity and access management, see [80].

Proving your identity is part of information sharing. Proving that you have the authority to do something is another component of identity and access management [17], and this subject can play a role in enhancing recovery during a disaster. Consider a firefighter from New Jersey who goes to Florida to help in the recovery from a hurricane, an emergency management technician from New Jersey who goes to California to help treat earthquake victims, or a policeman from New Jersey who goes to New York City to help control a terrorist standoff. How can these people convince the responsible people at the disaster scene that they are who they are, but more importantly that they have official credentials such as a security clearance or a permit to carry a weapon or a hazardous materials cleanup certificate? The tools of identity and access management can enable their smart phones to carry encrypted information about their credentials that will speed up the approval for their involvement by the local authorities [17]. This is an important, growing field that will help enhance trust and as a result enhance resilience in disaster situations.

9   Closing Comments

Today's world of big data, massive computing capacity, artificial intelligence, and machine learning makes it possible to learn how to build resilience into systems. The deluge of data from in-situ sensors, remote sensing, images, videos, recordings, makes it possible to observe changes in systems across temporal and spatial scales. These same sources of data should make it possible to develop tools for characterizing resilience. However, in addition to the challenges discussed in this paper, another critical one is that there are no agreed-upon metrics to measure whether a system has become more (or less) resilient, or many tools for improving a system's resilience.

As we have observed, resilience of a system can be enhanced by learning from the past to sense emerging risks. As more data becomes available, this learning can benefit. We can fuse massive amounts of data of different kinds, combining with machine learning tools for anomaly detection, to provide early warning that a system might be in danger. By providing tools for faster awareness of problems, data science can give systems time to take mitigating actions. This learning can only be useful, however, if we can identify appropriate features and indicators, determine how to measure them, and use them as input into tools of data science to learn which parameter configurations allow a system to recover to a healthy state if it has been disrupted.

Acknowledgement. The author thanks the National Science Foundation for support under grants DMS-1737857 and CCF-1934924 to Rutgers University.

References

1. Adem, A., et al.: Human well-being and the natural environment Appendix 1. In: Cozzens, M., Roberts, F.S. (eds.) Mathematical and Statistical Challenges for Sustainability, pp. 61–85. American Mathematical Society, Providence (2011)
2. Amin, M.: Powering the 21st century: we can - and must - modernize the grid. IEEE Power Energ. Mag. **3**, 93–95 (2005)
3. Amin, M., Schewe, P.: Preventing blackouts. Sci. Am. **296**, 60–67 (2007)
4. Amin, M., Stringer, J.: The electric power grid: today and tomorrow. Mater. Res. Soc. Bull. **33**, 399–407 (2008)
5. Amin, M., Wollenberg, B.: Towards a smart grid. IEEE Power Energ. Mag. **3**, 34–41 (2005)
6. Anand, S., Madigan, D., Mammone, R., Pathak, S., Roberts, F.: Experimental analysis of sequential decision making algorithms for port of entry inspection procedures. In: Mehrotra, S., Zeng, D.D., Chen, H., Thuraisingham, B., Wang, F.-Y. (eds.) ISI 2006. LNCS, vol. 3975, pp. 319–330. Springer, Heidelberg (2006). https://doi.org/10.1007/11760146_28
7. Arenilla, M.: Concepts in democratic theory. In: Rios Insua, D., French, S. (eds.) e-Democracy, pp. 15-30. Springer, Dordrecht (2010). https://doi.org/10.1007/978-90-481-9045-4_2
8. Baptista, A.T., Bouillet, E., Calabrese, F., Verscheure, O.: Towards building an uncertainty-aware personal journey planner. In: Proceedings 14th International IEEE Conference on Intelligent Transportation Systems (ITSC), pp. 378–383. IEEE (2011). https://doi.org/10.1109/ITSC.2011.6082962.
9. Barnosky, A.D., et al.: Approaching a state shift in earth's biosphere. Nature **486**, 51 (2012)
10. Bellwood, D.R., Hughes, T.P., Folke, C., Nystrom, M.: Confronting the coral reef crisis. Nature **429**, 827–833 (2004). https://doi.org/10.1038/nature02691
11. Boettiger, C., Hastings, A.: Early warning signals and the prosecutor's fallacy. Proc. R. Soc. Lond. B Biol. Sci. **279**, 4734–4739 (2012)
12. Boros, E., Fedzhora, L., Kantor, P.B., Saeger, K., Stroud, P.: A large-scale linear programming model for finding optimal container inspection strategies. Naval Res. Logist. (NRL) **56**(5), 404–420 (2009). https://doi.org/10.1002/nav.20349

13. Boros, E., Fedzhora, L., Kantor, P.B., Saeger, K., Stroud, P.: Large scale LP model for find-ing optimal container inspection strategies. Technical report RUTCOR 26–2006. Rutgers University Center for Operations Research (2006)
14. Boyens, J., Paulsen, C., Moorthy, R., Bartol, N.: Supply Chain Risk Management Prac-tices for Federal Information Systems and Organizations. NIST Special Publication 800-161, April 2015. https://www.dni.gov/files/NCSC/documents/supplychain/20190327-NIST-Sp-800-161.pdf. Accessed 14 Jan 2020
15. Brafman, R.I., Roberts, F.S., Tsoukiàs, A. (eds.): ADT 2011. LNCS (LNAI), vol. 6992. Springer, Heidelberg (2011). https://doi.org/10.1007/978-3-642-24873-3
16. Carpenter, S.R., et al.: Early warnings of regime shifts: a whole-ecosystem experiment. Science 332, 1079–1082 (2011). https://doi.org/10.1126/science.1203672
17. CCICADA: CCICADA launches ID verification project to speed responses to natural and terrorist disasters. CCICADA Center, Rutgers University, 22 March 2016. https://ccicada.org/2016/03/22/ccicada-launches-id-verification-project-to-speed-res ponses-to-natural-and-terrorist-disasters/. Accessed 2 June 2020
18. CCICADA: Fight against Zika virus to benefit from Ebola math models. CCICADA Center, Rutgers University, 5 May 2016. https://ccicada.org/2016/05/05/fight-against-zika-virus-to-benefit-from-ebola-math-models/. Accessed 1 June 2020
19. CCICADA: Expanding information-sharing environments to fight crime and terror is goal of Rutgers research team. CCICADA Center, Rutgers University, 6 April 2017. https://ccicada.org/2017/04/06/expanding-information-sharing-environments-to-fight-crime-and-terror-is-goal-of-rutgers-research-team/. Accessed 31 May 2020
20. Centers for Disease Control and Prevention, National Center for Environmental Health: Extreme Heat Events. https://www.cdc.gov/climateandhealth/pubs/ClimateChangeandExtre meHeatEvents.pdf. Accessed 1 June 2020
21. Cherlet, M., Hutchinson, C., Reynolds, J., Hill, J., von Sommer, S., Maltitz, G.: World Atlas of Desertification. Publication Office of the European Union, Luxembourg (2018)
22. CISA: Cybersecurity and Infrastructure Security Agency Information and Communications Technology Supply Chain Risk Management Task Force: Interim report: status update on activities and objectives of the task force, September 2019. https://www.cisa.gov/sites/def ault/files/publications/ICT%20Supply%20Chain%20Risk%20Management%20Task%20F orce%20Interim%20Report%20%28FINAL%29_508.pdf. Accessed 14 Jan 2020
23. Cozzens, M.B., Roberts, F.S. (eds.): Mathematical and Statistical Challenges for Sustainabil-ity. American Mathematical Society, Providence (2011)
24. CyberKeel: Maritime cyber-risks: Virtual pirates at large on the cyber seas. White Paper, CyberKeel, Copenhagen, 15 October 2014
25. Daki, H., El Hannani, A., Aqqal, A., Haidine, A., Dahbi, A.: Big Data management in smart grid: concepts, requirements and implementation. J. Big Data 4(1), 1–19 (2017). https://doi.org/10.1186/s40537-017-0070-y
26. Dalal, S.R., Jain, A., Kantor, P.B.: Creating configurations for testing radiation portal algo-rithms using factor covering combinatorial designs. Presented at the 2015 IEEE International Symposium on Technologies for Homeland Security, Boston, MA (2015)
27. Daugherty, P.R., Wilson, H.J.: Human + Machine: Reimagining Work in the Age of AI. Harvard Business Review Press, Boston (2018)
28. Deloitte: COVID-19: Managing supply chain risk and disruption. Coronavirus highlights the need to transform traditional supply chain models (2020). https://www2.deloitte.com/global/en/pages/risk/articles/covid-19-managing-supply-chain-risk-and-disruption.html. Accessed 28 Apr 2020
29. DiRenzo III, J., Goward, D.A., Roberts, F.S.: The little known challenge of maritime cyber security. In: Proceedings 6th International Conference on Information, Intelligence, Systems, and Applications (IISA), pp. 1–5. IEEE, Piscataway (2015)

30. DiRenzo, J., III., Drumhiller, N., Roberts, F.S. (eds.): Issues in Maritime Cyber Security. Westphalia Press, Washington, DC (2017)
31. Dobson, I., Carreras, B.A., Lynch, V.E., Newman, D.E.: Complex systems analysis of series of blackouts: cascading failure, critical points, self-organization. Chaos **17**, 026103 (2007). https://doi.org/10.1063/1.2737822
32. Dobson, I., Carreras, B.A., Newman, D.E.: A loading-dependent model of probabilistic cascading failure. Prob. Eng. Inf. Sci. **19**(1), 15–32 (2005)
33. D'Odorico, P., Bhattachan, A., Davis, K.F., Ravi, S., Runyan, C.W.: Global desertification: drivers and feedbacks. Adv. Water Res. **51**, 326–344 (2013)
34. Fair, K.R., Bauch, C.T., Anand, M.: Dynamics of the global wheat trade network and resilience to shocks. Sci. Rep. **7**, 7177 (2017)
35. FBI: FBI and Secret Service working against COVID-19 threats. FBI National Press Office, 15 April 2020. https://www.fbi.gov/news/pressrel/press-releases/fbi-and-secret-service-wor king-against-covid-19-threats. Accessed 30 Apr 2020. (A version of this appeared in the Washington Post online edition of 14 April 2020.)
36. Fefferman, N., Emergency shelter location and resource allocation. In: Lacy, C. (ed.), Report on the Development of the University Center for Disaster Preparedness and Emergency Response (UCDPER), pp. 50–86. Rutgers University, New Brunswick (2011). https://www.researchgate.net/publication/279336405_Development_of_the_Univer sity_Center_for_Disaster_Preparedness_and_Emergency_Response_UCDPER. Accessed 2 June 2020.
37. Gallagher, R., Bloomberg News: Hackers "without conscience" demand ransom from dozens of hospitals and labs working on coronavirus. Fortune, 1 April 2020. https://fortune.com/2020/04/01/hackers-ransomware-hospitals-labs-coronavirus/. Accessed 31 May 2020
38. Galloway, J.N., et al.: The nitrogen cascade. AIBS Bull. **53**(4), 341–356 (2003)
39. Gao, F., Masek, J., Schwaller, M., Hall, F.: On the blending of the Landsat and MODIS surface reflectance: predicting daily Landsat surface reflectance. IEEE Trans. Geosci. Remote Sens. **44**(8), 2207–2218 (2006)
40. Gasparini, L., Bouillet, E., Calabrese, F., Verscheure, O., O'Brien, B., O'Donnell, M.: System and analytics for continuously assessing transport systems from sparse and noisy observations: case study in Dublin. In: Proceedings of IEEE Conference on Intelligent Transportation Systems, pp. 1827–1832. IEEE (2011)
41. Gevaert, C.M., García-Haro, F.J.: A comparison of STARFM and an unmixing-based algorithm for Landsat and MODIS data fusion. Remote Sens. Environ. **156**, 34–44 (2015)
42. Greenberg, A.: Hackers reveal nasty new car attacks – with me behind the wheel. Forbes, 12 August 2013. https://www.forbes.com/sites/andygreenberg/2013/07/24/hackers-reveal-nasty-new-car-attacks-with-me-behind-the-wheel-video/#3fe5a27c228c. Accessed 31 May 2020
43. Greenberg M.: Willingness to pay for a sustainable shoreline: public reactions follow Superstorm Sandy in New Jersey, USA. In: Krope, J., Olabi, A.G., Goricanec, D. (eds.) Sustainable Energy and Environmental Protection, SEEP, Maribor, Slovenia, pp. 46–50 (2013)
44. Greenberg, M.R.: Energy policy and research: the underappreciation of trust. Energy Res. Soc. Sci. **1**, 152–160 (2014)
45. GTRI: GTRI NSTIC Trustmark Pilot. https://trustmark.gtri.gatech.edu/technical-framework/. Accessed 31 May 2020
46. Hood, P.: Sandy's wake. Columbia Magazine, Winter 2012–2013. https://magazine.columbia.edu/article/sandys-wake. Accessed 2 June 2020.
47. Jacob, K., Blake, R.: Indicators and monitoring. In: Climate Change Adaptation in New York City: Building a Risk Management Response. The New York City Panel on Climate Change 2010 Report. Annals of The New York Academy of Sciences, Chapter 7, vol. 1196, pp. 1–354 (2010)

48. Jacob, K., et al. (eds.): Responding to climate change in New York State: the ClimAID integrated assessment for effective climate change adaptation in New York State, pp. 299–369. Technical report 11-18, New York State Energy Research and Development Authority (2011)

49. Jewell, Z.C., et al.: Automated biometrics for biodiversity assessment: opportunities and challenges (2020, in preparation)

50. Kantor, P., Dalal, S., Jain, A., Nelson, C.: Optimal selection of configurations to test radiation detectors. Presented at the Informs Annual Meeting, San Francisco, CA (2014)

51. Kaper, H.G., Engler, H.: Modeling food systems. In: Kaper, H.G., Roberts, F.S. (eds.) Mathematics of Planet Earth: Protecting Our Planet, Learning from the Past, Safeguarding for the Future, pp. 267–296. Springer, Cham (2019). https://doi.org/10.1007/978-3-030-22044-0_10

52. Kumar, S., et al.: Deep learning framework for recognition of cattle using muzzle point image pattern. Measurement 116, 1–17 (2018)

53. Kumar, S., Singh, S.K., Singh, R.K, Singh, A.K.: Muzzle point pattern-based techniques for individual cattle identification. In: Kumar, S., Singh, S.K., Singh, R.K., Singh, A.K (eds.) Animal Biometrics: Techniques and Applications, pp. 111–135. Springer, Singapore (2017)

54. Lawrence, D., D'Odorico, P., Diekmann, L., DeLonge, M., Das, R., Eaton, J.: Ecological feedbacks following deforestation create the potential for a catastrophic ecosystem shift in tropical dry forest. Proc. Natl. Acad. Sci. U.S.A. 104(52), 20696–20701 (2007)

55. Liao, R., Fan, Z.: Supply chains have been upended. Here's how to make them more resilient. World Economic Forum, 6 Apr 2020. https://www.weforum.org/agenda/2020/04/supply-chains-resilient-covid-19/. Accessed 28 Apr 2020

56. Lobell, D.B.: The use of satellite data for crop yield gap analysis. Field Crops Res. 143, 56–64 (2013)

57. Lundstrom, M.: Hoarding in a pandemic: a problem of messaging, selfishness, or simply fear? FairWarning, 21 March 2020. https://www.salon.com/2020/03/21/hoarding-in-a-pandemic-a-problem-of-messaging-selfishness-or-simply-fear_partner/. Accessed 30 Apr 2020

58. Madigan, D., Mittal, S., Roberts, F.S.: Sequential decision making algorithms for port of entry inspection: overcoming computational challenges. In: Muresan, G., Altiok, T., Melamed, B., Zeng, D. (eds.) Proceedings of IEEE International Conference on Intelligence and Security Informatics (ISI-2007), pp. 1–7. IEEE Press, Piscataway (2007)

59. Madigan, D., Mittal, S., Roberts, F.S.: Efficient sequential decision-making algorithms for container inspection operations. Naval Res. Logist. 58, 637–654 (2011)

60. Méndez, F.J., Menéndez, M., Luceño, A., Losada, I.J.: Estimation of the long-term variability of extreme significant wave height using a time-dependent peak over threshold (POT) model. J. Geophy. Res. Oceans 111(C7) (2006)

61. Mohney, G.: Hospitals remain key targets as ransomware attacks expected to increase. ABC News, 15 May 2017. https://abcnews.go.com/Health/hospitals-remain-key-targets-ransomware-attacks-expected-increase/story?id=47416989. Accessed 1 June 2020.

62. National Counterintelligence and Security Center, Supply Chain Directorate: Supply Chain Risk Management: Best Practices. https://www.dni.gov/files/NCSC/documents/supplychain/20190405-UpdatedSCRM-Best-Practices.pdf. Accessed 14 Jan 2020

63. Norouzzadeh, M.S., et al.: Automatically identifying, counting, and describing wild animals in camera-trap images with deep learning. Proc. Natl. Acad. Sci. U.S.A. 115(25), E5716–E5725 (2018)

64. Pasternack, J., Roth, D.: Comprehensive trust metrics for information networks. In: Proceedings of the Army Science Conference (ASC), Orlando, Florida, December 2010.

65. Pasternack, J., Roth. D.: Knowing what to believe (when you already know something). In: Proceedings of International Conference on Computational Linguistics (COLING), pp. 877–885 (2010).

66. Pei, S., Kandula, S., Shaman, J.: Differential effects of intervention timing on COVID-19 spread in the United States. medRxiv preprint, posted 20 May 2020. https://doi.org/10.1101/2020.05.15.20103655. Accessed 31 May 2020

67. Pekeč, S., Venable, K.B. (eds.): ADT 2019. LNCS (LNAI), vol. 11834. Springer, Cham (2019). https://doi.org/10.1007/978-3-030-31489-7

68. Perry, J., Gupta, D., Feigenbaum, J., Wright, R.N.: Systematizing secure computation for research and decision support. In: Abdalla, M., De Prisco, R. (eds.) Security and Cryptography for Networks (SCN 2014). LNCS, vol. 8642. Springer, Cham (2014). https://doi.org/10.1007/978-3-319-10879-7_22.

69. Pluchinotta, I., Kazakçi, A.O., Giordano, R., Tsoukiàs, A.: Design theory for generating alternatives in public decision making processes. Group Decis. Negot. **28**(2), 341–375 (2019). https://doi.org/10.1007/s10726-018-09610-5

70. Rios Insua, D., French, S. (eds.): e-Democracy. Springer, Dordrecht (2010). https://doi.org/10.1007/978-90-481-9045-4

71. Roberts, F.S.: Computer science and decision theory. Ann. Oper. Res. **163**, 209–253 (2008)

72. Roberts, F.S.: From football to oil rigs: risk assessment for combined cyber and physical attacks. J. Benefit-Cost Anal. **10**, 251–273 (2019)

73. Roberts, F.S.: Measurement of biodiversity: richness and evenness. In: Kaper, H.G., Roberts, F.S. (eds.) Mathematics of Planet Earth: Protecting Our Planet, Learning from the Past, Safeguarding for the Future, pp. 203–224. Springer, Cham (2019). https://doi.org/10.1007/978-3-030-22044-0_8

74. Roberts, F.S.: Socially responsible facial recognition of animals (2020, in preparation)

75. Rose, A.: Economic consequence analysis of maritime cyber threats. In: DiRenzo, J.D., Drumhiller, N.K., Roberts, F.S. (eds.) Issues in Maritime Cyber Security, pp. 321–356. Westphalia Press, Washington, DC (2017)

76. Rosenzweig, C., Solecki, W.: Advancing Tools and Methods for Flexible Adaptation Pathways and Science Policy Integration. New York City Panel on Climate Change 2019 report. Annals NY Acad. Sci. 1439 (2019)

77. Rosoff, H., John, R.S., Burns, W., Siko, R.: Structuring uncertainty and conflicting objectives for life or death decisions following an urban biological catastrophe. Integr. Disaster Risk Manage. J. **2**(1), 1–21 (2012)

78. Rosoff, H., John, R.S., Prager, F.: Flu, risks, and videotape: escalation of fear and avoidance behavior. Risk Anal. **32**(4), 729–743 (2012)

79. Rossi, F., Tsoukias, A. (eds.): ADT 2009. LNCS (LNAI), vol. 5783. Springer, Heidelberg (2009). https://doi.org/10.1007/978-3-642-04428-1

80. Schwartz, M., Machulak, M.: Securing the Perimeter: Deploying Identity and Access Management with Free Open Source Software. APress, New York (2018)

81. Sturgis, L.A. Smythe, T.C., Tucci, A.E.: Port recovery in the aftermath of hurricane Sandy: improving port resiliency in the era of climate change. Center for New American Security, Washington, DC, August 2014

82. Tebaldi, C., Strauss, B.H., Zervas, C.E.: Modelling sea level rise impacts on storm surges along US coasts. Environ. Res. Lett. **7**, 014032 (2012)

83. Tendall, D.M., et al.: Food system resilience: defining the concept. Global Food Secur. **6**, 17–23 (2015)

84. The 9/11 Commission: The 9/11 Commission Report: Final Report of the National Commission on Terrorist Attacks Upon the United States (2014). https://fas.org/irp/offdocs/911commission.pdf. Accessed 31 May 2020

85. Turner, B.L., II.: Vulnerability and resilience: coalescing or paralleling approaches for sustainability science? Global Environ. Change **20**, 570–576 (2010)

86. Valletta, J.J., Torney, C., Kings, M., Thornton, A., Jmadden, J.: Applications of machine learning in animal behavior studies. Anim. Behav. **124**, 203–220 (2017)

87. Wagstaff, J.: All at sea: Global shipping fleet exposed to hacking threat. Reuters, 23 April 2014. https://www.reuters.com/article/2014/04/23/tech-cybersecurity-shipping-idUSL3N0N 402020140423. Accessed 21 Feb 2015

88. Zhao, W., Villaseca, F.E.: Byzantine fault tolerance for electric power grid monitoring and control. In: Proceedings of the 2008 International Conference on Embedded Software and Systems, pp. 129–135. IEEE Computer Society (2008)

89. Zhao, C., et al.: Secure multi-party computation: theory practice applications. Inf. Sci. **476**, 357–372 (2019). https://doi.org/10.1016/j.ins.2018.10.024

Chapter 8
Building Resilience into the Metadata-Based ETL Process Using Open Source Big Data Technologies

Peter Panfilov[1]([✉]) and Alexander Suleykin[2]

[1] National Research University – Higher School of Economics, School of Business Informatics, Moscow, Russia
ppanfilov@hse.ru
[2] Russian Academy of Sciences, V.A. Trapeznikov Institute of Control Sciences, Moscow, Russia

Abstract. Extract-transform-load (ETL) processes play a crucial role in data analysis in real-time data warehouse environments which demand low latency and high availability features for functionality. In essence, ETL- processes are becoming bottlenecks in such environments due to complexity growth, number of steps in data transformations, number of machines used for data processing and finally, increasing impact of human factors on development of new ETL-processes. In order to mitigate this impact and provide resilience of the ETL process, a special Metadata Framework is needed that can manage the design of new data pipelines and processes. In this work, we focus on ETL metadata and its use in driving process execution and present a proprietary approach to the design of the metadata-based process control that can reduce complexity, enhance resilience of ETL processes and allow their adaptive self-reorganization. We present a metadata framework implementation which is based on open-source Big Data technologies, describing its architecture and interconnections with external systems, data model, functions, quality metrics, and templates. A test execution of an experimental Airflow Directed Acyclic Graph (DAG) with randomly selected data is performed to evaluate the proposed framework.

Keywords: ETL-processes · Metadata management · Big Data · Open-source technologies · DAG-template

1 Introduction

A traditional extract, transform, and load (ETL) technology has proved itself useful when being applied to data integration in "normal" data warehouse environments [1]. Originally, it was designed to predominantly support batch processing with data updates happening during long breaks in normal business or organizational operational activities [2]. Thus, it was not intended to produce accurate results for near real-time data

© Springer Nature Switzerland AG 2021
F. S. Roberts and I. A. Sheremet (Eds.): Resilience in the Digital Age, LNCS 12660, pp. 139–153, 2021.
https://doi.org/10.1007/978-3-030-70370-7_8

analysis on continuous flows of streaming data coming from multiple sources. However, modern data management environment requires support from ETL system for such key environmental features as its high availability of streaming data, low latency of intervals between transactions and horizontal scalability for performance improvement [3]. Many data warehouses are vulnerable during operation. A built-in error handling functionality of the ETL tools can help data engineers develop a resilient and well instrumented ETL process. However, many desirable features of ETL systems such as fault tolerance, quick fault finding and easy resume after error, are not typically available and sometimes seem hard to achieve.

Therefore, what is needed in the era of Big Data is the resilient ETL process control frameworks which are capable of performing when things go wrong. Thus, to cope with new Big Data demands such as very big data volumes, continuous data streaming, multiple heterogeneous data types and sources, real-time user interactions, new powerful data analytics solutions and tools, certain changes to the control, management and maintenance part of ETL system should be introduced [4].

A staged analysis of the ETL processes and challenges of ETL in near real-time environment is presented in [3], followed by discussion of possible/suggested and existing solutions to meet those challenges. For the high availability and support of real-time streaming in ETL, many solutions are looking for new processors and server configurations to accommodate streaming data in combination with backup and replication techniques to ensure availability and minimize risk of data loss. An interesting attempt to capture and leverage insights from Big Data, represent solutions in [5] and [6] that apply updated semantic web technologies that support real-time streaming in ETL system. Low latency requirements in data warehouse environments can be satisfied through the framework development that combine streaming processors with change data capture (CDC) techniques, which support real-time data [2, 7]. Another approach is the *data warehouse-based data model* proposed for data analytics in [8]. This approach filters data required for analysis to feed them into a staging database of server for aggregation. Special architectures are proposed to satisfy the scalability requirement within the data warehouse environment.

Building efficient, flexible, dynamic data warehouse environments requires a number of technical advances. It is imperative to mention that, in this respect, a metadata model that could be used for ETL-processes, cycle runs, and cycle refresh monitoring in data warehouse environments plays an important role in the ETL system design and implementation. Here, the metadata framework can enable various activities from data integration, through data transformation and up to online analytical processing (OLAP) and data mining [9]. Different kinds of metadata can be collected in a data warehouse environment and different metadata models and frameworks can be built. In this research, we are mostly concerned with new technical solutions that facilitate the development and maintenance of the efficient, flexible, and possibly near real-time or highly responsive and dynamic data warehouse environments. The ETL metadata is the metadata to be used by the technical analysts for the ETL development and the data warehouse maintenance [10].

In this paper, we are mostly considering ETL metadata framework that is critical for the data warehouse environment management and operation.

The remainder of this paper is structured as follows. In Sect. 2, we discuss the use of metadata in ETL process control. Section 3 describes the metadata framework (MF) for automation of typical ETL and provides description of object types in the MF along with the set of functions and templates—various table operations, DAG management operations, source system and environment manipulations—to allow the user to perform certain operations within metadata of ETL-processes. A set of quality metrics for evaluating the proposed framework concludes the section. Section 4 presents an experimental study comparing the results of different ETL-process control practices and scenarios on performance, concurrency, and delay response. Section 5 concludes the study and discusses future works.

2 Metadata-Driven Resilient ETL-Process

Establishing a metadata framework at the planning stage is crucial to the success of the overall data warehousing project [11]. A metadata model that captures various information about data transfers and transformations from operational data source to the target data warehouse is useful both to business users and back-end support personnel. It can be used for different purposes such as extract-transform-load (ETL) process control, cycle runs, and cycle refresh monitoring.

Traditionally, two distinct types of metadata in a data warehouse environment are considered, that is, the logical type and the technical type [12]. The former is business-oriented, while the latter, also called the ETL metadata, is associated with the back-end processes that extract, transform, and load the data [13]. The focus of this work is on ETL metadata that is critical for ETL process development and control, batch cycle refreshes, and data warehouse maintenance.

The ETL process control defines the jobs to be run and maintains job times and job execution order. Introduction of the resilience capacities to the ETL process requires additional functionality such as detecting erroneous processes, diagnosing errors, and recovering processes from the errors (restart after failure). ETL metadata plays a fundamentally important role in this kind of "smart" process control by providing and maintaining information on object (process and/or resources) dependencies, process states and execution history [14].

As it is shown in [14], the choice of metadata models for process dependency and process state data has a great impact on the resilience of the ETL process. It was demonstrated that denormalized process dependencies may introduce unnecessary roadblocks after process failure and prevent from parallel execution of the process dependency graph (DAG). The metadata models for normalized process dependencies allows for parallel execution of multiple process handlers. It is suggested in [14], that process dependencies in metadata model can be expressed using resource dependencies that are easier to manage and are finer-grained.

Resource dependencies in metadata can be stored as process inputs and outputs, while process dependencies can be inferred by process handlers. Benefits of using resource dependencies in metadata include clarification of meaning of process dependencies and the possibility of reading these directly from process definitions. It also makes it easier to add new processes to the system.

At the same time, the metadata model for process state influences the restartability of the ETL process. It was shown that lightweight state metadata makes restart easier, where the lightweight state means the controller does not know much about processes at restart. A special metadata model for process execution is used to calculate average duration from recent execution history and uses branch weight in the process graph to predict good execution order adaptively.

Process controller components for the metadata driven resilient ETL process implementation would include the *lightweight state*, the *normalized process dependencies*, and a *process handler* that runs processes.

The resilient ETL process control as it is presented in [14] was implemented by the author Richard Swinbank in the Sprockit project [15] which is essentially a process controller for managing SSIS package and T-SQL stored procedure execution. Sprockit provides resilience features – fault tolerance, quick fault finding and easy resume after error – using only T-SQL and the SQL Server Agent, while at the same time supporting parallel processing, adapting to evolving workloads, providing a breadth of monitoring and diagnostic information and a host of other benefits [15]. Sprockit's process handlers need information about process dependencies to be able to execute processes in the correct order. Process dependencies are the arrows on the dependency graph. Sprockit describes dependencies in terms of resources – the set of SQL Server objects that make up the inputs and outputs of a process. By joining an output resource to its subsequent uses as an input resource, handlers infer process dependencies from the underlying resource dependencies.

In our approach, we also use metadata modeling to establish a framework for resilient ETL process development and control. Our solution is based on open- source Big Data technologies, such as Apache Spark/Hadoop framework. For process dependency graph (DAG) generation and design in our metadata framework, the Python programming language is used [16]. New job templates are generated from SQL-tables and transformed to DAGs. Then, DAGs are executed by process handlers. PostgreSQL relational database [17] is used as a main storage of main entities (metadata) of the Metadata Framework and job templates for python DAG synchronization using python. In addition, there are templates for running PostgreSQL jobs. HDFS distributed fault tolerant file system [18] is used as main data storage of raw data, and ETL-jobs are imitating the data movements and transformations between HDFS layers. Spark jobs [19] were created to run data transfers within HDFS layers. Apache Airflow universal scheduler [20] is used for ETL-steps orchestration and synchronization. In our project, a test implementation of the Metadata Framework is based on Airflow.

3   Metadata Framework

3.1   Overview, Architecture and Data Model

The MF is a framework for automation of typical ETL-tasks through automatic generation of Airflow DAGs based on the created data model. When Airflow DAG is generated using the Metadata Framework, it becomes active and ready for executing some particular ETL-jobs. Among the typical ETL-tasks, it can be any of the ETL-jobs, although in our research we have tested the following ETL-tasks based on the following Open Source

Big Data technologies: Apache Spark tasks, Shell commands, PostgreSQL commands. The Metadata Framework provides the following possibilities:

- Metadata management interface;
- Single entry point for managing metadata of DAG creation, which reduces the likelihood of error due to the human mistakes;
- Automatic construction of the load pipeline with support for dependencies of loading steps;
- Keeping architecture consistent with naming convention;
- Data model versioning;
- Synchronization of development environments;
- Avoidance of hardcode and extra configuration files;
- Reducing number of supported code and various languages.

The general architecture of the MMF and developed ETL-process templates are presented in Fig. 1. User is launching a DAG that consists of different steps which are the ETL-transformations and tasks. When a job is launched, DAG is extracting all metadata from the Metadata Framework, which is in essence, a PostgreSQL database with created objects and their connections. Based on the data model of the Metadata Framework, a set of SQL-objects (templates and ETL-jobs metadata) is being transformed to Airflow DAG using python scripts and finally launched as usual Airflow DAG.

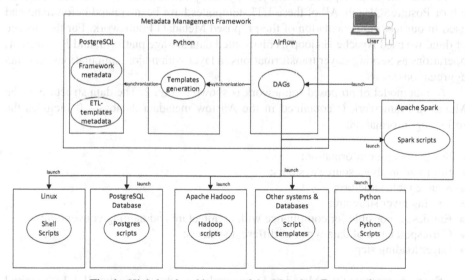

Fig. 1. High-level architecture of the Metadata Framework.

The following ETL-task templates and architectural components have been developed on the basis of Open-Source Big Data technologies (Table 1):

Table 1. ETL-task templates and architectural components for the Metadata Framework.

No.	Component	Definition
1	Python	The main programming language for DAGs generation and design [11] for the Metadata Framework. New templates are generated from SQL-tables and transformed to DAGs. Then DAGs are executed by users
2	HDFS	Distributed fault tolerant file system optimized for storage for processing large amounts of data, part of Apache Hadoop [12]. HDFS is used for main data storage of raw data and ETL-jobs are imitating the data movements and transformations between HDFS layers
3	Spark	Distributed in-memory framework for high-load data processing [13]. Spark jobs was created that run data transfers within HDFS layers
4	PostgreSQL	Relational database [14] for storage of the Metadata Framework's main entities (metadata) and job templates for python DAG synchronization using python. In addition, there are templates for running PostgreSQL jobs
5	AirFlow	Universal Scheduler [15], which is used for ETL-steps orchestration and synchronization. In our work, test implementation of the Metadata Framework is based on AirFlow

A task can be an Apache Spark job, python job, Linux shell command, Hadoop job or PostgreSQL job. All of these ETL-templates have been created beforehand and used in our test implementation of the proposed Metadata Framework. For the storage of data, we used Apache Hadoop as distributed data storage platform, and PostgreSQL operations as Serving Layer transformations (a layer with major computations and data aggregations).

A data model of proposed framework is shown in Fig. 2. The data structure of the Metadata Framework is contained in the Airflow metadata database. It includes the following information:

- System contour information;
- Information about source systems;
- Source table structure;
- Serving layer structure;
- Entities responsible for compliance with architecture and naming convention;
- Correspondence of data types of different systems;
- Layer loading steps.

The management of the Metadata Framework is conducted via the GUI. In the initial version, control flow occurs through functions in Postgres database. In the future, we plan to switch to an API and enter the metadata through configuration files.

3.2 API Functions and DAG Templates with Parameters

The Metadata Framework includes several types of objects. Among them are:

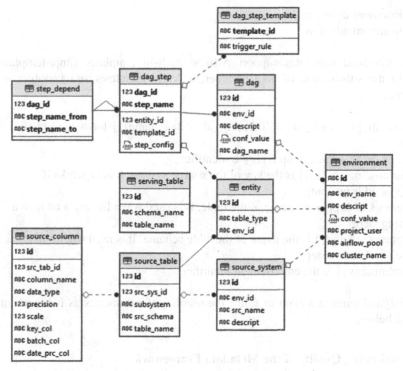

Fig. 2. Data model of the Metadata Framework.

- Environment – the logical contours of the project;
- DAGs – process pipelines;
- DAG steps – atomic boot steps (processes);
- Download dependencies (DAG step dependencies) – download dependency steps responsible for the order in which steps are run;
- DAG step templates – step templates on the basis of which each download step is formed individually;
- Entities – target entities of the serving layer and entities of source systems;
- Layer loading steps.

A developed set of functions allow user to perform the following operations within metadata of ETL-processes:

- Service Layer Tables management;
- DAG management;
- DAG steps management;
- DAG sequence management;
- Source table deletion;
- Source system addition;
- Environment duplication;
- Environment change;

- Environment deletion;
- Environment addition.

All designed templates support Airflow built-in templates (jinja-templates) to simplify the substitution of boot parameters. Valid templates and variables are the following:

- {{ti.xcom_pull (task_ids = 'lid', dag_id = dag_name)}} loads load id (lid) of the ETL;
- {{ti.job_id}} is the startup ETL job identifier;
- {{params.src_sys_id}} is the key of the source system. It only works if
- src_sys_id is present;
- {{params.table}} is the name of the table. It is used when linking a table to a
- loading step;
- {{params.schema}} is the name of the table schema. It is used when linking a
- table to a loading step;
- {{params.env}} is the environment identifier.

Designed templates need to fulfill the number of parameters as it is presented in Table 2 below.

3.3   Evaluating Quality of the Metadata Framework

In order to evaluate the effectiveness of the Metadata Framework for ETL automation in comparison to the traditional ETL-processes creation from scratch, some special quality metrics are needed that can value the Metadata Framework usage by users. We propose using the following metrics for the Metadata Framework evaluation:

- Number of used ETL-templates (ETL runs): This metric shows how many different ETL-jobs could be created using any tool and language. Thus, potentially each ETL-template run can represent some time saving and higher ETL-process quality for user.
- Number of created templates and sub-templates: Each template represents integration with different systems and run of some command in general, while sub- template can launch particular job, i.e. functions for data type conversions or data transfer with data enrichment etc. The more templates and sub-templates are created, the more functionality a framework will have.
- Number of failed processes run by users: If number is increasing, some conditions are not adapted for this particular case and template needs to be redesigned.
- Number of successful processes run by users. The greater this value, the more stable the framework.
- Number of fault-tolerant job templates created. If some node is failed during the execution, the process should be automatically restarted.
- Number of scalable job templates created. If there is a need to increase system performance, it should be possible to add a node for better computation.

Table 2. Parameters for templates.

Parameter	Description
bash	Run a bash script. Required parameter: cmd bash-command. Example: {"cmd": "echo end` date` "}.
py_get_lid	Initialize load_id.
stg2exch	Data transfer from the STG layer to EXCHANGE. Optional parameter: exec_cores – number of cores used by Spark. By default, it's 3.
exch2ods	Data transfer from the EXCHANGE to ODS layer (a table is required to create a step). Optional parameter: exec_cores. By default, it's 1.
ods2bv	Data transfer from the ODS layer to BV (a table is required). Optional parameter: exec_cores. By default, it's 4. Required parameter: load_method – a way to load data into the BV layer. Example: {"load_method": "full", "exec_cores": 4}.
bv2dds_stg	Data transfer from the BV layer to DDS_STG (a table is required). Optional parameter: exec_cores. By default, it's 2.
exch_clean	Clearing EXCHANGE directory (a table is required).
pg_func_run	Start a Postgres procedure. Optional parameter: src_sys_id – is used, if it is present in the procedure and the jinja-template "{{params.src_sys_id}}" is used in the procedure parameters. Required parameters: pg_func_name – procedure name, params – unnamed procedure parameters. Example: {"pg_func_name": "etl.f_gen_sk", "src_sys_id": "demo", "params": ["{{ti.xcom_pull (task_ids = 'lid', dag_id = dag_name)}}," {{ti. job_id}} "," {{params.src_sys_id}}, "{{params.table}} _ {{params.src_sys_id}} _ v"]}.
rest_call	Step to call rest-api. Required parameter is call_str – url call string api.
dummy_all_success	Dummy-step, which only starts upon successful completion of all the previous steps.
dummy_none_failed	Dummy-step, which only starts in the absence of failures of the previous steps.
dummy_all_done	Dummy-step, which only starts at the end of the previous steps, regardless of success.
bash_branch	A conditional step that defines the next step to execute. It executes a bash-command. The test is carried out on the first value of the result of the command. Required parameters: cmd – bash-command line, results – a list of values (in key-value format) in the output and the next steps to be performed based on the output. Supports the "else" option in the list. Example: {"cmd": "hadoop fs -count -q hdfs: // datapark / data / {{params.env}} / {{params.src_sys_id}} / stg / topics / sys__{{params.env}}__skim__{{ params.table}}__data|awk '{print $ 6}' ", "results":{"0":"all_success__public__{{params.table}}", "else": "stg2exch__public__{{params.table}}"}}. This example is similar to the py_branch_check_hdfs template, but the names of the steps that follow are more manageable.
pg_branch	Conditional step that defines the next step to be performed. It executes a sql-command, and the test is carried out on the first value and the leftmost field in the query result. The step does not contain commit. Required parameters: conn – name of the Airflow connector for connecting to PostgreSQL, sql – sql-command line, results – a list of values (in key-value format) in the output and the next steps to be performed based on the output. Supports the "else" option in the list.
bash_gen_param	Step that initializes the variable. It executes a bash-command, saves the first value of the result. In the future, to access the variable in the parameter text, the jinja-templates will be used: {{ti.xcom_pull (task_ids = '<STEP_NAME>', dag_id = dag_name)}}, where <STEP_NAME> - name of step that initialized the variable.
pg_gen_param	Step that initializes the variable. It executes a sql-command, saves the value of the first line, the left field in the query result. The step does not contain commit. Required parameters: conn – name of the Airflow connector for connecting to PostgreSQL, sql – sql-command line. Example: {"conn": "airflow_db: airflow@airflow","sql": "select nextval ('lid');"}. The example is similar to the py_get_lid step, but the step is now not necessary to call lid to get the value in the next steps.

4 Test Metadata Framework's DAG Execution

4.1 Experimental Setup

Test implementation of the ETL-process based on the Metadata Framework has been performed using created templates and data processing through different layers imitating data moves and transformations.

For the experiments, only Apache Spark tasks and PostgreSQL tasks were created as examples of templates.

All data processing within Apache Hadoop (Batch Layer) and to the PostgreSQL DDS_STG Layer have been accomplished using distributed Apache Spark cluster computing framework, while transformations from DDS_STG Layer to DM Layer were made by one-thread PostgreSQL commands.

The characteristics of the Open Source Big Data infrastructure used in test implementation of the proposed Metadata Framework, the description and versions of the services used are presented in Table 3.

Table 3. Experimental setup.

CPU/RAM	Role in experiment	Components and versions
12/32	Hadoop Name Node Active; YARN Resource Manager StandBy	HDFS Client 3.1.1.3.1 Metrics Monitor/Ambari Metrics 0.1.0 NameNode/HDFS 3.1.1.3.1 YARN Client 3.1.0 Zeppelin Notebook 0.8.0 ZKFailoverController/HDFS 3.1.1.3.1 ZooKeeper Server 3.4.9.3.1
12/32	Hadoop Name Node StandBy; YARN Resource Manager Active	HBase Master 2.0.0.3.1 HDFS Client 3.1.1.3.1 JournalNode/HDFS 3.1.1.3.1 Metrics Monitor/Ambari Metrics 0.1.0 NameNode/HDFS 3.1.1.3.1 Timeline Service V2.0 Reader ZKFailoverController/HDFS 3.1.1.3.1 ZooKeeper Server 3.4.9.3.1
12/32	Datanode HDFS; YARN Node Manager	DataNode/HDFS 3.1.1.3.1 HBase Client 2.0.0.3.1 RegionServer/Hbase 2.0.0.3.1 Hive Client 3.0.0.3.1 MapReduce2 Client 3.0.0.3.1 Metrics Monitor/Ambari Metrics 0.1.0 NodeManager/YARN 3.1.0 YARN Client 3.1.0
12/32	Datanode HDFS; YARN Node Manager	DataNode/HDFS 3.1.1.3.1 RegionServer/Hbase 2.0.0.3.1 HDFS Client 3.1.1.3.1 Hive Client 3.0.0.3.1 MapReduce2 Client 3.0.0.3.1 Metrics Monitor/Ambari Metrics 0.1.0 NodeManager/YARN 3.1.0 YARN Client 3.1.0
12/32	Datanode HDFS; YARN Node Manager	DataNode/HDFS 3.1.1.3.1 HBase Client 2.0.0.3.1 RegionServer/Hbase 2.0.0.3.1 HDFS Client 3.1.1.3.1 Hive Client 3.0.0.3.1 MapReduce2 Client 3.0.0.3.1 Metrics Monitor/Ambari Metrics 0.1.0 NodeManager/YARN 3.1.0

(*continued*)

Table 3. (*continued*)

CPU/RAM	Role in experiment	Components and versions
12/32	Datanode HDFS; YARN Node Manager	Atlas Metadata Server/Atlas 0.7.0.3.1 DataNode/HDFS 3.1.1.3.1 HBase Client 2.0.0.3.1 RegionServer/Hbase 2.0.0.3.1 HDFS Client 3.1.1.3.1 Infra Solr 0.1.0 Client Metrics Monitor/Ambari Metrics 0.1.0 NodeManager/YARN 3.1.0
12/32	Datanode HDFS; YARN Node Manager	DataNode/HDFS 3.1.1.3.1 HBase Client 2.0.0.3.1 RegionServer/Hbase 2.0.0.3.1 HDFS Client 3.1.1.3.1 Hive Client 3.0.0.3.1 MapReduce2 Client 3.0.0.3.1 Metrics Monitor/Ambari Metrics 0.1.0 NodeManager/YARN 3.1.0
8/32	Spark Edge Node; Airflow Worker	Airflow 1.10.5 Spark2 Client 2.3.0
8/32	Spark Edge Node; Airflow Worker	Airflow 1.10.5 Spark2 Client 2.3.0
8/32	Spark Edge Node; Airflow Worker	Airflow 1.10.5 Spark2 Client 2.3.0
8/32	Spark Edge Node; Airflow Worker	Airflow 1.10.5 Spark2 Client 2.3.0
8/32	Spark Edge Node; Airflow Worker	Airflow 1.10.5 Spark2 Client 2.3.0
8/16	PostgreSQL for Metadata Framework Airflow metadata	PostgreSQL 11.5
8/16	Airflow for DAGs launching and ETL-process visualization	Airflow 1.10.5
12/128	PostgreSQL for Serving Layer transformations	PostgreSQL 11.4

4.2 Test Scenarios

All test scenarios were based on services listed above. Apache Spark distributed jobs are launched from Airflow, and the particular job instance can be launched at any Spark Edge Node listed above. Each worker node in Airflow is getting a task according to the load, so an Edge Node with minimal load would be assigned for task execution, that makes mechanism scalable, reliable and fault tolerant.

Figure 3 depicts architecture of the test implementation.

As an input data, we used two entities with following characteristics presented in Table 4.

Each entity has 10000 records. We have developed and used the following job templates in test implementation:

- Check_hdfs_directory (entity name) – check if hdfs directory is not empty. If it is empty, all other jobs are skipped;
- STG2EXCH – data movements from STG directory to EXCH directory in Hadoop, where processing batch is fixed;
- EXCH2ODS – data transformation from XML data type to Parquet (Spark native format) for incremental data storage in compressed columnar type;
- ODS2BV – data aggregation from Parquet to Parquet data format where only relevant data from source systems are aggregated;

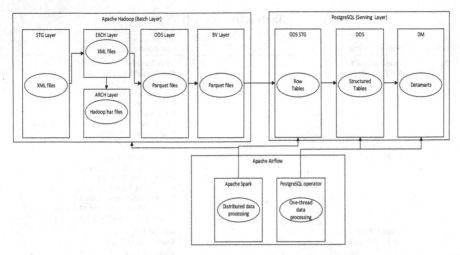

Fig. 3. Dataflows in the test implementation of the Metadata Framework.

Table 4. Data entries for the experiment.

Entity name	Attribute name	Data type
NOD	NAME1	CHAR
	NAME2	CHAR
	NAME3	CHAR
	NAME4	CHAR
	NAME5	CHAR
	NAME6	TIMESTAMP
DIR	NAME1	INTEGER
	NAME2	CHAR
	NAME3	CHAR
	NAME4	CHAR
	NAME5	CHAR
	NAME6	TIMESTAMP

- BV2DDS_STG – data load from Hadoop BV Layer (relevant data batch) to PostgreSQL dds_stg layer;
- Pg_(some function) – run of some PostgreSQL function;
- EXCH2ARCH – data copy and compression from EXH layer to Arch using Ha- doop har archive;
- EXCH_CLEAN – cleaning of exchange directory.

An example of DAG visualization for the Spark job is shown in Fig. 4. The total time is 0.7 s for the job that includes 2 stages.

Fig. 4. DAG of Spark job EXCH2ODS.

The resulting DAG implementation for two randomly selected entities (tables) is shown in Fig. 5.

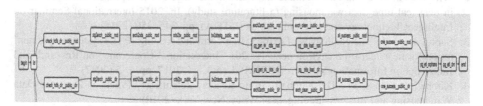

Fig. 5. Test Metadata Framework DAG execution.

5 Conclusion

Management of high loads of data within comprehensive data pipelines is an important task for those who have a solid number of ETL-processes. When the amount of data is considered increasing significantly in the future along with the amount of distributed ETL-processes, the human factor and complexity of each process are becoming crucial points.

We propose to use the Metadata Framework for creation and management of different types of ETL-processes. In our research, we have developed the architecture of a new framework, a data model, an API and different templates – a set of Apache Spark jobs, Hadoop jobs, Linux shell jobs and PostgreSQL jobs. In addition, the quality metrics were proposed for evaluation of the Metadata Framework effectiveness. In order to prove the applicability of the proposed framework based on two randomly selected tables, the experimental DAG run was performed, which moved data through different layers of the system using distributed Apache Spark jobs for Batch layer and one-thread PostgreSQL operations for Serving Layer. The successful implementation of DAG has shown applicability of the developed Metadata Framework for other cases and jobs such as python operations, R, shell and others.

For the next steps of framework development, more operations should be standardized and developed. A special Front End GUI for easier dataflow management should be designed. Finally, the RDBMC PostgreSQL for the Metadata Framework and Airflow must be made to be fault-tolerant, reliable and distributed, together with Airflow server and scheduler.

Acknowledgements. The reported study was partially supported by RFBR grant according to the research project No. 20-07-00958. The article was prepared within the framework of the HSE University Project Group Competition at the National Research University Higher School of Economics (HSE University) in 2020–2022 (Research Group on Decentralized Data).

References

1. Kimball, R., Ross, M.: The Data Warehouse Toolkit: The Complete Guide to Dimensional Modeling. Wiley, New York (2011)
2. Wibowo, A.: Problems and available solutions on the stage of extract transform and loading in near real-time data warehousing (a literature study). In: 2015 International Seminar on Intelligent Technology and its Applications (ISITIA), pp. 345–350 (2015)
3. Sabtu, A., et al.: The challenges of extract, transform and loading (ETL) system implementation for near real-time environment. In: 2017 International Conference on Research and Innovation in Information Systems (ICRIIS), Langkawi, 2017, pp. 1–5 (2017)
4. Kimball, R., Ross, M.: The Kimball Group Reader: Relentlessly Practical Tools for Data Warehousing and Business Intelligence. Wiley, New York (2010)
5. Bansal, S.K., Kagemann, S.: Integrating big data: a semantic extract-transform-load framework. Computer **48**(3), 42–50 (2015)
6. Nath, R.P.D., Hose, K., Pedersen, T.B., Romero, O.: SETL: a programmable semantic extract-transform-load framework for semantic data warehouses. Inf. Syst. **68**, 17–43 (2017)
7. Jain, T., Rajasree, S., Saluja, S.: Refreshing datawarehouse in near real-time. Int. J. Comput. Appl. **46**(18), 24–29 (2012)
8. Narendra, N., Ponnalagu, K., Tamilselvam, S., Ghose, A.: Goal-driven context-aware data filtering in IoT-based systems. Faculty of engineering and information sciences, January 2015, pp. 2172–2179 (2015)
9. Fan, H., Poulovassilis, A.: Using AutoMed metadata in data warehousing environments. In: Proceedings of the 6th ACM International Workshop on Data Warehousing and OLAP, New Orleans, Louisiana, USA, pp. 86–93 (2003)
10. Rahman, N., Marz, J., Akhter, S.: An ETL metadata model for data warehousing. J. Comput. Inf. Technol. **20**, 95–111 (2012)

11. Vetterli, T., Vaduva, A., Staudt, M.: Metadata standards for data warehousing: open information model vs. common warehouse metadata. ACM SIGMOD Rec. **29**(3), 68–75 (2000)
12. Zyl, J.V., Vincent, M., Mohania, M.: Representation of metadata in a data warehouses. In: Proceedings of IEEE 1998. IEEE Xplore (1998)
13. Shankaranarayanan, G., Even, A.: The metadata enigma. Commun. ACM **49**(2), 88–94 (2006)
14. Swinbank, R.: Design patterns for metadata-first ETL process control. In: SQLBITS 2019, Manchester, UK, 2 March 2019 (2019). https://sqlbits.com/Sessions/Event18/Design_pat terns_for_metadata-driven_ETL_process_control
15. Sprockit. https://RichardSwinbank.net/sprockit
16. Python.org. https://python.org
17. PostgreSQL: The World's Most Advanced Open Source Relational Database. https://www.postgresql.org
18. The Apache Hadoop project. https://hadoop.apache.org
19. The Apache Spark.org. https://spark.apache.org
20. Apache Airflow.org. https://airflow.apache.org

Applications

Chapter 9
Towards Democratizing Human–Building Simulation and Analytics

Muhammad Usman[1]([✉]), Brandon Haworth[5], Glen Berseth[2], Petros Faloutsos[1,4],
and Mubbasir Kapadia[3]

[1] York University, Toronto, Canada
{usman,pfal}@eecs.yorku.ca
[2] University of California, Berkeley, USA
gberseth@gmail.com
[3] Rutgers University, New Brunswick, NJ, USA
mk1353@cs.rutgers.edu
[4] UHN - Toronto Rehabilitation Institute, Toronto, Canada
[5] University of Victoria, Victoria, BC, Canada
bhaworth@uvic.ca

Abstract. This work addresses a key emerging issue for building resiliency in the digital age and the advent of "smart" environments, specifically the impact of AI on human-building interactions. We present herein a concise summary of the workflows we have developed over time to simulate human-movements and dynamics of human-building interactions. We discuss the applications of human behaviour simulation in the analysis of building environments. We then discuss the approaches which use dynamic human-aware simulations in improving environment designs. We highlight the challenges in existing simulation workflows, which are usually decoupled from environment modeling tools or often tightly coupled with any specialized modeling platform. Such workflows require significant infrastructure and domain expertise, hindering the users' abilities to seamlessly simulate, analyze, and incorporate dynamics of human-building interactions into their preferred design workflows. We introduce a democratized approach using an on-demand service-based workflow for human behaviour simulation and analysis of human-building interactions.

Keywords: Crowd simulation multi-agent system · Human-building interaction · Computer-Aided Design · Virtual environment · Built environment simulation-as-a-service

1 Introduction

Due to the advent of sophisticated sensing solutions and smart and connected environments, it is now possible for buildings and environments to passively monitor and actively interact with their human inhabitants. In order for buildings to be resilient in this

© Springer Nature Switzerland AG 2021
F. S. Roberts and I. A. Sheremet (Eds.): Resilience in the Digital Age, LNCS 12660, pp. 157–171, 2021.
https://doi.org/10.1007/978-3-030-70370-7_9

digital age of smart environments [50], it is imperative to consider how AI techniques and predictive analytics can be used to fundamentally inform the design and management of these spaces while accounting for and leveraging these innovations.

Fig. 1. Egress evacuation of an office environment. Three snapshots are presented in raster order of a real-time simulation of multi-agent navigation with a planning-based steering approach which uses an egocentric field for planning paths, optimized to reduce time-to-destination (e.g., twice as fast as its default configuration.

Estimating how an environment design impacts the movement and activities of its prospective inhabitants is a critical aspect in architecture design. It is essential to account for human occupancy and behavior in the design and management of buildings and environment spaces. While many established building performance evaluation methods in Computer-Aided Design (CAD) and Building Information Modeling (BIM) tools, such as energy, structure, and lighting, mostly rely on static environment representations. How an environment design will perform for the dynamic movement of people, its spatiotemporal impact on user experience, operational efficiency, and space utilization, is mostly left to de- signers and architects' experience and self-intuition. Predicting and accounting for Human-Building Interaction (HBI) is particularly challenging, if not impossible, to do unassisted in-built environments.

To this end, we advocate an approach for simulating HBI in semantically meaningful environments. We make use of crowd simulation techniques [23, 32, 43] in mimicking human-like movements in building environments. The simulation of human dynamics, from person-to-person interactions to global-scale transportation networks, affords a plethora of revolutionary predictive and analytical powers across several fields.

In research and industry, crowd simulation has afforded the power to predict and opti- mize the spaces and processes which drive the modern world. However, crowd simulation techniques present high integration costs into environment modeling pipelines. The early solutions developed required expertise in a particular simulation platform and present sophisticated technical and workflow challenges, such as loading building geometries, annotating buildings with space semantics, configuring crowd parameters, generating simulation results, and visualizing spatiotemporal data maps of space utilization.

In this work, we focus on the applications of human-behaviour simulation in the analysis of HBI, and how these predictive and analytical powers have and can be democ- ratized. The use of democratization in the context of technology has and does largely refer to the increase in access to sophisticated technologies. In general, this means the expansion of a technology's user base and its associated information production. That is, the ability for a wide range of users, primarily non-experts, to participate in the modification, use, and extension of specialized knowledge, techniques, and tools which transform or produce information or material. In this work, we focus on the use of a broad set of techniques, algorithms, and systems centered around human-movement and behaviour simulation. We then introduce an on-demand service-based platform and approach for removing or abbreviating the underlying barriers associated with big data production and analysis in the dynamic context of human movement simulation and its myriad uses, not limited to: virtual environment analysis, predictive architectural design, predictive urban design & planning, accessible design & accessibility analysis, safety-critical analysis, and forensic analysis of disasters. The proposed platform provides an exploratory and comparative analysis of HBI in semantically meaningful environments through informative visualizations in an interactive workspace.

The remaining sections of this chapter talk about our work in human-movement and behaviour simulations, HBI, the use of behaviour simulations to analyze and improve environment designs, and lastly, the proposed democratized workflow for the analysis of HBI in more detail.

2 Human–Movement and Behaviour Simulation

Human movement and behaviour simulation have a long and rich history in the literature [1, 23, 31, 32, 43]. The area is split among a few approaches. First, methods are largely either agent-based or cellular-automata. In this work, we focus on high fidelity agent-based models as they promise to capture high-fidelity phenomena at the microscopic and mesoscopic scales. Next, agent-based models are largely broken into several areas: physical force-based methods; geometric optimization-based methods; field-based methods; data-driven methods; planning methods; and machine learning methods. However, no list is exhaustive as the area of research is continually active. In this section, we will touch on two specific areas which move away from expertly defined or *ad hoc* rules and toward high-fidelity representation of humans–planning and machine learning methods. These methods either seek to solve for agent actions within target constraints or to learn policies from simulations and data.

2.1 Evidence for Fidelity and Diversity

Recent work has shown that single-particle methods, which comprise much of the human movement and behaviour simulation literature, has many drawbacks. In particular, the biomechanical modelling is extremely important, as stepping used in bipedal locomotion of humans is neither linear nor consistent across scenarios [39]. Most recently, it has been shown that modelling heterogeneous walkers at the footstep level impacts crowd behaviour and quantitative outcomes [18]. That is, diversity in mobility has a significant impact on simulation results. These results provide significant motivation toward the planning and machine learning approaches to human behaviour simulation.

Planning-Based Methods: Planning-based methods typically account for additional information to produce high fidelity short-term plans which resolve steering and collision avoidance behaviours. Often this information is biologically inspired. For example, an egocentric field of attenuating resolution can be used as the basis for planning paths, similar to how vision can be used in biological navigation [24]. Additionally, assuming not all situations require the same type of steering decisions, methods can be composed of several steering possibilities which are then integrated as a singular plan [40]. Very high-fidelity movement behaviours can be generated by moving beyond the single-particle linear time-step movements of prior models. By representing movement as the inverted pendulum of human bipedal walking, space-time plans of several steps can be found which solve the steering behaviour problem [5, 41]. That is, instead of making instantaneous movement decisions as the simulation updates, the model can plan any number of steps ahead, more akin to how humans navigate. These methods can be extended to model people with interesting or non-normative gaits, such as post-stroke patients [18].

Learning-Based Methods: More recently, machine learning methods have been proposed to alleviate the need for expert or ad-hoc rules and control paradigms used to produce movement and behaviour simulation previously. Vector Quantization has been used to model multi-agent pedestrian navigation [27]. Similarly, preliminary work has shown to successfully simulate small groups of navigating agents [7, 8]. A set of models have shown that this problem is both tractable and scalable [28, 30].

However, this approach requires scenario-specific training to converge on expected emergent behaviours. Reinforcement learning (RL) has been shown to map particularly well to the agent movement simulation problem, both conceptually and in practice [29, 44]. Models have learned continuous actions using a curriculum training approach, like prior expertly defined models [26]. However, these methods must overcome several hurdles related specifically to the Multi-Agent RL (MARL) problem, most serious of which is the non-stationary problem–the issue of learning updates among agents invalidating prior observations between those agents. More recently, the MARL problem, rules definition, and simplified underlying model representation have been address through multi-agent hierarchical reinforcement learning (MAHRL). This approach separates low-level skills related to locomotion form high-level skills like navigation and uses a biomechanically inspired action representation (footstep plans) to communicate between levels [3]. Figure 1 shows a simulation of multi-agent navigation for a planning-based approach which uses egocentric fields to plan navigation paths.

3 Modeling Human-Building Interactions

The maturity in modeling human movements and behaviours (Sect. 2) facilitates the investigation of how the design of semantically meaningful environments impacts the movement and occupancy of its inhabitants and is a precursor to informing the design of buildings with respect to human-centric performance criteria [36].

Low Density (LoS: B–C) High Density (LoS: E–F)

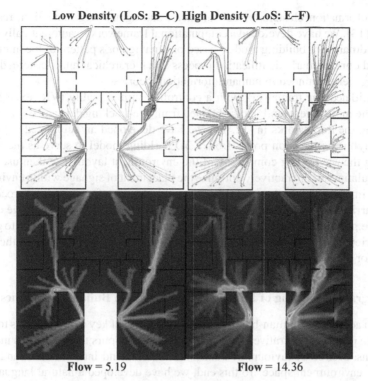

Flow = 5.19   Flow = 14.36

Fig. 2. Showing crowd-aware analytics for different crowd occupancy levels. Each column maps a different crowd occupancy level (e.g., Level of Service). Top row shows the color-coded crowd trajectories based on evacuation times (**T**) and traveled distances (**D**).The trajectories in *Red* show shorter traveled distances and evacuation times. Trajectories in *Blue* show longer distances and evacuation times. Average crowd flow values (**F**) for egress (i.e. occupants/second) are also shown. Bottom row shows crowd density heatmaps with high density in red (problematic areas – e.g., bottlenecks) and low density in blue. (Color figure online)

3.1 Wayfinding in Complex Environments

One of the most important functions of a building is its ability to inform how people can find their way in the building and is one of its prominent performance indicators. There are many aspects of the design of a building which contribute to human wayfinding such as its architectural complexity, the design and placement of signage, etc. Our research examines building models to investigate these aspects. We have conducted a study to investigate the effects of cues in the immediate environment and from other people on decision-making of human subjects during navigation through a virtual airport terminal. We observed that environment layouts with no visual cues led to shorter decision times and higher navigation accuracy compared to layouts with visual cues [54].

We have developed a biologically inspired computational model of human-signage interaction based on information theory. Our model allows for greater flexibility to modeling agent-signage interaction by adding different types of noise with respect to the environment (e.g., layout complexity, crowds, and other distractions), signage (e.g., multiple information clusters, visual salience), and agents (e.g., attention, reasoning, memory) [13]. We have developed a computational framework to automatically identify indoor landmarks for building models based on a navigator's pattern of locomotion. We formalized our landmark identification process as a hierarchical multi-criteria decision-making problem grounded in human information theories.

We validated our framework with a controlled virtual reality (VR) experiment to compare the most salient landmarks obtained from eye-tracking data and our framework [12]. Using the frameworks in [12, 13], we have developed an automated approach to extract wayfinding decision points from a 3D building model to serve as the basis for estimating the wayfinding complexity of the environment layout. We then used agent-based simulations to interactively optimize the placement of signage within environment design to improve wayfinding [11]. We have developed a framework to procedurally generate arrival and destination locations and times for virtual agents in large complex facilities (e.g., train station, airport, etc.). Our framework is expressive enough to generate a wide variety of crowds seen in real urban environments while maintaining the realism required for the complex, real-world simulations of a transit facility [34].

3.2 Integrated Modeling of Individuals, Crowds, and Building Semantics

In order to account for human-building interactions, one of key components is to be able to generate plausible "narratives" of human crowd behaviours that integrates individual motivations, desired behaviours of human movements and inter- actions, and semantics of the environment space. To this end, we have developed a natural language style interface to author collaborative and context-dependent virtual crowd behaviours in a given building environment to get insights on the mutual interactions between the people and the environment they inhabit [51]. We have also developed workflows (Fig. 3) to author complex, multi-agent behaviour narratives to satisfy time-varying building occupancy specifications and agent-level behaviour distributions using a prioritized resource allocation system to improve decision-making in designing a building layout. Such approaches can be used generate progressively more complex and plausible narratives that satisfy spatial, behavioral, and social constraints to modeling more realistic human-building interactions. We also presented a case study to highlight the effectiveness of this approach to seamlessly author behaviour narratives that can be used for visualizing, analyzing, and communicating how buildings may be used by their future inhabitants [52, 53].

3.3 Joint Modeling of Human-Building Interactions

It is important to consider the phenomenon like change in temperature with the presence of humans and propagation of sound caused by their movements, in an effort to jointly model the interaction between a building and the resulting behaviour of its inhabitants. To this end, we have developed a multi-paradigm approach to model event-based simulations of dynamic human behaviours in a building environment, which accounts for ecological conditions such as temperature changes, acoustics, sound propagation, human occupancy, and other environmental and occupancy phenomena that unfold at different

time scales [37, 38]. We have developed a node-based representation to jointly parameterize different spatial and human behavioural parameters to model human activities
and interactions in a building design [49].

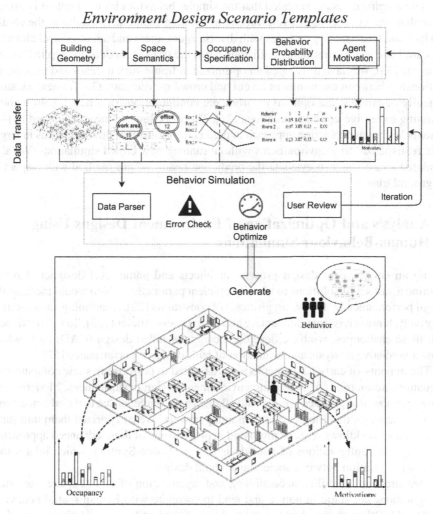

Fig. 3. A multi-constrained authoring of occupant behaviour narratives that accounts for building-
level occupancy specifications, zone-level behavior distributions, and occupant-level motivations.

3.4 Machine Learning for Human-Building Interaction

The use of advanced machine learning techniques allows learning data-driven models to
predict hard-to-interpret and complex factors governing human behaviour, such as the
amount of time it would take a crowd to evacuate a building, without needing to run

prohibitively expensive crowd-based simulations. We have developed a general imitation model to imitate the movement of expert agents in highly dense crowds. We trained our model using different learning techniques (e.g., Behavior Cloning and Generative Adversarial Imitation Learning) on a set of domain scenarios with diverse characteristics. The empirical results revealed that the simpler behavior cloning method is overall better than the more complex reinforcement learning method. In addition, the results also indicated that training samples with diverse agent-agent and agent-obstacle interactions are beneficial for reducing collisions when the trained models are applied to new scenarios [33]. We have developed an optimization framework to learn and understand relationship between environment layout and crowd movements. Our framework automatically determines the optimal environment configuration for a new layout without rerunning expensive crowd simulations [21]. The workflow we have developed in [42] presents an instant prediction approach to predict the movement flow of crowds in large-scale realistic building environments without running new crowd simulations. We also presented a case study to evaluate the prediction results of our method with respect to the ground truth.

4 Analysis and Optimization of Environment Designs Using Human-Behaviour Simulations

During an environment design process, architects and game-level designers have to examine a vast set of solutions to identify efficient parameters which would increase the design performance by following given set of constraints [22]. Examining each solution iteratively, however, is time-consuming and perhaps less efficient [35]. To help designers with these challenges, we have developed computer-aided design (CAD) tools which allow a predictive analysis and evaluation of built-designs' performance [52].

The majority of early CAD methods were limited to performing static computations of quantitative metrics for evaluating environment-design performances. Modern techniques can now also produce optimal and efficient environments due to the advancements in optimization methodologies and computing powers. We categorized them into static and dynamic workflows (e.g., as discussed in [46]). Some of these advanced approaches utilize spatial configurations of built-designs (e.g., Space-Syntax), which relates to a constructive relation between society and a built design.

Measures like visibility, accessibility, and organization of a built space from such configurations are static in nature and tend to correlate with human spatial behaviors [2, 20, 45]. Other approaches are more dynamic and utilize crowd simulations [23, 32], to account for how humans would act and interact with built designs. Measures like pedestrian flow, evacuation time, and travel distance from such approaches directly relate to HBI.

4.1 Integrated Computer-Aided Design Tools

We have developed several tools for environment analysis and optimization. We showed that optimization processes could produce the placement of architectural elements (e.g., doors and pillars) using human behavior simulations to improve pedestrian flow for

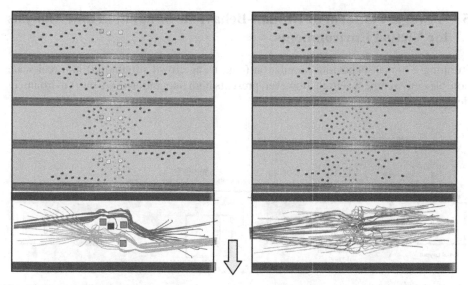

Fig. 4. Snapshots in raster order of two-way crossing scenario where two groups of agents move in opposite directions. The placement of pillars (left) at optimal locations improves the movement flow for both groups compared to the case without pillars (right).

not-yet-built environments [6, 14–16] (Fig. 4). We developed a user-in-the-loop approach to maximize the movement flow of occupants by optimizing the position of architectural obstacles in an Adaptive Mesh Refinement Approach [17]. We developed an environment optimization framework to automatically find optimal egress routes in a not-yet-built environment using human behavior simulations for safety-critical analysis and optimization [9]. Using another approach, we developed an analysis tool which allow architects and designers to analyze their designs with measures from Space-Syntax, as well as using dynamic human behaviour simulations [47]. Expanding on this approach we developed a human-centered AI approach that uses interactive optimization to analyze designs with measures from Space-Syntax and yield a diverse set of design recommendations for the users to choose from [4] (Fig. 5). Most recently, we have developed approaches [10, 19] which closes the loop between designers, stakeholders, and community by crowd-sourcing environment floorplans from the community by re-imagining the design process in a multiplayer game setting, Fig. 6.

4.2 Parametric Workflows

We have developed node-based frameworks using mainstream architecture modeling tools to parameterize environment and human-behavioral parameters for modeling human activities in not-yet-built environments. We showed occupants' trajectories and density heat maps for human-building interactions as analytics for designers and architects [49] (Fig. 2). Using the work in [49], we presented a case study to investigate joint parameter exploration and sequential parameter exploration workflows to identify the optimal set of environment and human behavioral parameters in a not-yet-built environment space [48].

5 A Single Platform to Human-Behaviour Simulation and Analysis for Virtual Environments

Running a human-behaviour simulation (e.g., using crowd simulation) in a real-scale complex environment setting, however, presents high integration costs into environment design pipelines.

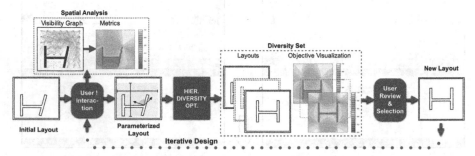

Fig. 5. With an initial environment design, the user specifies permissible alterations to the layout as bounds on the degree to which different environment elements can transform. The user then specifies one or more focal regions in the environment for which different spatial measures are computed to quantify visibility, accessibility, and organization of the space. A multi-objective hierarchical diversity optimization produces a set of diverse near-optimal solutions concerning user-defined optimality criteria, from which the user may select one and repeat the process as desired.

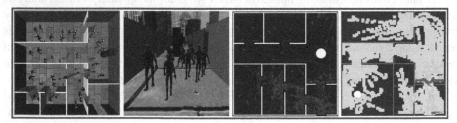

Fig. 6. Crowd-sourcing the environment floorplan from community by re-imagining the design process as a gamification approach, allowing game users to rapidly iterate on their designs while soliciting feedback from computer simulations of crowd movement and the designs of other players.

Prior solutions require expertise in a particular human simulation platform and present sophisticated technical and workflow challenges, such as loading building geometries, annotating environments with space semantics, configuring human-behaviour parameters, generating simulation results, and visualizing spatiotemporal data maps of space utilization. In addition, previous approaches have mostly been developed either as standalone systems or integrated in some particular environment design platform, limiting users' abilities to human-aware design of environments. The

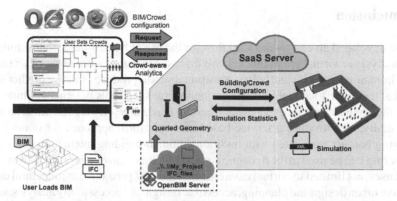

Fig. 7. A service-based cross-platform framework to simulate the dynamics of human-building interactions. It allows users to upload their environment models, set up human-behaviour parameters, runs the simulation and analyzes spatial visual and quantitative feedback for their environment designs.

goal is to democratize human-behaviour simulation and analysis of environments and have a single, integrated platform for researchers and industry experts from across disciplines to share environment models, analyze environments for human-behaviour simulations, crowd-source collaborative human-aware environment designs, and share simulation-driven analytics for environments with other users.

In this regard, we propose to use a cross-platform design-domain agnostic integration of dynamic human-behaviour simulation and analysis into environment design pipeline. To address the aforementioned challenges, we propose to adopt a Software-as-a-Service (SaaS) paradigm that is progressively gaining more traction in the industry because it separates the ownership, deployment, and maintenance of the software products from the end-users (e.g. clients).

Such a paradigm lets users utilize the software services on-demand by means of some client-side infrastructure (e.g. Application Program Interface (API), Web Interfaces, etc.) often via the internet [25]. It has several advantages both as a business model, but also for its users. It enables deep integration levels with other software in the work process to achieve targeted goals often in a cross-platform manner. In this way, specifically utilizing web-based or cloud services, allows tools to be used as needed on many platforms without re-configuring processes (Fig. 7).

We posit that such a platform would foster communication among design stakeholders across different disciplines. It would minimize the required expertise and hardware/software infrastructure dependencies for human-behaviour simulation analyses thus enabling the design of environments that are cognizant of the behaviour of the inhabitants in real-world conditions to ensure safety, productivity and satisfaction of the inhabitants.

6 Conclusion

We have developed an end-to-end workflow for the use of human-behaviour simulations in the analysis of virtual environments. We discuss the use of a broad set of techniques around human-movements and behaviour simulations to produce effective predictive and analytical tools. We then highlight the limitations for such tools in terms of limited user base as they require special expertise and certain hardware/software infrastructure to be used. Finally, we introduce a service-based cross-platform approach for removing the underlying barriers associated with traditional human-building interaction approaches, empowering it to be used in the dynamic context of human movement simulations and its myriad uses, not limited to: virtual environment analysis, predictive architectural design, predictive urban design and planning, accessible design and accessibility analysis, safety-critical analysis, and forensic analysis of disasters.

Acknowledgements. This research has been partially funded by grants from the NSERC Discovery, ISSUM, OGS, and in part by NSF IIS-1703883 and NSF S&AS-1723869.

References

1. Ali, S., Nishino, K., Manocha, D., Shah, M.: Modeling, simulation and visual analysis of crowds: a multidisciplinary perspective. In: Ali, S., Nishino, K., Manocha, D., Shah, M. (eds.) Modeling, Simulation and Visual Analysis of Crowds. TISVC, vol. 11, pp. 1–19. Springer, New York (2013). https://doi.org/10.1007/978-1-4614-8483-7_1
2. Bafna, S.: Space syntax: a brief introduction to its logic and analytical techniques. Environ. Behav. **35**(1), 17–29 (2003). https://doi.org/10.1177/0013916502238863, https://eab.sag epub.com/cgi/content/abstract/35/1/17
3. Berseth, G., Haworth, B., Kapadia, M., Faloutsos, P.: Multi-agent hierarchical reinforcement learning for humanoid navigation. In: Deep Reinforcement Learning Workshop at NeurIPS (2019)
4. Berseth, G., et al.: Interactive architectural design with diverse solution exploration. IEEE Trans. Vis. Comput. Graph. (2019)
5. Berseth, G., Kapadia, M., Faloutsos, P.: Robust space-time footsteps for agent-based steering. Computer Animation and Virtual Worlds (2015)
6. Berseth, G., Usman, M., Haworth, B., Kapadia, M., Faloutsos, P.: Environment optimization for crowd evacuation. Comput. Anim. Virtual Worlds **26**(3–4), 377–386 (2015)
7. Casadiego, L., Pelechano, N.: From one to many: simulating groups of agents with reinforcement learning controllers. In: Brinkman, W.-P., Broekens, J., Heylen, D. (eds.) IVA 2015. LNCS (LNAI), vol. 9238, pp. 119–123. Springer, Cham (2015). https://doi.org/10.1007/978-3-319-21996-7_12
8. Bastidas, L.C.: Social crowd controllers using reinforcement learning methods. Master's thesis, Universitat Politecnica de Catalunya (2014)
9. Cassol, V.J., et al.: Evaluating and optimizing evacuation plans for crowd egress. Comput. Graph. Appl. **37**(4), 60–71 (2017)
10. Chakraborty, N., Haworth, B., Usman, M., Berseth, G., Faloutsos, P., Kapadia, M.: Crowd sourced co-design of floor plans using simulation guided games. In: Proceedings of the Tenth International Conference on Motion in Games, pp. 1–5 (2017)

11. Dubey, R.K., Khoo, W.P., Morad, M.G., Hoelscher, C., Kapadia, M.: Autosign: a multi-criteria optimization approach to computer aided design of signage layouts in complex buildings. Comput. Graph. (2020)
12. Dubey, R.K., Sohn, S.S., Thrash, T., Hoelscher, C., Kapadia, M.: Identifying indoor navigation landmarks using a hierarchical multi-criteria decision framework. In: Motion, Interaction and Games, p. 11 (2019)
13. Dubey, R.K., Thrash, T., Kapadia, M., Hoelscher, C., Schinazi, V.R.: Information theoretic model to simulate agent-signage interaction for wayfinding. Cogn. Comput. 18 (2019)
14. Haworth, B., Usman, M., Berseth, G., Kapadia, M., Faloutsos, P.: Evaluating and optimizing level of service for crowd evacuations. In: ACM SIGGRAPH Conference on Motion in Games, pp. 91–96. ACM (2015)
15. Haworth, B., Usman, M., Berseth, G., Khayatkhoei, M., Kapadia, M., Faloutsos, P.: Towards computer assisted crowd aware architectural design. In: CHI Conference Extended Abstracts on Human Factors in Computing Systems, pp. 2119–2125. ACM (2016)
16. Haworth, B., Usman, M., Berseth, G., Khayatkhoei, M., Kapadia, M., Faloutsos, P.: Using synthetic crowds to inform building pillar placements. In: 2016 IEEE Virtual Humans and Crowds for Immersive Environments (VHCIE), pp. 7–11. IEEE (2016)
17. Haworth, B., Usman, M., Berseth, G., Khayatkhoei, M., Kapadia, M., Faloutsos, P.: Code: crowd-optimized design of environments. Comput. Anim. Virtual Worlds 28(6), e1749 (2017)
18. Haworth, M.B.: Biomechanical Locomotion Heterogeneity in Synthetic Crowds. Ph.D. thesis, York University, Toronto, Canada, November 2019
19. Haworth, M.B., et al.: Gamification of crowd-driven environment design. IEEE Comput. Graph. Appl. (2020)
20. Hillier, B., Hanson, J.: The Social Logic of Space. Press Syndicate of the University of Cambridge, Cambridge (1984)
21. Hu, K., Yoon, S., Pavlovic, V., Faloutsos, P., Kapadia, M.: Predicting crowd egress and environment relationships to support building design optimization. Comput. Graph. (2020)
22. Kalay, Y.E.: Architecture's New Media: Principles, Theories, and Methods of Computer-aided Design. MIT Press, Cambridge (2004)
23. Kapadia, M., Pelechano, N., Allbeck, J., Badler, N.: Virtual crowds: Steps toward behavioral realism. Synthesis Lectures Visual Comput. Comput. Graph. Anim. Comput. Photogr. Imaging 7(4), 1–270 (2015)
24. Kapadia, M., Singh, S., Hewlett, W., Faloutsos, P.: Egocentric affordance fields in pedestrian steering. In: Interactive 3D Graphics and Games, pp. 215–223. ACM (2009)
25. Laplante, P.A., Zhang, J., Voas, J.: Distinguishing between software-oriented architecture and software as a service: What's in a name? (2008)
26. Lee, J., Won, J., Lee, J.: Crowd simulation by deep reinforcement learning. In: Proceedings of the 11th Annual International Conference on Motion, Interaction, and Games, p. 2. ACM (2018)
27. Martinez-Gil, F., Lozano, M., Fernández, F.: Multi-agent Reinforcement Learning for Simulating Pedestrian Navigation. In: Vrancx, P., Knudson, M., Grześ, M. (eds.) ALA 2011. LNCS (LNAI), vol. 7113, pp. 54–69. Springer, Heidelberg (2012). https://doi.org/10.1007/978-3-642-28499-1_4
28. Martinez-Gil, F., Lozano, M., Fernandez, F.: Marl-ped: a multi-agent reinforcement learning based framework to simulate pedestrian groups. Simul. Model. Pract. Theory 47, 259–275 (2014)
29. Martinez-Gil, F., Lozano, M., Fernández, F.: Strategies for simulating pedestrian navigation with multiple reinforcement learning agents. Auton. Agent. Multi-Agent Syst. 29(1), 98–130 (2014). https://doi.org/10.1007/s10458-014-9252-6

30. Martinez-Gil, F., Lozano, M., Fernandez, F.: Emergent behaviors and scalability for multi-agent reinforcement learning-based pedestrian models. Simul. Model. Pract. Theory **74**, 117–133 (2017)
31. Nasir, F.M., Sunar, M.S.: A survey on simulating real-time crowd simulation. In: 2015 4th International Conference on Interactive Digital Media (ICIDM), pp. 1–5. IEEE (2015)
32. Pelechano, N., Allbeck, J.M., Kapadia, M., Badler, N.I.: Simulating Heterogeneous Crowds with Interactive Behaviors. CRC Press, Boca Raton (2016)
33. Qiao, G., Zhou, H., Kapadia, M., Yoon, S., Pavlovic, V.: Scenario generalization of data-driven imitation models in crowd simulation. In: Motion, Interaction and Games, p. 11 (2019)
34. Ricks, B., Dobson, A., Krontiris, A., Bekris, K., Kapadia, M., Roberts, F.: Generation of crowd arrival and destination locations/times in complex transit facilities. Vis. Comput. **36**(8), 1651–1661 (2019). https://doi.org/10.1007/s00371-019-01761-z
35. Rittel, H.: Some principles for the design of an educational system for design. J. Archit. Educ. **26**(1–2), 16–27 (1971)
36. Schaumann, D., Kapadia, M.: Modeling social and spatial behavior in built environments: current methods and future directions. Soc.-Behav. Model. Complex Syst. 673–695 (2019)
37. Schaumann, D., et al.: Join: an integrated platform for joint simulation of occupant-building interactions. Archit. Sci. Rev. 12 (2019)
38. Schaumann, D., et al.: Toward a multi-level and multi-paradigm platform for building occupant simulation. In: Proceedings of the Symposium on Simulation for Architecture and Urban Design, pp. 169–76 (2019)
39. Seitz, M.J., Dietrich, F., Koster, G.: A study of pedestrian stepping behaviour for crowd simulation. Transp. Res. Procedia **2**, 282–290 (2014)
40. Singh, S., Kapadia, M., Hewlett, B., Reinman, G., Faloutsos, P.: A modular framework for adaptive agent-based steering. In: Interactive 3D Graphics and Games, p. 9. ACM (2011)
41. Singh, S., Kapadia, M., Reinman, G., Faloutsos, P.: Footstep navigation for dynamic crowds. Comput. Anim. Virtual Worlds **22**(2–3), 151–158 (2011)
42. Sohn, S.S., Moon, S., Zhou, H., Yoon, S., Pavlovic, V., Kapadia, M.: Deep crowdflow prediction in built environments. arXiv preprint arXiv:1910.05810 (2019)
43. Thalmann, D., Musse, S.R.: Springer (2013)
44. Torrey, L.: Crowd simulation via multi-agent reinforcement learning. In: Proceedings of the Sixth AAAI Conference on Artificial Intelligence and Interactive Digital Entertainment, pp. 89–94. AIIDE 2010, AAAI Press (2010). https://dl.acm.org/citation.cfm?id=3014666.3014683
45. Turner, A., Penn, A.: Making isovists syntactic: isovist integration analysis. In: 2nd International Symposium on Space Syntax, Brasilia. Citeseer (1999)
46. Usman, M.: Towards Static and Dynamic Analysis of Architectural Elements. Master's thesis, York University, Toronto, Canada, September 2016
47. Usman, M., Schaumann, D., Haworth, B., Berseth, G., Kapadia, M., Faloutsos, P.: Interactive spatial analytics for human-aware building design. In: Motion, Interaction, and Games, p. 13. ACM (2018)
48. Usman, M., Schaumann, D., Haworth, B., Kapadia, M., Faloutsos, P.: Joint exploration and analysis of high-dimensional design-occupancy templates. In: Motion, Interaction and Games, p. 35. ACM (2019)
49. Usman, M., Schaumann, D., Haworth, B., Kapadia, M., Faloutsos, P.: Joint parametric modeling of buildings and crowds for human-centric simulation and analysis. In: Lee, J.-H. (ed.) CAAD Futures 2019. CCIS, vol. 1028, pp. 279–294. Springer, Singapore (2019). https://doi.org/10.1007/978-981-13-8410-3_20
50. Whyte, J.K., Hartmann, T.: How digitizing building information transforms the built environment (2017)

51. Zhang, X., Schaumann, D., Faloutsos, P., Kapadia, M.: Knowledge-powered inference of crowd behaviors in semantically rich environments. In: Proceedings of the AAAI Conference on Artificial Intelligence and Interactive Digital Entertainment, vol. 15, pp. 202–208 (2019)
52. Zhang, X., Schaumann, D., Haworth, B., Faloutsos, P., Kapadia, M.: Coupling agent motivations and spatial behaviors for authoring multiagent narratives. Comput. Anim. Virtual Worlds **30**(3–4), e1898 (2019)
53. Zhang, X., Schaumann, D., Haworth, B., Faloutsos, P., Kapadia, M.: Multiconstrained authoring of occupant behavior narratives in architectural design. Simul. Ser. **51**(8), 177–184 (2019)
54. Zhao, H., Thrash, T., Grossrieder, A., Kapadia, M., Moussaad, M., Holscher, C., Schinazi, V.R.: The interaction between map complexity and crowd movement on navigation decisions in virtual reality. Royal Soc. Open Sci. **7**(3), 191523 (2020)

Chapter 10
The Adequacy of Artificial Intelligence Tools to Combat Misinformation

Nadejda Komendantova[1]([✉]), Love Ekenberg[1,2], Wolfgang Amann[3], Mats Danielson[1,2], and Vasilis Koulolias[2]

[1] International Institute for Applied Systems Analysis (IIASA), Laxenburg, Austria
komendan@iiasa.ac.at
[2] Stockholm University, Stockholm, Sweden
[3] Institute for Real Estate, Construction and Housing Ltd., Vienna, Austria

Abstract. We discuss a computationally meaningful process for evaluating misinformation detection tools in the context of immigration in Austria, admitting for the wide variety of qualitative and quantitative data involved. The evaluation machinery is based on a library of tools to support the process in both the elicitation and evaluation phases, including automatized preference elicitation procedures, development of result robustness measures as well as algorithms for co-evaluating quantitative and qualitative data in various formats. The focus of our work is on the Austrian limited profit housing sector, which makes up 24% of the total housing stock and more than 30% of the total of new construction, with a high share of migrants as tenants. We describe the results from workshops analysing the existing misinformation on migration issues in Austria, where we also introduced a co-creation phase. To better understand the stakeholder ecosystem and the lifecycle of misinformation towards social conflicts, we applied a software for integrated multi-stakeholder-multi-attribute problems under risk subject to incomplete or imperfect information, based on the evaluation machinery. Perceived countermeasures of importance turned out to be institutional and regulatory measures in combination with the creation of info-points, measures to raise awareness and stimulate critical thinking, production of tools to deal with misinformation, provision of reliable sources of information, and creation of a culture of thinking.

Keywords: Misinformation · Migration · Austria · Limited profit housing sector · Social media · Preconditions · And social conflicts

1 Introduction

1.1 Misinformation and Resilience in the Digital Age

Misinformation and its dissemination to the general public is one of the most pressing issues facing our world today. It has existed for a long time, but modern and emerging communications technologies and the rise of social media have facilitated the spread of

© Springer Nature Switzerland AG 2021
F. S. Roberts and I. A. Sheremet (Eds.): Resilience in the Digital Age, LNCS 12660, pp. 172–198, 2021.
https://doi.org/10.1007/978-3-030-70370-7_10

misinformation to unprecedented levels, which has the potential to lead to social and political conflicts on a global scale.

The impact of the spread of misinformation has become central to politics and greatly influences electoral outcomes, health, environment, and foreign policy. It has become a common part of our digital media environments, and it is compromising the ability of members of human societies to form fact-based opinions and policies. The World Economic Forum listed digital misinformation as a key challenge to modern societies. Misinformation influences public perception. Further, our conceptualization and formulation of policies are heavily influenced by public perception. Perception affects people's recognition and interpretation of information, and how they respond to this information. The increasing omnipresence of misinformation generates greater misperceptions, affecting policymaking in many domains.

For example, one actual instance of this impact is currently found in the perceptions within the socially constructed immigration discourse, influenced by factors such as socialization, experience, awareness as well as general sentiments in the media reporting. Misinformation about such socially disputed issues can influence existing prejudice towards migrants that is frequently influenced by preconditions, resulting from information flows.

More precisely, misinformation is defined as false or inaccurate information that is spread either intentionally or unintentionally (Antoniadis et al. 2015), while fake news usually means that much of information which people receive about current events or policy debates are unvetted. There are different types of mis and disinformation (Koulolias et al. 2018):

- satire or parody when there is no intention to cause harm, but there is potential to fool a consumer of the information as to its truth,
- misleading content with misleading use of information to frame an issue or individual,
- imposter content when genuine sources are impersonated,
- fabricated content when new content is 100% false, designed to deceive and do harm,
- false connection when headlines visuals or captions do not support the content,
- false context when genuine content is shared with false contextual information,
- manipulated content when genuine information or imagery is manipulated to deceive the audience.

There are no simple solutions for combatting misinformation, but for establishing systems through which people are fully informed and the counter-mechanisms to misinformation are well-anchored in a variety of ways. Citizens, journalists, and policymakers must be empowered with socio-technical solutions to increase the overall societal resilience against misinformation, to support a misinformation-resilient society by creating more informed behaviours and policies for exposing confirmation-biased networks to different perceptions and corrective information. A part of this is to provide policymakers with elaborated misinformation analysis tools to support their policy making and validation processes and the aim of this paper is to investigate desirable features of tools for the purpose of rapid dissemination of misinformation.

For such tools to be effective, they must be well-integrated in a user context. Therefore, we base our methodology on the concept of co-creation, in the sense that affected parties co-create together towards mutually shared goals or values. We discuss the applicability of such tools in the context of immigration in Austria with a focus on the Austrian limited profit housing sector (LPHS) - a key pillar of the Austrian policy on socio-economic development and political stability.

An active citizen involvement in a co-creative process to gain acceptability and promote a user capacity in social innovations and co-creation, can increase efficiency of decision-support tools in frames of participatory modelling (Komendantova et al. 2014). Co-creation, while involving representatives of various stakeholders' groups, can also increase the legitimacy of decision-making processes and support the design of compromise solutions for contested policy options (Komendantova et al. 2018). Herein, we used such methods in stakeholder workshop settings to both better understand the stakeholder ecosystem and the lifecycle of misinformation towards social conflicts in an environment considering contextual and cultural variances. Co-creation can also be beneficial in development of new tools while adapting the features of these tools to the requirements of various stakeholders' groups in order to increase their usage and usefulness (Joshi et al. 2018), why we also apply a co-creative framework for desception of desirable features of the combatting tools as such.

There are indeed several automatic detection tools for misinformation, many times using machine learning techniques – a sub-category of the frequently hyped term artificial intelligence (AI). Such automated digital tools have often been useful in dealing with the phenomena of misinformation and for measuring and developing trust-ensuring capacities. Earlier examples are, for instance, (Golbeck 2005; Adali et al. 2010; Canini et al. 2011). More recently, and for obvious reasons, there is an abundance of approaches that have been suggested for the social media areas, such as (Jia et al. 2017; Jiang et al. 2014; Pichon et al. 2014; Zhao et al. 2016). These tools are useful for several reasons. First such tools can become neutral arbiters of information trustfulness measuring. Second, they might allow for evaluation of information based on algorithms while (potentially) avoiding some biases in judgment connected with human reasoning. Third, many messages are operating with emotions rather than with ration and can more systematically be detected using statistical data or other types of scientific evidence. Fourth, such tools can provide comprehensible interfaces making them attractive to people without interest in the details of the detection algorithms and deliberations behind them. However, it is, as always, an open question which features here are perceived as useful for a more general audience. A main aim of this article is therefore to investigate which features of such tools that are desirable.

1.2 Participatory Processes

Various discourses exist in the literature and policy debate about the usefulness and organisation of co-creation processes and participatory processes. An early, but still mature survey, was provided where a large set of participatory modelling and processes, as well as several problematic issues involved, are discussed. Quite recently, (Porwol et al. 2016) has provided an informed coverage of e-participation and requirements for social software infrastructure. There is also a field discussing the many intrinsically problematic issues in the underlying overall concepts of democracy, were some examples are (Dahlberg 2011; Hansson et al. 2014; Orihuela and Obi 2012; Pirannejad and Janssen

2017). There are also numerous approaches to open government and participatory effects (Al-Jamal and Abu-Shanab 2016; Komendatova et al. 2018) as well as an abundance of overviews with different definitions, theories, and methods, for instance (Freschi 2009; Macintosh et al. 2009; Medaglia 2007; Sæbø et al. 2008; Sanford and Rose 2007; Medaglia 2012; Hansson and Ekenberg 2018; Naranjo-Zolotov et al. 2018).

Independent of the manifold of research in the area, the participatory practice is not always as developed as might be desired. Generally, public discourses recognise public engagement and co-creation only as a feature to reach public and social acceptance. This discourse takes, for instance, place in frames of the so-called Not-in-My-Backyard or "NIMBY" thinking. The NIMBY attitude has had a strong influence in shaping how industry, policymakers and media think about public engagement and address sceptical responses. Many social scientists argue even that the NIMBY discourse is a misleading, inaccurate, and pejorative way of understanding objections (Wolsink 2006). Another practice discourse is the so-called "decide-announce-defend" (DAD) model. In this model, policy solutions are developed by scientists together with government officials and are then communicated to the general public.

Herein, we argue for a contradictory view to such discourses, under the assumption that an integration of views of also lay people and public values, and not only from "educated experts", can lead to enhanced legitimacy of decision-making process and trust. This idea been expressed by many, such as, e.g., (Renn 2008).

However, participation must be formalised to be effective. Participatory modelling is an integrated part of a co-creation methodology and is the process which allows taking into consideration facts, but also values by asking questions and collecting feedback from stakeholders (Forester 1999). It requires the active participation of stakeholders and two-way communication, where the feedback is collected, analysed and implemented (Funtowicz and Ravetz 1994). The process of stakeholder interaction leads to an enhanced understanding of the different points of view, criteria, preferences and trade-offs involved in decision-making (Antunes et al. 2006). Such processes can nevertheless be meaningless in an unstructured format, and the actual processes involved must admit for the wide variety of qualitative and quantitative data involved, requiring significant computational efforts for the evaluations; which is why we have developed a library of tools to support participatory processes in both the elicitation and evaluation phases. This includes automatized preference elicitation procedures, development of result robustness measures as well as algorithms for co-evaluating quantitative and qualitative data in various formats. An important technical component is adequately representation and evaluation of second-order information to facilitate decision making based on incomplete input data using second-order distributions of belief in the basic utilities, probabilities, and criteria weights. This practice then allows for better and more transparent discrimination between the resulting values of the decision alternatives.

1.3 Misinformation and Migration

Migration is not a new phenomenon in Austria since it has already been considered a country of migration for many decades. The migration always showed a character of waves that were frequently connected to political events outside of Austria or to political decisions inside Austria. Furthermore, migration inflows varied significantly in the past.

These inflows were strongly connected with political interventions, such as the invitation of guest workers in the 1970s, and political events, such as the fall of the Iron Curtain and Yugoslavia wars in 1990s and the Middle East crisis in 2015. The annual balance of immigration and emigration for 2018 shows that the consistency rate of the net migration rate is positive, which means that Austria remains an immigration country. Notably, in the year 2015 Austria ranked as the 4th largest receiver in the EU of asylum seekers, with most of the refugees originating from the Middle East, Central Asia, or African countries (Migration Council for Austria 2016).

Currently, 16% of the Austrian population are migrants and 23% are people with migration backgrounds. Migrants also bring their culture and traditions which enrich interaction in everyday life situations. This is more evident in the multifamily housing sector where people interact daily; consequently, the background transforms into a more heterogeneous one in terms of cultural, ethnic and religious backgrounds.

Austria has significant experience in the integration of migrants. The majority of Austrians welcome customs, traditions as well as the national languages that are brought in, especially from southern and far-eastern countries, and identify them as an enrichment. Such examples are folk-dancing groups who meet in the community rooms or festivals celebrated with traditions from different countries (Brech and Feigelfeld 2017). Another example is the integration of migrants in the limited profit housing where the city of Vienna integrated a high share of migrants, up to 50% of inhabitants, through projects such as the Interethnic Neighbourhood Housing Model and the Liesing "Globaler Hof" (Global Estate).

The issue of integration regained its actuality at the start of 2015 with the arrival of a new wave of refugees from the Middle East and North African countries. Research on migration and societal attitudes in Austria in late 2015 shows the dominance of the "welcoming culture" in the country, which was characterized by the large involvement of civil society (De Jong and Atac 2017). Also, interviews with refugees in 2015–2016 reveal that only a few respondents reported experiences of xenophobic attitudes towards them (Kohlbacher 2015). However, Rheindorf and Wodak (2019) show that some elements of extreme-right discourse are being channelled through social media and that these elements are frequently based on misinformation. Further, considering that technological innovations are increasing the speed and spread of misinformation, the development of tools to address the phenomena of misinformation becomes important.

2   Background

2.1   The Austrian Limited Profit Housing Sector and Migration

The focus of our work is on the Austrian limited profit housing sector (LPHS) for three reasons. First, this sector is a key pillar of the Austrian policy on socio-economic development and political stability. The owners in the sector are municipalities, the finance sector, trade unions, charity organizations, private pensions, etc. Currently, the sector makes up 24% of the total housing stock and more than 30% of the total of new constructions (IIBW 2016).

Secondly, this sector has a high share of migrants as tenants. Migrants make up a significant share of the inhabitants in the Austrian limited profit housing sector because the Austrian General Act on Equal Treatment prohibits discrimination regarding access to public goods and services for any reason such as gender, ethnicity, or age. For example, in Sozialbau, which is the leading Austrian limited profit housing association, the share of residents with a migration background, such as foreign nationals or Austrian citizens born abroad, reached 38% according to the data for the year 2015, among them 15% of residents came from Turkey, 14% from Bosnia, 8% from Poland, and 7% from Croatia, followed by 4% from Serbia, 3% from Germany, and 2% each from Bulgaria, Macedonia, Montenegro and Romania (Ludl 2017).

Thirdly, this sector cannot be compared to social housing in other countries, which are mainly oriented towards low-income families. In Austria, LPHS hosts both low- and middle-income families. A further characteristic of this sector is that migrants are more strongly orienting themselves towards local conventions and middle-class forms of everyday interaction than in municipal housings (Brech and Feigelfeld 2017). Also, the hurdles to closer contacts with migrants within LPHS are not so high.

More than 50% of the people in this housing sector maintain intercultural contacts which go beyond saying "hello." Also, more than 70% of the residents have an intention towards having closer contact with neighbours beyond polite gestures (Brech and Feigelfeld 2017). But conflicts still exist. In the year 2016 alone, more than 243 mediation cases in one housing estate were recorded by external and in-house mediators. Around 40% of all complaints were about the behaviour of children and teenagers while more than 50% were about the lack of cleanness and the presence of noise (Ludl 2017). These conflicts are getting intensified in the summer when windows are open and balconies, terraces, and other communal places are used more intensively. No correlation has been established between frequent reasons for conflicts such as noise, the behaviour of children, and perceptions of cleanness and interethnic background (Brech and Feigelfeld 2017). Although more than 60% of all respondents see contacts with neighbours of different cultural backgrounds and perceive different cultural symbols as enrichment, less than 30% would like to have a high share of migrants (50%-50%) in the housing estate (Ludl 2017).

Statistics show that complaints are getting intensified with age. Examples collected by Sozialbau show that the older a resident is, the more likely he or she will register a complaint, as well as become concerned about migrants. This can be connected to the feeling of place attachment and representatives of other cultures affecting it. Evidence shows that place attachment gets stronger with age (Kohlbacher et al. 2015).

Concerns about people with Muslim backgrounds were mentioned more frequently, whereas less frequent concerns were about people from Balkan and Eastern European countries (Brech and Feigelfeld 2017a).

Security concerns were never a matter of these complaints, neither the religion itself. However, religious expressions, such as a headscarf and its visibility in everyday life, caused questions. During a survey conducted at the Global Estate, of all characteristics of migrants the religious symbols have the greatest impact, because of their visibility. This frequently resonates with the feelings of Austrians, because due to the political processes in the recent past, the religious symbols have largely lost their significance in building an identity. In contrast, many migrants integrate religious symbols into their appearances, such as certain types of beards or cloths.

Currently, it is not so much the cultural background but the religious background which became a prominent topic in public and political discourses (Schmiedel and Schmidt 2018). This is mainly connected to the fact that previous waves of migrants were from secular or Catholic countries. In comparison to the 1960s, when almost 90% of Austrians were Roman Catholic, by the year 2016 this proportion dropped to 64%. Currently, the majority of migrants are predominantly Muslims (Castles et al. 2015). Nowadays, religion also plays an important role in sustaining migrants through their journey (Brech and Feigelfeld 2017b) and their adaptation and integration in the host society (Brech and Feigelfeld 2017c).

2.2 Perceptions of Migration and Impacts of Media

Previous research shows that it is not everyday situations that are influencing attitudes to migrants, but rather opinions and perceptions developed about migrants (Observatory of Public Attitudes to Migration 2018). Perceptions towards migration are frequently based on a subjectively perceived collision of interests. Therefore, it is a characteristic that is socially constructed and influenced by several factors such as socialization, experience, awareness, and many others. It is also a social construct that defines what can be seen as improper behaviour and what cannot. For example, it is a cultural construct regarding values such as cleanness or noiselessness.

These perceptions can be frequently influenced by preconditions such as preconceived attitudes towards migrants. These preconditions can be a result of information flow or personal experience. Without being addressed or without further information, preconditions can form prejudices. Prejudices are frequently formed at the societal level and their effects can be serious for the coexistence in the housing communities. Preconditions also frequently appear in situations with limited information or experience. For example, migrants from countries with unfamiliar cultures are confronted with more preconditional judgements because of their appearance, clothing, or form of communication.

Importantly, the perception of foreign characteristics is frequently determined by general sentiments in the media reporting. Dorostkar and Preisinger (2017) analysed online discourses about migration in forums such as derStandard.at. Der Standard is an Austrian liberal newspaper that has one of the widest circulations. It was also one of the first newspapers offering a digital platform for discussions. On average, the forums of the newspaper have 20,000 new reader postings per day. The forums for reader commentaries are institutionally framed by the forum rules, which have ethical standards and discursive practices such as rational argumentation and respect. There are also criteria such as limits on text length, anonymity, and moderation. The editors of the forums respond to violations of these rules by deleting the postings or accounts in question.

Dorostkar and Preisinger (2017) follow the assumption that an online reality created in internet discussion forums is not the mirror of reality but that both are domains of social reality and interact with each other. They found out that anonymity and the lack of social mechanisms for sanctioning facilitate the production of discriminatory language towards other groups of people. Their results show elements of prejudice discourse in such forums. They derive these results by using macro codes such as authority, justice, history, homogeneity in terms of conformity and culture, as well as usefulness, victim, responsibility. They found the following elements of discriminatory discourse:

- "Austrians on paper but not in reality" is a discourse which supports that immigrants differ from locals in terms of cultural characteristics, and as such these immigrants are not "true Austrians" even after receiving citizenship and thus cause problems to the society of the receiving country.
- The "good and bad migrants" discourse has key elements on education and welfare of migrants saying that if a person is highly skilled in a professional field, such as a scientist or skilled worker, or if the person is a member of the upper class, this is a useful migrant.
- The discourse about migration and education includes elements such as the proportion of pupils of a first language other than German which negatively influences education and German in schools. This discourse uses the generalisation that if persons have a first language other than German, then they don't know German or they are less intelligent than native speakers. It also reflects in the discourse that "if fewer pupils with migration background attend a given school, the higher is the level of education in this school".
- Elements of the rejection of justified criticism, such as "because certain statements are seen as politically incorrect, certain factual problems in our society cannot or can only inadequately be articulated and thus also solved".

Little evidence exists about the spread of misinformation regarding migration in social media. However, because misinformation has existed already for a long time and that today new technologies and social media enable its rapid spread, the need to deal with misinformation gains its actuality. Additionally, even though Austria has in general, a welcoming culture towards migrants, some elements of discriminative discourses still exist in online forums. This demonstrates the importance of creating and providing tools that can address the issues of misinformation regarding migration and migrants.

3 Methodology

3.1 Empirical Data Collection Through Stakeholders' Process

The methodology of this paper includes three steps. The first one was a comprehensive analysis of the existence of misinformation and migration issues in Austria. This review was compiled by interviews with key stakeholders from the limited profit housing sector. Interviews and literature reviews helped to identify stakeholders for two participatory workshops. The workshops aimed to discuss the issues of misinformation and expectations and preferences about the features of proposed artificial intelligence tools to deal with the phenomena of misinformation.

Several stakeholders from the Austrian decision-making processes on migration and housing expressed their interest in the project and the workshop. Among them were the Austrian Chamber of Labour, LPH companies "Neues Leben," "Siedlungsgenossen-schaft Neunkirchen," "Heim," "Wohnbauvereinigung für Privatangestellte", Housing Service of the Municipality of Vienna, as well as the Austrian Association of Cities and Towns, which has 252 members among the total of 2100 local authorities representing 55% of the total population in Austria. The announcement about the workshop was also published in social media such as Facebook, Twitter, and LinkedIn, and 38 citizens expressed their interest in participation. Consequently, three groups of stakeholders (decision-makers, journalists/fact-checkers, and citizens) were established. Each group included 7 participants.

The first stakeholder workshop was organized by IIASA (International Institute of Applied Systems Analysis) at the premises of the Ministry of Economy and Digitalization of the Austrian Republic on the 28th of March 2019 in Vienna. The workshop included several innovative methods of stakeholder dialogue such as games based on word associations, participatory landscape mapping, as well as wish lists for policy-makers and interactive online "fake news" games.

The roundtable discussion during the first workshop included the following questions:

1. How do you define misinformation regarding migration and migrants? What is misinformation "spread" in housing regarding migration and migrants?
2. When or in which cases do misinformation on social conflicts arise? Why and how does misinformation about migration in social media lead to social conflicts?
3. Which are the most common reasons for spreading misinformation? Either in general, in all media, or in social networks in particular? Which are the most common reasons for spreading disinformation or misinformation?
4. Has misinformation ever been unpleasant or dangerous for you personally? Why?
5. Which are the challenges for you personally to deal with misinformation in a private or professional context?

The sessions included co-creation activities and the collection of stakeholders' perceptions about misinformation, sessions on everyday practices to deal with misinformation, co-creation activities on challenges connected with misinformation, and discussions about the needs to deal with misinformation and possible solutions.

The second workshop was organised by IIASA on the 20th of November 2019 at the premises of the Ministry of Economy and Digitalization of the Austrian Republic. The goal of the workshop was to discuss the features of misinformation and to conduct decision-making experiments with application of Multi-Criteria Decision Analysis (MCDA) to evaluate preferences of various stakeholders' groups, including journalists, fact checkers, policymakers and citizens, regarding features of online tools to address misinformation in social media.

Following a very similar lifecycle to the one proposed by Gouillart and Hallet (2015), the second workshop aimed at applying co-creation methods to better understand the stakeholder ecosystem (Beierle 2002; Blicharska et al. 2011) and the life cycle of misinformation towards social conflicts (Cook and Kothari 2001). We identified relevant stakeholders from the groups of decision-makers, citizens, and journalists/fact-checkers. We also built the environment considering contextual and cultural variances, to assess the needs of each stakeholder group and create something together that would be useable and useful to each stakeholder. These types of co-creation efforts will specifically target design engagement and resilience methods with respect to misinformation and the online tools to be developed (Fiorino 1990; Newig et al. 2013).

During the workshop, participants discussed the features of tools to deal with misinformation. Additionally, the participants suggested the desired features of the tools and possible extensions thereof. The participants also reviewed the positive and negative sides of the options available. As a result, a list of features important to the participants was developed.

These features were ranked in a decision-making experiment. The participants ranked the features of the tools under each of the three pre-determined criteria and were free to suggest other possible tools or extensions to the existing ones. Ensuing the feature ranking, the criteria were ranked in the same way as the tool features. Before commencing the criteria ranking, each criterion was discussed to make sure that the participants agreed on their definitions. The participants could also change or add further criteria if deemed necessary by the stakeholder groups.

Overall, the following 13 features were selected for ranking:

- *Awareness*: I want the Browser Plug-In to make me aware of misinforming content that I come across when I am online; for example, a news article, in the browser tab I am currently using.
- *Why, who and when*: I want to know why a claim has been flagged as misinforming; and I want to know who has flagged it and when.
- *How it spread and who*: I come across something that I find misinformative. I would like to know how this information has spread online and who has shared it.
- *Life cycle or timeline*: I want to know the life cycle (timeline) of a misinforming post/article; for example, when was it first published, how many fact-checkers have debunked it, and when was it reshared again?
- *Share over time*: I want to be able to quickly understand how much misinformation people have shared over time through an overall misinformation score.
- *How misinformative an item is*: I want to be able to quickly understand how much misinformation a news item or tweet may contain through the provision of an overall "misinformation score".
- *Instant feedback on arrival*: when I encounter a tweet from someone else, which contains misinformative content, I want to be informed.
- *Inform on consistent accounts*: I want the Co-Inform system to inform me which accounts (within my network) consistently generate/spread misinformation.
- *Self-notification*: I want the Co-Inform tools to notify me whenever I repeatedly share misinformation.
- *Credibility indicators*: I want to see credibility indicators that I will immediately understand, or I want the credibility indicators to look very familiar, like other indicators online.
- *Post support or refute*: I want to be able to post links to reputable articles and data that support or refute the story or claim.
- *Tag veracity*: I want to be able to tag the veracity of an element (tweet, story, image or a sentence/claim) in the current tab I am seeing.
- *Platform feedback*: I want to be able to receive feedback about what the platform is doing and has done with the tags and evidence I have submitted.

These features were ranked in three rounds (the procedure is described in more detail below) for three overarching questions (criteria) why tools to address misinformation are needed:

- Building trust
- Thinking twice
- Transparency

Afterward, the three criteria were ranked according to their importance as most, medium, and least.

The results from both workshops formed a basis for the development of two artificial intelligence tools, vis-à-vis a browser plug-in to raise awareness of citizens about misinformation and dashboards for fact-checking journalists and policymakers. These tools aim to show detected misinformation and its origins.

3.2 Elicitation and Analyses of Multi-stakeholder-Multi-criteria Problems

The method of analysis of stakeholder preferences was based on a multi-criteria decision analysis (MCDA) framework which is a decision analytical approach for co-creation in a multi-stakeholder/multi-criteria environment (Ekenberg et al. 2017; Pluchinotta et al. 2019). MCDA allows analysing and solving decision problems with multiple criteria and stakeholders by specifying a set of attributes that represents the relevant aspects of the possible outcomes of a decision. Value functions are then defined over the alternatives for each attribute and a weight function is defined over the attribute set.

Thus, the entire background framework was a decision analytical approach for co-creation in a multi-stakeholder/multi-criteria environment, supported by elaborated decision analytical tools and processes:

- a framework for elicitation of stakeholder preferences;
- a decision engine for strategy evaluation;
- a set of processes for negotiation;
- a set of decision rule mechanisms;
- processes for combining these items;
- various types of implementations of the above.

These components apply to decision components, such as:

- agenda settings and overall processes;
- stakeholders;
- goals;
- strategies/policies/sub-strategies/part-policies, etc.;
- consequences/effects;
- qualifications and sometimes quantifications of the components;
- negotiation protocols;
- decision rules and processes.

A variety of methods for analysing and resolving decision problems involving several criteria and stakeholders have been proposed in recent decades (Amerasinghe 2008; Berry et al. 2003; Hashim et al. 2010). These methods were applied for evaluation of participation in environmental assessment (Diduck and Sinclair 2002; Dietz and Stern 2008), environmental governance (Newig and Fritsch 2009) and environmental management (Reed 2008), as well as land-use policy (Koontz 2005; Schwilch et al. 2009; Stringer et al. 2007), agriculture (Pretty 1995) and forest management (Valente 2013). Internet, electronic participation and e-governance are the new areas of research and the volume of scientific works in this area is growing constantly (Pirannejad and Janssen 2017; Wimmer 2007). This includes citizen electronic participation (Alathur et al. 2014), e-democracy (Anttiroiko 2003; Bindu and Kumar 2019) and open government (Al-JamalEmad and Abu-Shanab 2016), as well as the question of big data (Bright and Margetts 2016).

A widespread method in common use is to make preference assessments by specifying a set of attributes that represent the relevant aspects of the possible outcomes of a decision (Amerasinghe 2008; Habitat 2009, Sharma et al. 2003). Value functions are then defined over the available courses of action for each attribute and a weight function is then defined over the attribute set. An option is to define a weighting function with fixed numbers on a normalised scale and then define numerical functions over the alternatives, where these are also mapped to fixed values, after which the numbers are aggregated and the total score for each alternative is calculated.

One of the problems with many standard models, is that, in practice, numerically accurate information is rarely available, and most decision-makers experience difficulties in providing realistic information when, for instance, eliciting weights. The general and ubiquitous lack of even remotely complete information greatly increases this problem. Several attempts have been made to solve it. For the analyses here, we used a method and software for integrated evaluation of multi-stakeholder-multi-criteria problems subject to incomplete or imprecise information. The software originates from our previous work on the evaluation of decision situations of that kind, cf., e.g., (Danielson et al. 2019). For the decision structure, we omit exact numbers and instead use rankings, relations and interval statements. To alleviate the problem of overlapping results, we use a new method of evaluation based on the beliefs in the resulting weighed average intervals, but without attempting to introduce further complicated aspects into the decision situation. Due to the complexity of these calculations, we use the software DecideIT for the analyses (Danielson et al. 2020). Versions of DecideIT have been used successfully in a variety of decision contexts, such as large-scale energy planning (Komendantova et al. 2018), allocation planning (Larsson et al. 2018), demining (Ekenberg et al. 2018), financial risks (Danielson and Ekenberg 2018), gold mining (Mihai et al. 2015), and many others (Ekenberg et al. 2017).

The stakeholder workshops were conducted according to a blank card convergence (BCC) method. Each stakeholder group (decision-makers, citizens, and journalists/fact-checkers) were given the cards denoting the same 13 tool features described above. The purpose of each session was to rank these features by creating a preference order from most desired to least desired. The groups had a ranking scale at their disposal where they could place the features. The most important features were to be placed on top and the least important at the bottom. If two features were perceived to be almost as important, they occupied the same step, while if the difference was small but clearly noticeable, they occupied adjacent steps. In this way, the distance between two features showed the perceived difference in importance. The group was also given blank cards to occupy/make up steps where no feature resided. If, for example, there was a large perceived difference between features F2 and F7, two blank cards could be placed in between them. There were several rounds, and in each round, each group member got to change a predefined number of cards a certain number of steps or insert blank cards if needed. For each round, the movements became more restricted until the ranking converged. The final placements of the cards became the group's ranking of the features under the criterion being processed. See Fig. 1 for an example of such a ranking.

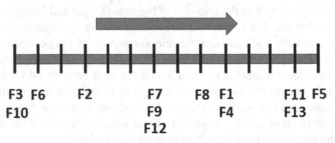

Fig. 1. An importance scale with features F1–F13 arranged in decreasing order

This BCC procedure was then repeated for the other two criteria, resulting in three feature rankings for each stakeholder group. In the next step, the groups were asked to rank the importance of the criteria, i.e. which aspect of the AI tools were of greater or lesser importance to the responding participants than others. There were three criteria, and they were ranked by a similar BCC method, the main difference being that it converged much faster due to there being only three criteria compared to 13 features in the previous step. These visual ranking scales (both features and criteria) were then entered into the DecideIT decision tool which generated aggregated preferences for each stakeholder group individually and for the groups combined.

The results of the process were (i) a detailed analysis of each option's performance compared with the others, and (ii) a sensitivity analysis to test the robustness of the result. During the process, the DecideIT tool considers the entire possible range of values of the features presented across all criteria, as well as how plausible it is that a feature will be able to outrank other ones, and thus provides a robustness measure of the results. The outcome of the DecideIT analysis will be discussed next.

4   Results

Our results show that there is no consensus among the stakeholders concerning the definition and nature of misinformation. Several definitions exist and we heard about definitions such as "unchecked information", "rumour", "unconscious human reaction to redirect inner states of mind" or "information which deviates from reality for different reasons, but mainly because of the lack of proper information". During the workshop, it became clear that stakeholders can differentiate between misinformation and disinforma-tion as "accidental spread of incorrect information" or "spread of incorrect information with an intent to cause damage".

While speaking about misinformation on migrants and its potential to lead to con-flicts, there was an opinion that misinformation can lead to such a risk in situations where conflicts or prejudices already exist. This position was expressed by one of the participating decision-makers as follows:

> It leads to conflicts in a situation with existing prejudices, flaccid use of language, understanding problems of either language or even word definitions. Also, the atmosphere of lack of trust and suspicion creates a fertile environment for the dissemination of rumours. Social conflicts usually arise when someone is feeling disadvantaged or overlooked. Fears also frequently lead to the building of rumours and misinformation. This is an emotional reaction, some kind of feeling, when someone feels him/herself being threatened by something foreign, unknown or different. The lack of information in such a situation leads to a tendency to believe in rumours, especially if they cause strong emotions".

However, prejudice alone does not necessarily lead to conflict. Conflict relates to the feeling of being disadvantaged or threatened, and the feeling of deprivation also frequently leads to conflict. Social conflicts appear from feelings of being threatened by something foreign, but this is a question of what is perceived as being foreign. For different persons, it could be different things including migrants from another country, another region, or another city. Social conflicts are also frequently connected with the feeling of lack of fairness in the distribution of resources or benefits and the fear of losing these benefits.

During the workshop, we identified the following reasons for spreading misinfor-mation:

– Boredom, as the spread of misinformation or conspiracy story sparks joy when bored.
– Lack of awareness that an individual is actually spreading misinformation.
– Confirmation of preconceived options when fact-checking information is not con-nected with the wish to stay in the comfort zone of their own beliefs.
– Need to emphasize one's own importance, when sharing something that is shocking and attracts attention.
– Superficiality, low willingness to read and the lack of time to check the correctness of misinformation.

Most of the workshop participants mentioned that they were most frequently affected by misinformation which relates to political issues. The majority of participants did not feel that they must do something to correct misinformation on political issues however they felt much more active engagement in case s that misinformation was connected to areas of their professional activity. In such instances, many felt an obligation to provide the correct information. The misinformation which is spread about migrants is mainly in the context of social services and fears that migrants are using social services to a larger extent than other groups of the population. Misinformation could also be spread as a reaction to perceived unfair distribution of economic benefits such as:

"In a social house in the 16th district, somebody started to spread misinformation that the housing company is employing only Turkish families. This was obviously misinformation and should have been corrected immediately".

The workshop participants also identified the following challenges to correct misinformation. Firstly, many participants think that they can control the spread of misinformation, especially if it is coming from the professional area and is being spread by the networking circle or by an employee of the same organization. In this case, several participants suggested to check facts or to use statistics as a form of corrective information. Secondly, the major challenge in this regard for them would be to quickly recognize the misinformation and to quickly recognize the source of that information. This quick reaction was perceived by many as a barrier for corrective measures since some participants mentioned that someone really must be an expert to be able to correct misinformation in a particular area. Another challenge is that the more exciting and contradictory the misinformation is, the faster it is being spread around. Thirdly, corrections might also be difficult because people are reading less and less. And the less they read, the more corrections should take place in person. So, a main issue here is also the time needed to work with people on the correction of misinformation. Also, to be able to correct misinformation, especially with people who cannot read, close contact is needed as well as great personal integrity.

The participants recommended the following ways to deal with misinformation about migration:

– Statistics and scientific articles, which are perceived as trusted sources of information, however, they are not always suitable for the general public;
– Personal communication where people with authority and integrity are involved and could be communicators of correct information. Such people should also enjoy a certain level of trust;
– Publication in trustful sources of information. Following characteristics were mentioned of trustful sources of information: neutrality, legal mandate, professional appearance, which includes accurateness of presentation and writing style and if there is institutional capacity behind;
– Fact-checkers were also mentioned as a trustful source of information however this source is not yet common and available to everybody.

The expectations of stakeholders on tools to deal with misinformation were different. The expectations of the *decision-makers* were mainly connected with the creation of a reliable environment through the development and enforcement of regulations, stimulation of the culture of critical thinking, and strengthening the capacities of statistical offices as well as making statistical information available and understandable to everybody. They recommended:

- *Institutional and regulatory measures* including the introduction of regulations for social media regarding misinformation, the introduction of measures to guarantee the independence of media and research institutions, and the introduction of an institution of online journalism and fact-checking practices in traditional media.
- *Channels of communication* including the creation of info points and service points to provide information about migration, providing information about migration in Wikipedia and printed traditional media as well as in their online forums.

The expectations of the *journalists and fact-checkers* were mainly connected with the development and availability of tools for verification of information. They recommended:

- *Measures to raise awareness* such as the implementation of events of awareness-raising about misinformation and media literacy, measures to strengthen the awareness that behind every news item there could be a special political agenda, and implementation of events on sensibilisation in social media about misinformation and measures to stimulate critical thinking about from whom and why misinformation is originating.
- *Tools to deal with misinformation* such as the usage of plug-ins in browsers, cross-checking by using fact-checking sites, blacklisting of information sources that provide misinformation, and providing easily accessible tools that show sources of information online.

The expectations of the *citizens* were mainly connected with the role of the decision-makers who should provide them with credible sources of information at the official websites and organize information campaigns among inhabitants about the challenges of misinformation and how to deal with it. The citizens recommended the following tools:

- On *awareness-raising* such as public events about reliable sources of information and to raise awareness about misinformation, media reports about "from whom comes bad information" and recommendations in traditional media about reliable sources of information.
- On *critical thinking* such as the creation of a culture of thinking where people don't rush to conclusions but rather search for alternative information.

The rankings of the features of AI tools to deal with misinformation allowed us to identify which features were the most important for decision-makers, journalists, and citizens respectively, and to also understand why they demand such tools.

The results of the preferences in the group of decision-makers show that they desire such tools to become aware of misinformation, on the one hand, and to understand why and when misinformation was shared. Sharing over time was also important as well as the credibility indicators.

It seems that tag veracity is the least important criterion together with platform feedback. Lifecycle (timeline) and self-notification are also not significant to the decision-makers.

Further, decision-makers think that the tools are needed for reasons of transparency, on the one hand, and to make them think twice. The reasons for building trust are the least important (Fig. 2).

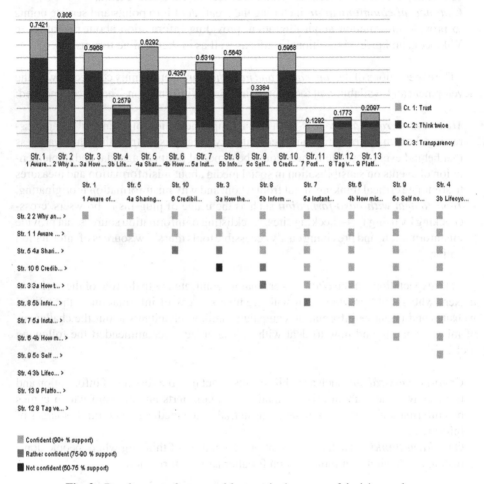

Fig. 2. Results on preferences of features in the group of decision-makers

In the figures the robustness of the opinions are color-marked. Green means that there is a significant difference between the features, and that there must be substantial changes in the input data for it to change. Yellow means that there is still a difference, but it is more sensitive to input data. Black means that there is no significant difference between the desirability of the features. The exact details of the semantics of the color-markings are provided in (Danielson et al. 2019). The identified options have the following meaning:

1. Awareness: I am aware of existing misinformation online.
2. Why and when: I want to know why a claim has been flagged as misinforming. And I want to know who has flagged it and when.

3. How they spread and who: I come across something that I find misinformative. I would like to know how this information has spread online and who has shared it.
4. Lifecycle (timeline): I want to know the lifecycle (timeline) of a misinforming post/article, for example, when it was first published, how many fact-checkers have debunked it, and when was it reshared again.
5. Sharing over time: I want to be able to quickly understand how much misinformation people have shared over time through an overall misinformation score.
6. How misinformative an item is: I want to be able to quickly understand how much misinformation a news item or tweet may contain through the provision of an overall misinformation score.
7. Instant feedback on arrival: When I encounter a tweet from someone else, which contains misinformative content, I want to be informed that it is misinformative.
8. Inform on consistent accounts: I want the Co-Inform system to inform me of which accounts (within my network) consistently generate/share/create misinformative content.
9. Self-notification: I want the Co-Inform tools to notify me whenever I repeatedly share misinformation.
10. Credibility indicators: I want to see credibility indicators that I will immediately understand, and I want the credibility indicators to look very familiar, like other indicators online.
11. Post-support or refute: I want to be able to post links to reputable articles and data that support or refute the story or claim.
12. Tag veracity: I want to be able to tag the veracity of an element (tweet, story, image, or sentence/claim) in the current tab I am seeing.
13. Platform feedback: I want to be able to receive feedback about what the platform is doing and has done with the tags and evidence I have submitted.

For the group of journalists and fact-checkers, the feature of awareness about misinformation was also the most important one. It was followed by the feature of how misinformative an item is and why and when misinformation was shared as well as credibility indicators.

Post support or refute together with platform feedback were the least important criteria. Also, information on consistent accounts and lifecycles (timelines) had a low level of importance. For journalists, tools are needed to make them think twice and to create trust. Transparency has the lowest level of importance (Fig. 3).

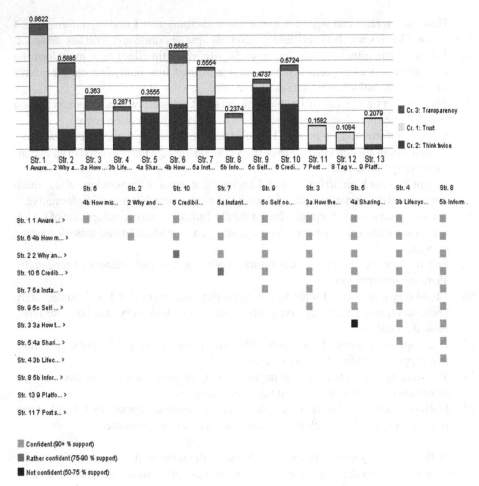

Fig. 3. First set of results for the group of journalists and fact-checkers

There was a conflict of opinions within the group of journalists and fact-checkers. Thus, we developed two sets of rankings to reflect the various preferences. However, the preferences on the criteria (the main questions) were the same since they perceived that AI tools are needed mainly to think twice and to create trust. The reason for transparency had the lowest value of importance. Also, in the second set of results, the awareness about misinformation was the most important criterion, followed by the criterion of how misinformative an item is and credibility indicators. The self-notification had a higher rank in this group. The two least important criteria were the same such as post support or refute and platform feedback (Fig. 4).

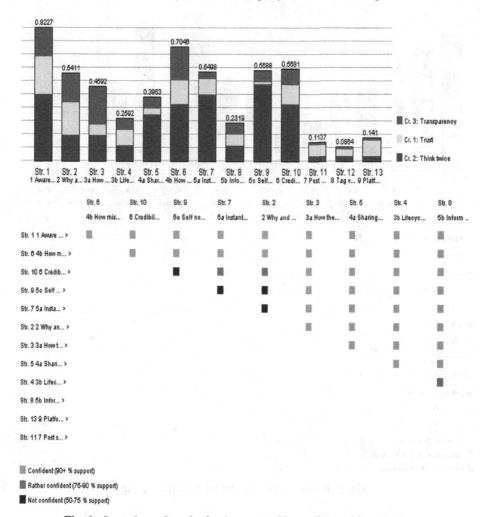

Fig. 4. Second set of results for the group of journalists and fact-checkers

Interestingly, for the group of citizens, the criterion to make them think twice had the lowest level of importance. They thought that tools are in the first place needed to create trust and secondly for reasons of transparency. The most important features were tag veracity and awareness about misinformation, as well as credibility indicators and why and who spread misinformation. The least important features were post support or refute and how misinformative an item is (Fig. 5).

In the next analysis step, the rankings of all three stakeholder groups were combined with an equal emphasis on each of them. The combined results for all groups show that awareness about misinformation is the most important feature for the combined stakeholders along with why and who shared misinformation and credibility indicators. The least important features are platform feedback and lifecycle (timeline) (Fig. 6).

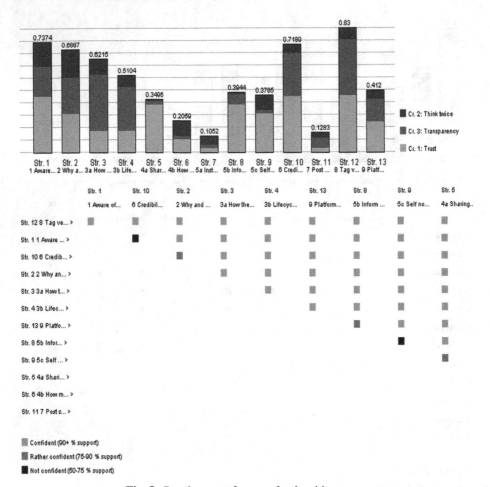

Fig. 5. Results on preferences for the citizen group

Our results allow us to draw conclusions about the rather passive attitudes toward the usage of artificial intelligence tools to address misinformation. People would like to be alerted and made aware of misinformation, however, only a few of them would like to use the tools to prevent misinformation from further spreading. Participants expressed their readiness to apply tools when it comes to misinformation about migration but for their own usage. They did not express a willingness to deal actively with misinformation about migrations and migrants online and enter correcting information. Only when it was connected to their professional activities did they feel an obligation to do so. These results also correspond with the first workshop when all three groups recommended the development of tools to raise awareness about existing misinformation about migration.

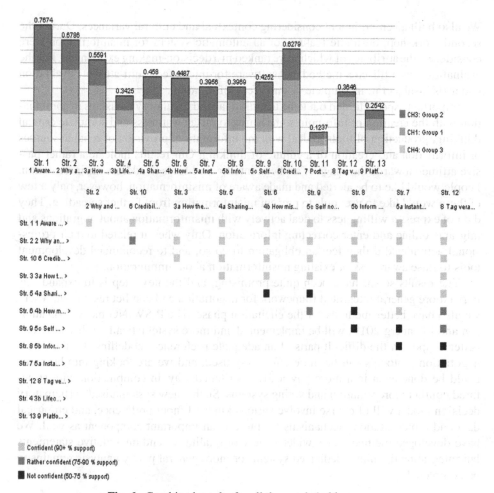

Fig. 6. Combined results for all three stakeholder groups

5 Conclusions

The work here is a part of the EU project Co-Inform and describes a methodology to evaluate machine learning based products designed within the framework of the Co-Inform project. The methodology is based on a multi-stakeholder-multi-criteria method-ology developed over some years and is here used for evaluating software solutions, with an emphasis on online misinformation on immigrants and refugees. The main idea behind the methodology is to empowering citizens, journalists, and policymakers with co-created socio-technical solutions, to increase resilience to misinformation.

As a part of this effort, we have presented herein desirable features of tools for rapid dissemination of misinformation in the context of immigration in Austria. The focus of our work is on the Austrian limited profit housing sector (LPHS), which is a key pillar of the Austrian policy on socio-economic development and political stability. We identified relevant stakeholders including decision-makers, citizen and journalists/fact-checkers.

We also built an environment considering contextual and cultural variances. During the second workshop, desirable features of an automatic system for misinformation were considered, the attributes of which were ranked in a decision-making experiment. For the evaluations, we utilised a method and software for integrated multi-attribute evaluation under risk, subject to incomplete or imperfect information.

Important aspects turned out to be institutional and regulatory measures in combination with the creation of info-points, measures to raise awareness and stimulate critical thinking, production of tools to deal with misinformation, provision of reliable sources of information and creation of a culture of thinking. Our results indicate a rather passive attitude towards the usage of artificial intelligence tools to address misinformation. People would like to be alerted and made aware of misinformation, however, only a few of them would like to use tools to prevent misinformation from further spreading. They did not express a willingness to deal actively with misinformation about migrations and migrants online and enter correcting information. Only when it related to their professional activities did they feel an obligation to do so, and to recommend development tools to raise awareness of existing misinformation about immigration.

The results so far have been quite promising, and the next step is to expand this into a more general integrated framework for negotiation and conflict resolution, where we also have better methods for the elicitation phase. The P-SWING method (Danielson and Ekenberg 2019) will be implemented and more systematically utilised to get a better support in the difficult parts of an adequate preference modelling. Furthermore, negotiation protocols can be more effectively used, and we are looking into how this could be done even in a more physically distributed way, in combination with structured conflict representation and voting systems. Such a new systematised participatory decision model will of course involve various kinds of input preference, and empirical data and representation mechanisms for these is an important component as well. We have developed methods for a wider variety of qualitative and quantitative statements but integrating them in a dedicated system for more general policy analysis remains to be completed.

Acknowledgment. This research was supported by the H2020 project "Co-Creating Misinformation-Resilient Societies" (Co-Inform, number 770302). We would like to express our gratitude to all stakeholders from the Austrian Limited Profit Housing Sector for their generosity with time and knowledge as well as all stakeholders who participated at our workshops and interviews. We are especially grateful to Gerlinde Gutheil-Knopp-Kirchwald from the Austrian Federation of Limited Profit Housing Associations and to Christian Zenz from the Federal Ministry for Digital and Economic Affairs of Austria.

References

Adali, S. et al.: Measuring behavioral trust in social networks. In: Proceedings of the IEEE International Conference on Intelligence and Security Informatics (ISI), pp. 150–152, May 2010

Al-JamalEmad, M., Abu-Shanab, E.: The influence of open government on e-government website: the case of Jordan. Int. J. Electron. Gov. 8(2), 159–179 (2016)

Alathur, S., Ilavarasan, V., Gupta, M.P.: Determinants of Citizens' Electronic Participation: Insights from India. Transform. Gov. People Process Policy **8**(3), 447–472 (2014)

Amerasinghe, M.: Enabling environmental justice: assessment of participatory tools. Environmental Department, United Nations Institute for Training and Research (2008)

Antoniadis, S., Litou, I., Kalogeraki, V.: A model for identifying misinformation in online social networks. In: Debruyne, C., et al. (eds.) OTM 2015. LNCS, vol. 9415, pp. 473–482. Springer, Cham (2015). https://doi.org/10.1007/978-3-319-26148-5_32

Anttiroiko, A.-V.: Building strong E-democracy - The role of technology in developing democracy for the information age. Commun. ACM **46**(9), 121–128 (2003)

Antunes, P., Santos, R., Videira, N.: Participatory decision-making for sustainable development – the use of mediated modeling techni- ques. Land Use Policy **2006**(23), 44–52 (2006)

Beierle, T.C.: The quality of stakeholder-based decisions. Risk Anal. **22**(4), 739–749 (2002). https://doi.org/10.1111/0272-4332.00065

Berry, T., et al.: We are all stakeholders: participatory decision-making and corporate sustainability. University of Technology, Sydney Australia, Institute for Sustainable Futures (2003)

Bindu, N., Prem Sankar, C., Satheesh Kumar, K.: From conventional governance to e-democracy: tracing the evolution of egovernance research trends using network analysis tools. Gov. Inf. Q. 36, 385–399 (2019)

Blicharska, M., Isaksson, K., Richardson, T., Wu, C.-J.: Context dependency and stakeholder involvement in EIA: the decisive role of practitioners. J. Environ. Plan. Manage. **54**(3), 3 (2011)

Brech, J., Feigelfeld, G.: Ethnic dimensions of coexistence. In: Ludl, H.: Integration im Wohnbau. Modelle fuer ein Soziales Zusammenleben. Birkhauser, Basel (2017)

Brech, J., Feigelfeld, G.: Current relevance of an initial project. Integration in the interethnic neighbourhood housing model. In: Ludl, H. (ed.) Integration im Wohnbau. Modelle fuer ein Soziales Zusammenleben. Birkhauser, Basel (2017a)

Brech, J., Feigelfeld, G.: Living together on housing estate. empirical survey of newer Sozialbau housing estates in Vienna. In: Ludl, H. (ed.) Integration im Wohnbau. Modelle fuer ein Soziales Zusammenleben. Birkhauser, Basel (2017b)

Brech, J., Feigelfeld, G.: Everyday life together. In: Ludl, H. (ed.) Integration im Wohnbau. Modelle fuer ein Soziales Zusammenleben. Birkhauser, Basel (2017c)

Bright, J., Margetts, H.: Big data and public policy: can it succeed where e-Participation has failed? Policy Internet **8**, 218–224 (2016). https://doi.org/10.1002/poi3.130

Canini, K.R., Suh, B., Pirolli, P.L.: Finding credible information sources in social networks based on content and social structure. In: Proceedings of the IEEE 3rd International Conference on Privacy, Security Risk Trust (PASSAT), IEEE 3rd International Conference on Social Computer (SocialCom), pp. 1–8, October 2011

Castles, S., de Haas, H., Miller, M.: The Age of Migration. International Population Movements in the Modern World. Palgrave Maximilian, London (2015)

Cook, B., Kothari, U.: Diversity and constructive conflict in stakeholder dialogue: considerations for design and methods. Policy Sci. **45**(1), 23-46 (2001). https://doi.org/10.1007/s11077-011-9141-7 Participation: the new tyranny? Zed Books, London, UK. Cuppen, E. 2012

Dahlberg, L.: Re-constructing digital democracy: an outline of four 'positions.' New Media Soc. **3**(6), 855–872 (2011)

Danielson, M., Ekenberg, L.: Efficient and sustainable risk management in large project portfolios. In: Zdravkovic, J., Grabis, J., Nurcan, S., Stirna, J. (eds.) Perspectives in Business Informatics Research. BIR 2018. Lecture Notes in Business Information Processing, vol. 330. Springer, Cham (2018). https://doi.org/10.1007/978-3-319-99951-7_10

Danielson, M., Ekenberg, L.: An Improvement to swing techniques for elicitation in MCDM methods. Knowl. Based Syst. (2019). https://doi.org/10.1016/j.knosys.2019.01.001

Danielson, M., Ekenberg, L., Larsson, A.: A second-order-based decision tool for evaluating decisions under conditions of severe uncertainty. Knowl. Based Syst. (2019). https://doi.org/10.1016/j.knosys.2019.105219

Danielson, M., Ekenberg, L., Larsson, A.: Evaluating multi-criteria decisions under strong uncertainty. In: de Almeida, A., Ekenberg, L., Scarf, P., Zio, E., Zuo, M.J.: Multicriteria Decision Models and Optimization for Risk, Reliability, and Maintenance Decision Analysis - Recent Advances. Springer, Heidelberg (2020)

De Jong, S., Atac, I.: Demand and deliver: refugee support organisations in Austria. Soc. Inclusion 5(2), 28–37 (2017)

Diduck, A., Sinclair, A.J.: Public involvement in environmental assessment: the case of the nonparticipant. Environ. Manage. 29(4), 578–588 (2002). https://doi.org/10.1007/s00267-001-0028-9

Dietz, T., Stern, P.C.: Public Participation in Environmental Assessment and Decision-Making. National Academies Press, Washington (2008)

Dorostkar, N., Preisinger, A.: 'Cyber hate' vs. 'cyber deliberation'. The case of an Austrian newspaper's discussion board from a critical online-discourse analytical perspective. J. Lang. Politics 16(6), 759–781 (2017)

Ekenberg, L., Fasth, T., Larsson, A.: Hazards and quality control in humanitarian demining. Int. J. Qual. Reliab. Manage. 35(4), 897–913 (2018). https://doi.org/10.1108/IJQRM-01-2016-0012

Ekenberg, L., Hansson, K., Danielson, M., Cars, G.: Deliberation, Representation, and Equity: Research Approaches, Tools, and Algorithms for Participatory Processes, p. 384. Open Book Publishers (2017). ISBN 978-1-78374-304-9

Fiorino, D.J.: Citizen participation and environmental risk: a survey of institutional mechanisms. Sci. Technol. Hum. Values 15(2), 226–243 (1990). https://doi.org/10.1177/016224399001500204

Forester, J.: The Deliberative Practitioner. Encouraging Participatory Planning Process. MIT Press, Cambridge (1999)

Freschi, A.C., Medaglia, R., Nørbjerg, J., et al.: eParticipation in the institutional domain: a review of research: analytical report on eParticipation research from an administration and political perspective in six European countries. In: Freschi, A.C., Medaglia, R., Nørbjerg, J., et al. (eds.) DEMO-Net Consortium, Bergamo (2009)

Funtowicz, S., Ravetz, J.: The worth of a songbird: ecological economics, as a post-normal science. Ecol. Econ. 10, 197–207 (1994)

Golbeck, J.A.: Computing and applying trust in Web-based social networks. Ph.D. dissertation, University of Maryland, Department of Computer Science, College Park, MD, USA (2005)

Gouillart, F., Hallett, T.: Co-Creation in Government. Stanf. Soc. Innov. Rev. 13, 40–47 (2015)

Habitat. Participatory decision-making indicators measuring progress on improving urban management decision-making processes. UNCHS (2009)

Hansson, K., Ekenberg, L.: Embodiment and gameplay: situating the user in crowdsourced information production. In: Manoharan, A.P. (ed.) Innovative Perspectives on Public Administration in the Digital Age, pp. 239–255. IGI Global (2018)

Hansson, K., Belkacem, K., Ekenberg, L.: Open government and democracy: a research review. Soc. Sci. Comput. Rev. 33(5), 540–555 (2014)

Hashim, F., et al.: Information and communication technology for participatory based decision-making-E-management for administrative efficiency in Higher Education. Int. J. Phys. Sci. 5(4), 383–392 (2010). Faculty of Education, 50603 Kuala Lumpur, MALAYSIA

IIBW. Third United Nations Conference on Housing and Sustainable Urban Development (HABITAT III) - Case Study – The Austrian System of Social Housing (in cooperation with the Austrian Federal Ministries for Europe, Integration and Foreign Affairs; for Transport, Innovation and Technology; of Agriculture, Forestry, Environment and Water Management; of Science, Research and Economy; the Austrian Economic Chamber) (2016)

Jia, J., Wang, B., Gong, N.Z.: Random walk based fake account detection in online social networks. In: Proceedings of the 47th Annual IEEE/IFIP International Conference on Dependable System Network (DSN), pp. 273–284, June 2017

Jiang, W., Wang, G., Wu, J.: Generating trusted graphs for trust evaluation in online social networks. Future Gener. Comput. Syst. **31**, 48–58 (2014). https://www.sciencedirect.com/science/article/pii/S0167739X1200146X

Joshi, S., et al.: Co-creation framework – building a sustainable ecosystem. Co-Inform Consortium (2018)

Kohlbacher, J., Reeger, U., Schnell, P.: Place Attachment and social ties – migrants and natives in three urban settings in Vienna. Popul. Space Place, Special Issue Paper (2015). https://doi.org/10.1002/psp.1923

Komendantova, N., et al.: Multi-hazard and multi-risk decision support tools as a part of participatory risk governance: Feedback from civil protection stakeholders. Int. J. Disaster Risk Reduction **8**, 50–67 (2014)

Komendantova, N., Ekenberg, L., Marashdeh, L., Al Salaymeh, A., Danielson, M., Linnerooth-Bayer, J.: Are energy security concerns dominating environmental concerns? Evidence from stakeholder participation processes on energy transition in Jordan. Climate **6**(4), 88 (2018)

Koontz, T.M.: We finished the plan, so now what? Impacts of collaborative stakeholder participation on land use policy. Policy Stud. J. **33**(3), 459–481 (2005). https://doi.org/10.1111/j.1541-0072.2005.00125.x

Koulolias, V., Jonathan, G., Fernandez, M., Sotirchos, D.: Combatting Misinformation: An Ecosystem in Co-Creation. Organization for Economic Cooperation and Development, April 2018 (2018)

Larsson, A., Fasth, T., Wärnhjelm, M., Ekenberg, L., Danielson, M.: Policy analysis on the fly with an online multi-criteria cardinal ranking tool. J. Multi-Criteria Decis. Anal. **2018**, 1–12 (2018). https://doi.org/10.1002/mcda.1634

Ludl, H.: Integration in housing models for social cohesion. SOZIALBAU AG (2017)

Macintosh, A., Coleman, S., Schneeberger, A. (2009), "eParticipation: The research gaps", Electronic Participation, Vol. 9 No. 1, pp. 1–11.

Medaglia, R.: The challenged identity of a field: The state of the art of eParticipation research. Inf. Polity **12**(3), 169–181 (2007)

Medaglia, R.: eParticipation research: moving characterization forward (2006–2011). Gov. Inf. Q. **29**(3), 346–360 (2012)

Migration Council for Austria. Understanding migration – managing migration. Migration Council for Austria and Austrian Federal Ministry of the Interior (2016)

Mihai, A., Marincea, A., Ekenberg, L.: A MCDM Analysis of the Roşia Montană Gold Mining Project. Sustainability **2015**(7), 7261–7288 (2015). https://doi.org/10.3390/su7067261

Naranjo-Zolotov, M., Oliveira, T., Casteleyn, S.: E-participation adoption models research in the last 17 years: a weight and meta-analytical review. Comput. Hum. Behav. **81**, 350–365 (2018)

Newig, J., Adzersen, A., Challies, E., Fritsch, O., Jager, N.: Comparative analysis of public environmental decision-making processes—a variable-based analytical scheme. Discussion Paper No. 37/13. Institut Für Umweltkommunikation, Lüneburg, Germany (2013). https://doi.org/10.2139/ssrn.2245518

Newig, J., Fritsch, O.: More input - better output: does citizen involvement improve environmental governance? In: Blühdorn, I. (ed.) In Search of Legitimacy: Policy Making in Europe and the Challenge of Complexity, pp. 205–224. Barbara Budrich, Opladen, Farmington Hills (2009)

Observatory of Public Attitudes to Migration. Public attitudes on migration: rethinking how people perceive migration. An analysis of existing opinion polls in the Euro-Mediterranean region. Observatory of Public Attitudes to Migration – Migration Policy Centre, European University Institute, Florence (2018)

Orihuela, L., Obi, T.: E-democracy: ICT for a better relation between the state and their citizens. In: Mishra, S.S. (ed.) E-Democracy Concepts and Practices by Mishra, Santap Sanhari, 31 December 2012, Hardback. SBS Publishers (2012)

Pichon, F., Labreuche, C., Duqueroie, B., Delavallade, T.: Multidimensional approach to reliability evaluation of information sources. Wiley Online Library. Inf. Eval. **30**, 129–159 (2014)

Pirannejad, A., Janssen, M.: Internet and political empowerment: towards a taxonomy for online political empowerment. Inf. Dev. **35**(1), 80–95 (2017)

Pluchinotta, I., Kazakçi, A.O., Giordano, R., Tsoukiàs, A.: Design Theory for Generating Alternatives in Public Decision-Making Processes. Group Decis. Negot. **28**, 341–375 (2019). https://doi.org/10.1007/s10726-018-09610-5

Porwol, L., Ojo, A., Breslin, J.G.: Social Software Infrastructure for e-Participation. Gov. Inf. Q. **35**, S88–S98 (2016)

Pretty, J.N.: Participatory learning for sustainable agriculture. World Dev. **23**, 1247–1263 (1995). https://doi.org/10.1016/0305-750X(95)00046-F

Reed, M.S.: Stakeholder participation for environmental management: a literature review. Biol. Cons. **141**(10), 2417–2431 (2008). https://doi.org/10.1016/j.biocon.2008.07.014

Renn, O.: Copying with Uncertainty in a Complex World, p. 455. Earthscan, London (2008)

Rheindorf, M., Wodak, R.: "Austria First" revisited: a diachronic cross-sectional analysis of the gender and body politics of the extreme right. Patterns Prejudice **53**(3), 302–320 (2019)

Sæbø, Ø., Rose, J., Skiftenes Flak, L.: The shape of eParticipation: characterizing an emerging research area. Gov. Inf. Q. **25**(3), 400–428 (2008)

Sanford, C., Rose, J.: Characterizing eParticipation. Int. J. Inf. Manage. **27**(6), 406–421 (2007)

Schmiedel, U., Schmidt, G.: Religion in the European Refugee Crisis. Palgrave, Cham (2018)

Schwilch, G., Bachmann, F., Liniger, H.P.: Appraising and selecting conservation measures to mitigate desertification and land degradation based on stakeholder participation and global best practices. Land Degrad. Dev. **20**(3), 308–326 (2009). https://doi.org/10.1002/ldr.920

Sharma, et al.: Participatory administration and collective decision making. Strengthening of State Administrative Training Institute in India (2003)

Stringer, L.C., Twyman, C., Thomas, D.S.G.: Combating land degradation through participatory means: the case of Swaziland. Ambio **36**(5), 387–393 (2007). https://doi.org/10.1579/0044-7447(2007)36[387:cldtpm]2.0.co;2

Valente, S.: Stakeholder participation in Sustainable Forest Management in fire-prone areas. Dissertation, University of Aveiro, Portugal (2013)

Wimmer, M.A.: Ontology for an e-participation virtual resource centre. In: Proceedings of the 1st International Conference on Theory and Practice of Electronic Governance - ICEGOV 2007, Macao, China, pp. 91–101 (2007)

Wolsink, M.: Invalid theory impedes our understanding: a critique on the persistence of the language of NIMBY. Trans. Inst. Br. Geogr. **31**(1), 85–91 (2006)

Zhao, L., Hua, T., Lu, C.-T., Chen, R.: A topic-focused trust model for Twitter. Comput. Commun. **76**, 1–11 (2016)

Author Index

Printed in the United States
By Bookmasters